EXCELLING AT CHESS

JACOB AAGAARD

EVERYMAN CHESS

Everyman Publishers plc   www.everyman.uk.com

First published in 2001 by Everyman Publishers plc, formerly Cadogan Books plc, Gloucester Mansions, 140A Shaftesbury Avenue, London WC2H 8HD

British Library Cataloguing-in-Publication Data
A catalogue record for this book is available from the British Library.

ISBN 1 85744 273 3

Distributed in North America by The Globe Pequot Press, P.O Box 480, 246 Goose Lane, Guilford, CT 06437-0480.

All other sales enquiries should be directed to Everyman Chess, Gloucester Mansions, 140A Shaftesbury Avenue, London WC2H 8HD
tel: 020 7539 7600 fax: 020 7379 4060
email: dan@everyman.uk.com
website: www.everyman.uk.com

EVERYMAN CHESS SERIES (formerly Cadogan Chess)
Chief advisor: Garry Kasparov
Commissioning editor: Byron Jacobs

Typeset and edited by First Rank Publishing, Brighton.
Production by Book Production Services.
Printed and bound in Great Britain by The Cromwell Press Ltd., Trowbridge, Wiltshire.

CONTENTS

ACKNOWLEDGEMENTS

There are a few people who have had considerable influence on this book and I would like to take this opportunity to thank them. First there is Finn Nøhr who, besides being my pupil, also helped by reading through much of the book and suggesting improvements. Then there is Coach Dalsberg, who helped me when I was still trying to be somebody as a player, and who pointed out a serious weakness in terms of attitude at the board. Mikael Franck contributed beyond what anyone would expect – he manages the gym that I have been attending during the last two years, and my momentary success could not have been achieved without his help. I would like to thank Ivo Timmermans both for his friendship and for buying my books when I ran out of free copies!

Thanks also go to Byron Jacobs for pleasant business manners and to Kim Røper Jensen and Dan Östergaard for helping me in creating an excuse for a website. Their work is a brilliant reflection of my limited ideas.

Finally, Donald Holmes deserves a special mention for giving me shelter when I needed to finish the book – it has become a tradition to finish in his office (there is no better place to work).

This book is dedicated to three important chess teachers in my life: Henrik Mortensen, Grandmaster Henrik Danielsen and International Master Mark Dvoretsky.

BIBLIOGRAPHY

I came across the books mentioned below when writing my own book. There may well be equally important works but I cannot remember either who wrote them or how they are specifically relevant, and some titles are omitted as they featured only one or two good ideas alongside lengthy list of false statements.

Actually, I am not a fan of attaching a bibliography to a chess book, the usual policy of quoting a book, without having read it from cover to cover, and then including it in the bibliography appearing rather artificial.

What I have written in this book is, to the best of my knowledge, true. When I quote others it is often from memory, and I decided quite early in this project that I would not waste too much time 'confirming' my memory (it has no previous history of failing me).

The list of books below is – besides constituting part of the foundations for this book – a list of recommended reading.

Chess Books

Elie Agur: *Fischer – His Approach to Chess*
A truly remarkable work, the idea is a middlegame handbook based on examples from Fischer – no full games, but many critical situations. Probably the best book ever written about Fischer.

Jonathan Rowson: *The Seven Deadly Chess Sins*
A great read. Rowson has read the most important books about the mind, and uses this knowledge in his book. What I particularly like about his writing is that he knows where his knowledge ends and does not try to go further. I do not know if this book will make you a better player, or whether his theories are correct, but you will enjoy reading it.

John Watson: *Secrets of Modern Chess Strategy*
This book is very well structured and features numerous good examples. However, sometimes I feel that Watson's line of argument insufficiently self-critical.

Mark Dvoretsky: *Technique for the Tournament Player, Positional Play, Attack and Defence* and *Training for the Tournament Player.*
The Master of chess literature. The greatest chess teacher of our time. These books concentrate on the endgame, prophylaxis, calculation and more general topics respectively.

Jonathan Tisdall: *Improve your Chess now*
Combining the first two chapters of this work with Dvoretsky's *Attack and Defence* is the right approach to calculation training.

Israel Gelfer: *Positional Chess Handbook*
Simply a wonderful collection of examples.

***New In Chess Magazine* (1992 and 2000)**
I like to get into the heads of the top players. No other place do you get there as often as in NIC.

Alexei Shirov: *Fire on Board*
Shirov annotates his games and talks about his ideas. The best games collection of the 1990s (together with Xie Jun's autobiography), unlike the quickly manufactured books about Anand, Sokolov, Khalifman and Kramnik.

Mikhail Tal: *Tal-Botvinnik 1960*
When Tal talks about his experience of playing the match you no longer care for variations and the correctness of ideas – you are reminded that chess is a game!

Chess Informant No.80
I found a good example here. I did not use the other books in the series.

Chessbase Magazine
A useful periodical. I recommend acquiring the annually updated Mega Database.

Performance psychology books

Will Railo: *Den nye Bedst når det gælder*
A practical book in Danish.

Garfield: *Peak Performance*
A classic, but now difficult to find.

Technical books about the brain

Gilles Fauconnier: *Mappings in Thought and Language*

FOREWORD

I wrote this book as a kind of personal test. I wanted to make some sense of the various ideas I came across during a period (1999-2000) when I was trying to improve my playing strength. I found that this was not as easy as I had originally believed, leading to a loss of confidence that resulted in difficulties finishing the book.

As the book evolved it became clear that I wanted to write about understanding in chess, no doubt as an antidote to the way too many players sit in front of computers. Of course it is true that computers help, but only if we question and interpret their results rather than accept them as truths.

It is interesting that while writing this book – during the first eight months of 2001 – I realised that I no longer had the same desire to be involved in competitive chess, a feeling that is partly a result of actually writing down my thoughts as to how chess should be played.

I truly believe that this book can help you in improving your chess if you adapt the ideas and training methods outlined in these pages. I have tried them all in practise with my pupils, and the results have been good.

My primary ambition when beginning work on this book was to write something that people would find to be a good read. The conversational style is intended as a means to shake up the more abstract parts and generally aid in getting my point over. Additionally I did not want to waste time doubting my own views, and I have tried to support them as well as I can with arguments and examples. I gave my best shot. If you have a feeling that I am incorrect you might be right – my mind is not made up and set in stone, but I did not want to waste your time by presenting precautions every third paragraph.

All in all I believe this is my best work, and I hope you will find it of some use.

Jacob Aagaard
Glasgow, Amsterdam and Copenhagen
October 2001

CHAPTER ONE

Think Like a Human – and Excel at Chess

You are reading this book in the hope that it will be worth your time and money. So what is the book about?

Let us start at the beginning. In 1997 and 1998 I worked on my first chess book, *The Easy Guide to the Panov-Botvinnik Attack,* trying to find my own approach. After spending three months on the first chapter I was running short of both pages and time, and the rest of the book ended up being rather standard. Ever since this I have felt that I was basically right in my way of structuring the positional issues in the chapter, and I continued to think along these lines for years until I met my current editor, Byron Jacobs, on the Internet Chess Club. We agreed that I should do an opening book, and I was invited to write a book on whatever subject I would find appropriate. For a couple of months I came up with new ideas every week, sending Byron long e-mails describing my chaotic brainstorms. Finally I settled on one basic idea, that humans are not computers – a 'discovery' so simple it seems unnecessary to mention

but, as with most basic ideas, a subject that can fill a book, since the observation contains more than meets the eye.

I have noticed how more and more people analyse with computer tools such as Fritz, Junior or Crafty, taking these computerised conclusions to heart without ever doubting them. The same people have a tendency to decline in playing strength and become frustrated. They have a belief that they should calculate better, but do not have the time or discipline to learn to do so. If you are one of those, please do not be sad – it would not do you that much good anyway, unless you really know what to calculate...

I also see – all too often – that people tend to suggest variations in positions which can be evaluated by a brief glance – 'But what about...' is heard so often after showing a position and explaining why, for example, this or that side has the advantage. I experienced such an example recently when a friend of mine analysed a game that he had won rather easily after sacrificing an exchange for a pawn. His opponent's remaining minor piece was a bishop, which shared the same colour squares as all his pawns, while there were no files for his rooks (and no way to open any) and no attack or counterplay. My friend would – by force – get a passed pawn on the sixth rank, without giving up any of these advantages. The opponent simply failed to realise that he was completely lost and he kept trying different moves – I stress: moves – not ideas. My friend's numerous attempts to explain the important characteristics of the position merely met with another move. I watched the last hour of this session, my friend's patience being worn thin by his opponent, the irony being that this unpleasant situation was a result of a lack of understanding rather than intentionally stubborn behaviour. I am not sure that I could have explained it to him, and I did not want to try – it would have been much easier to hand him this book...

The argument in this book is that chess is based on rules. Ten years ago, as a junior, I believed that there were no other rules in chess than the facts you could discover from analysing a position – in other words, every position is governed by its own set of rules. I had read this in a New In Chess magazine and was impressed, and the fact that the statement was somehow linked to the violent chess of Garry Kasparov did nothing to diminish this thought. Now, older – and hopefully wiser – I know that the former world champion would never say such nonsense. In fact he would offer the opposite argument, as I

have discussed in Chapter 2.

During the last six or seven years I have been convinced that chess is built on dynamic rules, in the same way as physics and biology. I believe that most tournament games are not won by superior calculation or imaginary power, as I used to think, but rather due to superior understanding of the very basics of the game. This point of view is a key argument put forward in this book, set out mainly in Chapters 2 and 3. The former offers some examples from top level competition of superior understanding, a topic that poses few difficulties in terms of explanation. In *No rules?* I try to provide a more abstract suggestion as to how these rules are organised. Of course this chapter features assumptions which may later be refuted but, nevertheless, I feel that it is a step in the right direction.

I know that a book filled with nothing but theoretical discussions would not be very interesting. I have already lived enough of my life in the intense world of academia at the University of Aarhus, where I study Cognitive Semiotics, so I do not want to impose such suffering on others – it would be like giving blank bullets to a soldier.

This book also aims to offer suggestions on how to improve one's knowledge of chess fundamentals and, subsequently, how these should be implemented in practical play. Whatever your ambition, from earning promotion from first board of the second team to tenth board of the first to gaining international success, I honestly believe that this book will help you achieve both. Of course, if you read it only once and then put it away your improvement will be considerably limited, but if you use the book to become better aware of how you think about chess, then who knows...

I remember David Norwood claiming that Grandmasters calculate less than amateurs. Basically, they do not need to because they know what to calculate, or so his argument goes, at least. In fact I believe he is correct. In my teens, when my calculation powers were superior to my opponents', I often impressed my higher rated opponents with numerous fancy lines, yet this did not lead to winning many points. And in Jonathan Rowson's interesting recent work, *The Seven Deadly Chess Sins*, the author talks about his six game match against Michael Adams, the Homer Simpson of chess (a positive comparison). After the games it always turned out that Adams had seen only a fraction of the lines addressed by Rowson but, somehow, these were the relevant lines! Adams won the match 5-1. However, perhaps Adams is the extreme example of this way of playing chess. Nobody has ever been able to tell me what Adams is thinking. A friend proposed that he just looks at one of his pieces and asks: 'Well, my little friend, where are we going tonight?' – an exaggeration, of course, but not completely, since I believe it does actually contain an element of truth.

Beyond the mere discussion of how you should think about chess, I have included some chapters on achieving the appropriate frame of mind. I am not a professional psychologist or physicist,

but I have spent a lot of time investigating these issues, and I also have the advantage of having implemented my theories in practice. This leads us directly to the main question that any critic should come up with – why does an International Master believe that he can contribute anything relevant to chess theory? This is to say beyond using annotations of others, asking computer tools such as *Fritz* for advice and then forming a structured model from an enormous mass of information – as is the case when working on books that concentrate on opening theory.

Well, I am happy you asked – in order to have faith in what I say you should know a little about who I am. I started playing chess at the age of twelve and was never a prodigy. I had talent but I was not the most talented junior in the club. Rather I was the most eager. At the age of sixteen my elo rating was 2100 and I was club champion. The following year I rose to 2370. Now my rating is 2360, the lowest in seven or eight years.

I came close to the international master norm a number of times, but always failed in the final round. In 1996, when I was twenty-three years old, I had some training sessions with Grandmaster Henrik Danielsen. In a few months I had made two International Master norms, the second being a full point above the required score. In March 1997 I made my final norm, and in the summer I was already playing for grandmaster norms. The closest I have been was probably the tournament in Groningen 1998, where I reached the following position:

White to play and win

Here I could have made the Grand-master-norm had I played the spectacular 50 ♖h8!! instead of 50 ♔f5+, securing a perpetual check. Note that 50 ♕e4?? fails to 50...♕xd5+!! 51 ♕xd5 ♖c5. After 50 ♖h8 ♗g6 (50...♔xh8 51 ♔h6! and mate, or 50...♖c2 51 ♕h1!, while 50...♕xd5+? this time leaves the bishop hanging on e8) 51 ♖g8+! ♔xg8 52 ♔h6 White soon mates.

Anyway, in 1999 I had the following painful experience in the Copenhagen Open, being Black (to move) in the following position:

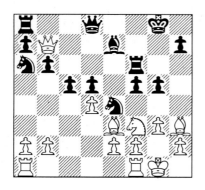

Black to play and win

This time an old habit came back to haunt me. Emotionally I realised I was probably winning, and something peculiar happened – I started to feel strange, my hands began to shake, I felt rather hot... Then I found myself playing 17...b5?? and after 18 ♘e5 White had a decisive advantage. I realised immediately that 17...cxd4 wins on the spot because White is forced to take on a6 in view of the threat 18...♘ac5, winning the queen.

It was due to the money I could win that I had reacted in this way, displaying a form of accelerated nervousness. I have later discovered the phenomenon in cognitive literature – it is known as an *agmygdala* attack. Basically it is a survival mechanism, which was very useful back in the days we were hunted by predators. It works the following way: Normally any consciousness event happens in what we call Pöbel time, named after the German Neurologist who discovered this phenomena, which is roughly three seconds. Every 30 milli-seconds we acquire knowledge and every 3 seconds we act on it. In order to react any faster it needs to be automatic not conscious. Pöbel time is seen every day in the human world. 4/4 in music is normally 3 seconds, the pentameter in poetry usually takes three seconds to read, a normal sentence in a conversation usually has a 3 seconds duration. When somebody says something to you and you reply 'Sorry', only to realise a split second later what the person really meant, you have experienced reacting before being consciously aware. Faster than Pöbel time that is.

Anyway, when a predator attacks you,

you need to react immediately. So in the case of danger approaching your central nerve system will alarm the brain. There the agmygdala will take over in the case immediate action is needed, and you will react on instinct only. A lot of people loose their heads this way, mainly in petty arguments, but sometimes also in performance situations like chess. This is what happened to me on a lot of occasions. I basically could not take the pressure in the situation and my play collapsed. A pity the cavemen did not keep his cool more often.

After losing this game I was devastated. I sincerely thought about giving up chess and getting on with my life. When I felt most sure that this was the correct choice I remembered something I had experienced over the board about a year earlier, which at the time had been something of a revelation to me.

Mortensen-Aagaard
Danish Rapidplay Championship 1998
Ruy Lopez

First you need to know about the tournament. Thirty-two players are invited – the sixteen highest rated players in the country, all correspondence grandmasters, some local players and the winner of the previous year's qualifier. I was ranked about 20th and invited mainly because I had been ranked 9th the year before. (In 2000 and 2001 I was no longer invited, as the organiser had realised I was no longer in the top...)

1 e4 e5 2 ♘f3 ♘c6 3 ♗b5 f5?

At the age of twenty I spent much of the year studying this line, concluding

that it is completely useless, and that White is close to winning (if he knows what to do). But then again, how many people would find it worthwhile intensely investigating White's position? I know one who did, but only after losing too many blitz games against me!

4 d4?

I do not want to give too much away, but this is not the test.

4...fxe4 5 ♗xc6 bxc6!? 6 ♘xe5 ♕h4!

A logical move but, for some reason, still a new one. After 6...♘f6 7 ♗g5 White is known to have a large advantage. The difference in this line is clear. The queen is poorly placed on d8, but after the light-squared bishop has disappeared it is very well placed on the kingside.

7 ♘c3 ♗b4!? 8 ♕e2 ♘f6 9 0-0 ♗xc3 10 bxc3 0-0 11 ♗a3

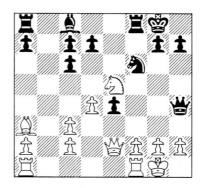

Here I thought for some time. I felt that 11...d6 was the best move but I was not sure that I could prove compensation for the c6-pawn. Consequently I was about to play 11...♖e8 when something struck me. Here I am in a rapidplay tournament – where a finish among the top ten would be a good result – and I am afraid of sacrificing a pawn? Basically I had so much doubt in myself and my judgement that I did not have the courage to play what I thought to be correct. Seeing it like this made it easy to make the best continuation, but at the same time I felt ashamed. I realised I had wasted so much of my life being 'safe', never achieving anything of significance. I was afraid of losing the nothing I had. Need I say that I promised myself never to do this again?

11...d6! 12 ♕c4+?

12 ♘xc6 ♗d7 13 ♕c4+ ♔h8 with unclear play is preferable. Now it seems that White is already much worse.

12...♘d5! 13 ♘xc6?

13 ♕xc6 ♗e6 14 ♘c4 ♘xc3 15 ♘e3 ♘e2+ 16 ♔h1 ♖ac8 gives Black a clear advantage. Now it is a forced win.

13...♗e6 14 g3

14 ♗c1 ♘f4 15 ♕a6 ♘xg2 16 ♕e2 is the best Fritz can suggest. Any defence here is of course hopeless: in reply to 14 ♕e2 ♘f4 15 ♕e3 Black has 15...♕g5!! 16 g3 (16 ♕xe4 d5) 16...♘h3+ followed by a sacrifice on f2 winning the queen.

14...♕g4!

Freeing h3 for the knight.

15 f3!? exf3 16 ♕d3 ♘f4 17 ♕e3

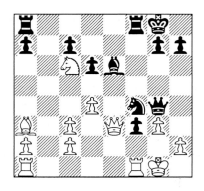

17...f2+! 0-1

As I said, this was a magical moment for me. Not only did I learn something about myself and doing the right thing, I also won a nice game against a strong opponent in very few moves. The confidence gained from this victory, combined with some luck, gave me 1½/2 from the closing rounds and thus a share of second place, in front of five Grandmasters (the best result I have ever achieved).

I decided to give my chess ambition one last try. I hired my friend, Coach – who had some experience with Neuro Linguistic Programming (NLP) and meditation, as well as physical training – and started working with my weaknesses. After six months I could look back at thirty games with an average performance of 2587. In all but one of these games I had sacrificed something and gone for the full point with heart and soul, and none of these were drawn. I drew one final round game in Hamburg in forty-four moves after a tough positional battle, but then nobody is perfect.

Unfortunately I performed best in the Danish and Swedish leagues, which are not FIDE-rated, so I remained around 2400. Nonetheless, I was confident and sure that the future would be good, even though there were some problems.

Although I was improving my physical and mental abilities, I was lazy with chess itself. I did not have enough interest in the game. I wanted to prove that my ideas were right, but I was more interested in reading James Ellroy than studying chess. Consequently I would soon hit a barrier, and to further complicate matters I met a nice girl and fell in love! So, eventually, I played poorly again, and I did not care so much for the results. I became frustrated, fired my friend and instead started a rock band with him, as I had learned that working with him was in fact what I really wanted.

In the year 1999-2000 I read a lot of books about the mind and body and did a lot of thinking about what it means to be a serious chess player. I found that the conclusions helped me a great deal in the short period of success I experienced. I have tried to put as much of this knowledge as possible into this book.

The other reasons why I feel that I have the right to write such a book, and to suggest to others that it is worth reading, are the following: I am well educated in how the mind works, and through my education I have trained the ability to analyse basic human behaviour. I have about twelve years of experience in teaching chess and communicating chess knowledge to others. And finally, I am not afraid of being wrong. This final point is, in my opinion, the most important, not only because I will argue my case with all my heart, but also because I will not defend it as I would defend myself. I will tell you what I think and I believe that I am right more often than not. But it is not the main point for me to be right, it is much more important to make you, the reader, think about these things, and find your own truth.

The final game I want to include in this introduction is the best game I played among these thirty. My opponent is also, incidentally, the strongest opposition I have ever faced. The game has no right to be in the book, of course, or at least none other than making the author happy. It is not connected to any kind of argument, but it does have a story.

It also seemed to have made an impact on my opponent, as he went on to win the next ten games he played (three in this tournament and the first seven in the next).

Shabalov–Aagaard
Hamburg 1999
Nimzo-Indian Defence

During the tournament I was staying in a flat with Coach. Every day we took a twenty minute journey on the subway to the playing hall. Whoever finished first would often go directly home, not waiting for the other to finish.

Before this game I asked Coach for the keys so I would not need to disturb his game when I had lost. The moment I had spoken the words I realised how awful they were. Coach smiled and asked me to sit next to him and pretend I was still sitting in my seat. I did so. He asked me what Jacob needed in order to play well.

I do not remember how the conversation continued, but I do remember how strong and confident I felt during the game, and how well deserved it was that I won. If I could play and feel like this in every game I might have held a high level of motivation. As it is, I chose not to. I am a happy amateur and nothing else, although this game will live in my heart for a long time.

1 d4 ♘f6 2 c4 e6 3 ♘c3 ♗b4 4 e3 0-0
5 ♗d3 d5 6 ♘f3 c5 7 0-0 cxd4 8 exd4
dxc4 9 ♗xc4 b6 10 ♕e2 ♗b7 11 ♖d1
♘bd7 12 ♗f4 ♗xc3! 13 bxc3 ♘d5 14
♗d2 ♖c8! 15 ♖ac1 ♕c7 16 ♗b5 a6!?
17 ♗xd7

Taking the pawn with 17 ♗xa6?
♗xa6 18 ♕xa6 gives Black good compensation after 18...♕c4.

**17...♕xd7 18 c4 ♘f6 19 ♘e5 ♕a4!?
20 ♖b1 b5 21 ♗e1! ♗e4 22 ♖b4 ♕c2
23 ♖d2 ♕c1 24 c5?**

This is a positional error. Shabalov is trying to attack my queen but is too ambitious. After the alternative 24 cxb5 I would have a lot of play for the pawn, but White might still have kept a small edge.

24...♕a3 25 ♖b3 ♕a4! 26 g4!?

The usual Shabalov style – burning bridges before crossing them.

**26...♗d5 27 g5 ♘e4 28 ♖dd3! b4 29
♖xb4 ♕e8!**

After this apparent surprise Black suddenly takes over the initiative.

30 ♕g4 ♘xg5 31 ♘c4?

After 31 ♕xg5! f6 32 ♕e3 fxe5 33 ♕xe5 the black pieces will find it difficult to get to the white king, although it looks promising.

31...f6 32 ♘d6 ♕g6 33 ♕g3

33 ♖g3!? ♖cd8 (33...♗f3? 34 ♘xc8!)
34 ♔f1 is a stronger defence.

**33...♖cd8 34 ♔f1 a5 35 ♖a4 ♕h5 36
♖aa3 f5 37 h4**

This loses. After 37 f4!? ♘e4 38 ♕h3
♕xh3+ 39 ♖xh3 ♘xd6 40 cxd6 ♖xd6
41 ♗xa5 ♗c4+ 42 ♔e1 ♖xd4 43 ♗c7
Black remains firmly placed in the driving seat.

**37...♘e4 38 ♘xe4 fxe4 39 ♖dc3 ♖f6
40 ♕g5 ♕f7 41 ♖g3?**

41 c6 ♖f8 42 ♖c2 ♗xc6 43 ♖xa5 offers more resistance, but Black must be well on the way to gaining the full point.

**41...♖f8 42 ♔g1 h6! 43 ♕d2 ♕h5 44
♖xa5 ♕xh4 45 ♖a7**

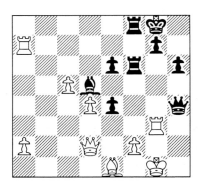

45...♕xg3+ 46 fxg3 ♖f1+ 0-1

CHAPTER TWO

Real Chess Players

Korchnoi used to say that 'Chess you don't learn, chess you understand.' I must say I could not disagree more. As I see it there are three kinds of talent for chess, music, mathematics or any other discipline in which we see prodigies. First there is a very limited group of naturals. In chess we mainly talk about Capablanca, Reshevsky, Karpov and, more recently, perhaps Radjabov. These people really understand chess; they do not have to learn it. They can improve, of course, but the basics are very natural to them. Then we have the majority of people, who have to work to achieve any real ability. We need to learn about chess and, fortunately, we can. Finally there are people who will never learn chess, no matter how hard they try. Some of these people still enjoy the game but the positional basics will forever be foreign to them.

If we assume that we can always improve our understanding of chess then we are optimistic (and we should always be optimistic). Let Korchnoi doubt us if he likes – we are not playing chess for his sake, but for ourselves.

Now, so far, so good. But what should we try to learn? In my search for the answer to this question I have read many interviews with top Grandmasters, deciding to follow the path laid out by Garry Kasparov and his notion of 'Real Chess Players.' Kasparov said in the mid-1990s that there were only 5-6 'real' chess players in the world. His definition of a 'real' player has nothing to do with rating (even though ratings naturally illustrate who is 'real' and who is not), calculating power or opening knowledge. No, it is far subtler. *A Real Chess Player is someone who knows where the pieces belong.*

With this notion in mind I have come to realise that most games – even among the top players – are decided on a superiority in the understanding of positional play. And the funny thing about it all is that when you analyse this it is happening on a very simple level. I believe that 'Real Chess Players' would never put a piece on awkward squares; only lesser players do so. When someone like Kasparov or Kramnik calculate I believe that they do not consider a lot of moves. Instead they penetrate deeper into a few minor differences in the possibilities, since these can prove important. They are also guided much more in their calculation by this positional understanding. If the pieces start going to the wrong squares, then the line is unfavourable and should be abandoned.

Below we have a game between two grandmasters that helps illustrate my point. White has a rating of 2515 while Black, at 2650, was ranked 20th in the world at the time (and a few years later – in 1999 – finished second in the FIDE world championships).

Rivas Pastor–Akopian
Leon 1995
Semi-Slav Defence

1 d4 d5 2 c4 c6 3 ♘f3 ♘f6 4 e3 e6 5 ♘bd2 ♘bd7 6 ♗d3 c5 7 b3 cxd4 8 exd4 b6 9 ♗b2 ♗b7 10 0-0 ♗d6

After 10...♗e7 we have a normal theoretical position usually arising after 1 d4 ♘f6 2 c4 e6 3 ♘f3 b6 4 e3 ♗b7 5 ♗d3 d5 6 0-0 ♗e7 7 b3 c5 8 ♗b2 cxd4 9 exd4 ♘bd7 10 ♘bd2, although there it is Black to move! Alas, Black has lost a tempo in the opening. Now let us jump forward a few moves:
11 ♕e2 0-0 12 ♘e5 ♕e7 13 ♖ad1 ♖ac8 14 ♗b1 ♖fd8 15 ♘df3 ♘e4 16 ♘xd7 ♖xd7 17 cxd5 exd5 18 ♘e5 ♖dc7 19 f3 ♘c3 20 ♗xc3 ♖xc3

In the diagram position Black already has the advantage. The two bishops will give him a lasting edge in the endgame and, as we are about to see, it is not too difficult to convert the win. I am certain

that Rivas Pastor was fully aware of this but, somehow, he did not demonstrate the same ability as his opponent to manoeuvre pieces, and thus found himself in this unpleasant situation.

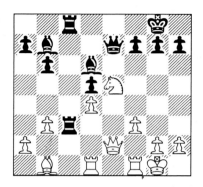

Akopian, certainly, in no way calculated better than his opponent. He had not foreseen all White's moves, rather he was searching for optimum coordination between his pieces. I do not think Akopian is on Kasparov's list of 'real' players but he did say that Khalifman, Akopian and a few others were serious players when commenting on the 1999 Las Vegas event, while others among the final eight or sixteen players were 'tourists.'

Let us return to the diagram position (after 20...♖xc3) and ask how Black has engineered such promising prospects. What has he done? The answer is: not much, really, simply posting his pieces on rather obvious squares. What really happened was that White weakened his c-file, allowed the enemy knight to come to e4 and c3 and added to his troubles by misplacing his pieces.

Let us take a look at the moves White played. First I believe the rooks should have been on c1 and e1 instead of d1 and f1, but this is not such a serious problem. Secondly, and this is far worse, the bishop looks stupid on b1, being better on d3 – there is simply no attack. And why, oh why, did White exchange on pawns d5 and open the c-file? This seems utterly pointless. Additionally, the knight had no real reason to go to f3. White actually used four moves with his knights to achieve what Black did with one move, to obtain an outpost in the middle of the board (and Black's knight had a future, while it is hard to see where White's is going).

If asked about the merits of White's knight manoeuvres Rivas Pastor would himself explain that White did nothing good for his position in this way, that you should not exchange pieces that have moved more times than their opposite numbers (an old Nimzowitsch dictum, which is obviously limited – see Chapter 3). But would he be able to suggest a good alternative plan for White? I do not believe so. This is where the difference between the two players would be apparent. Akopian would have some suggestions, but Rivas Pastor would most likely not – at least not at the time the game was played because (I assume) he would have tried something else. Perhaps there were doubts surrounding any possible option(s) considered by Rivas Pastor.

Akopian, on the other hand, was probably never in doubt, as what he played made perfect sense. Incidentally, to those of you unaware of Akopian's history, he is an Armenian player educated in the final years of the Soviet Union, affording him a chess education

of forgotten times, the likes of which we will not see in the future.

If you cannot fully appreciate that Black is a lot better after 20...♖xc3 you might want to have a discussion with yourself and/or a friend in order to acquire a better understanding of the differences between the respective set-ups. The game continued:

21 ♖fe1 f6 22 ♘d3 ♕xe2 23 ♖xe2 ♔f7 24 ♖ee1 h5 25 g3 a5 26 ♖c1 ♗a6 27 ♖xc3 ♖xc3 28 ♖d1 g5 29 ♔f2 h4 30 ♔g2 ♗b5 31 g4 ♗a6 32 h3 a4 33 bxa4 ♖a3 34 ♘c1 ♗f4 35 ♗c2 ♗c4 36 ♗b3 ♗xb3 37 ♘xb3 ♖xa2+ 38 ♔f1 ♖b2 39 ♖d3 ♖a2 40 ♖c3 ♖xa4 0-1

Even games between the world's elite are decided by similar positional factors. The following game is a modern classic, mainly due to Kasparov's annotations in *New In Chess* magazine. It is interesting that Movsesian, after Kasparov's 'tourists' remark (which included the youngster), wrote an open letter to *The Week in Chess*, attacking Kasparov's statement. However, after their game was played it transpired that Kasparov had not even read the letter! Anyway, this is how the game went. The quotes are taken from Kasparov's own account in *NIC* magazine.

Movsesian–Kasparov
Sarajevo 2000
Sicilian Defence

1 e4 c5 2 ♘f3 d6 3 d4 cxd4 4 ♘xd4 ♘f6 5 ♘c3 a6 6 ♗e3 e6 7 f3 b5 8 ♕d2

Here Kasparov notes that 8 g4! is more precise, forcing Black to play either 8...h6 or 8...♘fd7. Now Black has time to develop his pieces more naturally.

8...♘bd7 9 0-0-0 ♗b7 10 g4 ♘b6 11 ♛f2 ♘fd7

Kasparov writes: 'It struck me that he played all this without paying much attention to the correct move order. This position we had analyzed quite extensively'.

12 ♔b1 ♖c8 13 ♗d3?

'But we never analyzed this...'

(Note Kasparov's poetic use of the -yze endings)

13...♖xc3 14 bxc3 ♛c7

Kasparov is not completely happy about this move, which he calls an inaccuracy. His argument is based on logic. Black will play ...♘a4, ...♗e7 and ...0-0 no matter what but, depending on White's moves, it is not altogether clear where he should place his queen. Sometimes on c7, as in the game, and sometimes on a5.

15 ♘e2 ♗e7 16 g5

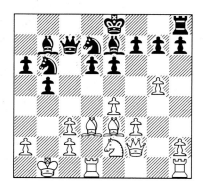

16...0-0!

Black is now fully developed and it is time to evaluate the position. Again we turn to Mr. Kasparov: 'After the game Movsesian told me that he had played a lot of games with this line on the ICC *(Internet Chess Club)* against Van Wely, investigating the position. But Van Wely never castled. From my perspective it's a matter of chess culture. If you take on c3 and the knight goes to a4, then Black is fine. Black need not look for an immediate approach. You castle, you put your knight on e5 and the queen on c7 or a5, and you have many options. Sometimes you strive for d5 or even for f5. The exchange means very little, since we both have such attacks going, the quantity of pieces is often more important than their quality. I was surprised that Movsesian didn't realise this. Unless you exchange queens you play with equal material, plus the black pawn structure is better and the white king is more exposed.'

And so he continues for another long paragraph. The important thing about these words is that in no way is he backing up his move with variations. It is a matter of Chess Culture. Movsesian apparently had a great advantage in knowing the position from all the 'blitz' games, but in practice it did not help him at all. Of course Kasparov has an enormous amount of opening knowledge, and (of course) he wins some games in the opening, but I believe that his greatest gain from analysing his openings so exhaustively – as is clearly the case – is a deep feeling for both where the pieces belong and how they should co-ordinate. Many people see Kasparov as mostly a tactical player, but this underestimates the extent of his talent. It is true that Kasparov plays better in dynamically charged positions, but this might have more to do with his personality than with his understanding of chess – please do not forget that such things are also important.

The rest of the game illustrates Kasparov's claims quite well:
17 h4 ♘a4 18 ♗c1 ♘e5 19 h5 d5 20 ♕h2 ♗d6 21 ♕h3 ♘xd3 22 cxd3 b4 23 cxb4 ♖c8 24 ♔a1 dxe4 25 fxe4 ♗xe4 26 g6 ♗xh1 27 ♕xh1 ♗xb4 28 gxf7+ ♔f8 29 ♕g2 ♖b8 30 ♗b2 ♘xb2 31 ♘d4

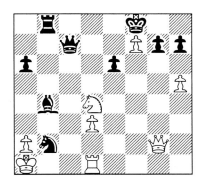

31...♘xd1 32 ♘xe6+ ♔xf7 0-1

Now for another example from Kasparov:

Shirov–Kasparov
Dortmund 1992
King's Indian Defence

1 d4 ♘f6 2 c4 g6 3 ♘c3 ♗g7 4 e4 d6 5 f3 0-0 6 ♗e3 e5 7 ♘ge2 c6 8 ♕d2 ♘bd7 9 0-0-0 a6 10 ♔b1 b5 11 ♘c1 exd4 12 ♗xd4 ♖e8

This was the first game at this level with the immediate capture 11...exd4. Later Kasparov preferred the alternative continuation 12...b4! hitting the white knight, when after 13 ♘a4 c5 Black obtains full equality.

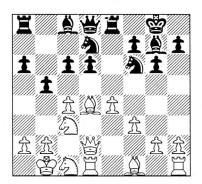

13 ♗xf6?!

This move looks risky, but I do not have the certainty of Kasparov. In NIC he wrote: 'Frankly speaking this decision amazed me. In my previous calculations I had not even considered this exchange, which wins a pawn by force. The value of the dark-squared bishop is too great (especially since White has castled queenside) to swap it for such a trifle. And there is more: up to this moment Black was objectively the weaker side; objectively he has no grounds for playing ambitiously. So it will not be long before he will be confronted. On the other hand my intuition says that when my King's Indian bishop remains, while its counterpart is gone, Black cannot be completely bad'.

Kasparov has no doubt that Black is doing fine despite the fact that he is losing a vital pawn in his structure, since the dark-square domination his bishop provides is far more important. This is the way to think about chess. Of course, you constantly need to calculate variations, but these should be based on such evaluation schemes.

13...♕xf6!

Neither the bishop nor the knight has

anything to do on f6, so Black decides to go for the exchange of queens as this is the only line that does not ruin the harmony of his pieces.

14 ♕xd6 ♕xd6 15 ♖xd6 ♘e5 16 f4?

This is too ambitious. Kasparov writes: 'Now, after this optimistic advance, can we really speak of an advantage for Black for the first time. With sensible and modest play by White it would only have been a matter of sufficient compensation for the pawn.'

Now, why does Kasparov consider this move to be poor? There are some positional advantages to the move which should be mentioned. White is trying to close down Black's bishop as well as improve his own on f1 by placing his pawns on dark squares. Additionally White is limiting the pressure on c4, as 16...♘xc4? 17 ♗xc4 bxc4 18 e5 is out of the question for Black. But these 'advantages' are superficial. Black will soon be able to free his bishop with ...f7-f6, which at the same time will open the e-file for his rook. And the bishop on f1 is not really gaining any freedom because Black can soon reach f2 with his knight, depriving White of the d3-square. Moreover it is the bishop on c8 that benefits from the advance of the white pawns, by gaining control of the f5-b1 diagonal. Finally White does have the c4-pawn to consider. This is true, but after Kasparov's suggested 16 cxb5 the problem is also out of the way. Others then arise, but these are less significant. Kasparov's annotations in NIC suggest that the position is more or less in balance.

16...♘g4 17 e5 ♘f2 18 ♖g1 ♗f5+ 19 ♔a1 b4 20 ♘a4 f6!

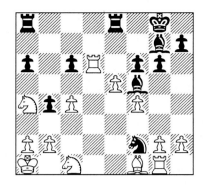

Based on the tactic 21 exf6 ♖e1!. Here Shirov returns the pawn, entering an ending with absolutely no drawing chances.

21 e6?

Kasparov writes the following: 'Next morning when this game had already receded into the past, Shirov came up to me and suggested that he could have 'maintained his advantage' if he had played 21 g4!? ♗xg4 22 ♗g2.' The difference between the players becomes quite apparent here. Shirov, being mainly a calculating player with a very imaginative style, was at this point in his career less strong on purely positional judgements. I find it weird to speak of an advantage for White with knights on a4 and c1, a rook on g1 and a bishop on f1. Of course the bishop is improved by 21 g4, but it is nevertheless difficult to believe that White should be better. Kasparov continues: 'Fortunately I also like to analyse my games at home, so I was able to console Alexei and demonstrate a beautiful win for myself: 21 g4 ♘xg4! 22 ♗d3 (22 ♗h3 ♘e3 23 ♗xf5 ♘xf5 24 ♖xc6 fxe5 also favours Black – J.A) 22...fxe5!! (22...♘h6 is less convincing...) 23 ♗xf5 gxf5 24 h3 exf4 25 hxg4 f3 26 gxf5 (26 ♘d3 fxg4 27 ♖xg4 ♖e1+!! 28 ♘xe1 f2, or 26 ♖d2 fxg4 27 ♖xg4 ♖ad8! 28 ♖xd8 ♖xd8 29 ♖g1 f2 30 ♖f1 ♖d2 31 ♔b1 ♗d4 32 ♘b3 ♖e2 33 ♘xd4 ♖e1+). With this position in our minds we parted at the time, but later I came to the conclusion that 21 e5 is absolutely worthless. The continuation 21 g4 is not just much more interesting, it is also objectively stronger. After 26...f2 27 ♖f1 ♖e1 28 ♖d1 ♖ae8 White keeps his drawing chances alive by playing 29 ♘d3 ♖xd1+ 30 ♖xd1 ♗d4 31 ♔b1 ♖e2 32 ♖h1 ♖e4 33 ♔c2 ♖g4. I do not see a clear win for me here anyway. Still, there is no doubt about Black having the advantage.'

Actually I think Kasparov is underestimating his position here. In the near future White will have to give up his best knight for Black's passed pawn, after which the material situation is equal. The ♘a4 is obviously useless and the h-pawn is an important asset. I believe Black is winning, but it is true that in practical play this is not always so important. For this reason we might as well call it an enormous black advantage.

21...♖xe6

After this Shirov failed to put up any kind of convincing resistance in the rest of the game.

22 ♖xe6 ♗xe6 23 ♗e2 f5 24 ♘b3 ♗f7 25 ♘a5 ♖d8 26 ♖f1 ♘g4 27 ♖d1 ♖xd1+ 28 ♗xd1 ♘e3 29 ♗f3 ♘xc4 30 ♘xc6 a5 31 ♘d8 ♘d2 32 ♗c6 ♗h6 33 g3 ♘f1 34 ♘b6 ♘xh2 35 ♘d7 ♗g7 36 ♘e5 ♗xe5 37 fxe5 ♔f8 38 e6 ♗e8 39 ♗xe8 ♔xe8 40 ♘c6 ♘f1 0-1

How Kasparov managed to win this game is not too important for our discussion, rather the difference in understanding described by Kasparov. It seems obvious to me that Kasparov is correct. It is an advanced example along the lines of the Movsesian game, where how the pieces play is more important than their numeric value. In my opinion Kasparov is the greatest master of understanding the dynamics in chess. His understanding of positional compensation is unchallenged. Shirov, on the other hand, is a great calculating player, far greater than Kasparov, but with a slightly lesser understanding of the deepest aspects. Actually, Shirov writes in his excellent book on his own games, *Fire on Board*, that he believes the endgame to be his strongest phase because he is able to use his calculating powers to a maximum when there are only few pieces remaining.

So the difference between the two players in this game, and in all their other encounters, seems to be Kasparov's superior understanding – not his preparation or his imagination, but the foundation on which these are built. Actually, although Kasparov is known for his fantastic preparation – which has often won the games for him – he claims that statistics show that he generally does not do well in the opening against his strongest adversaries. I have some doubts concerning this claim, but the following game illustrates very well that some of the success he does have in the opening is due to a great understanding and not to the assistance of this or that particular piece of computer software.

The next game is taken from one of the all-time highs of Kasparov's career.

His long-time desire to blow Karpov off the board and break his prophylactic style apart never succeeded as well as in this game. In my opinion this is the first time that Kasparov was Karpov's complete superior. In 1990, the last match they played, he had won 13-11 playing some very impressive games. But then Karpov managed, at times, to achieve success by breaking down the games to dry, positional exercises, an area of the game in which he was far stronger than Kasparov. As argued in Chapter 5 Kasparov does not have a great feel for chess; he is not a natural. But his determination has always more than compensated for this. Obviously he is talented, but more for the dynamics and the direct than for structural, long-term features. Anyway, in this game Karpov produced an idea that was relatively new at the time, and for which Kasparov had nothing prepared. But simply by choosing the obvious line of action Kasparov breaks down White's position until only ruins remain, forcing all the white pieces to retreat to the back rank. There is a demonstration here that excellent opening play and understanding far outweigh opening preparation – but only in this game, of course. I do not want to make a general argument about the opening, only show that a good understanding of a particular position – the Kings Indian Defence in this case – is often just as important as having prepared a new idea. Let's face it, there are not so many direct wins hidden in the opening these days, since what players have missed when analysing by themselves, they tend to find when the help of computers is enlisted.

Karpov-Kasparov
Linares 1993
King's Indian Defence

1 d4 ♘f6 2 c4 g6 3 ♘c3 ♗g7 4 e4 d6 5 f3

The Kings Indian was Kasparov's best choice during the 1990s, until he had problems dealing with 5 ♘f3 0-0 6 ♗e2 e5 7 0-0 ♘c6 8 d5 ♘e7 9 b4 ♘h5 10 ♖e1, just like everyone else. The King's Indian has lost a number of followers over the last few years simply due to the problems presented to Black by this line. After a bad loss against Kramnik, Kasparov went home and worked on the Tartakower variation of the Queen's Gambit Declined and the Nimzo-Indian. Unfortunately he also worked on the Grünfeld Defence, which never seemed to work quite well for him in practise and also cost him the second game in his match with Kramnik.

5...0-0 6 ♗e3 e5 7 ♘ge2 ♘bd7 8 ♕d2 c6 9 ♖d1?

Normal is 9 0-0-0. The idea behind the text is to put pressure on the d6-pawn and retain the possibility of kingside castling. Unfortunately this is not a very logical idea. Black is already practically fully developed, the c8-bishop having no better square, nor the a8-rook. Black's other rook could be on e8, but not before the tension in the centre evaporates; for now it is fine where it is. White, on the other hand, is now far away from castling. All his ideas will be carried out with the king in the centre, and such a strategy is simply too risky to promise any kind of advantage. Every time White has to make a decision there is also the matter of king safety to consider. White also has to develop somehow, and it is not easy to see how. Had he (correctly) castled queenside the h1-rook would suddenly be perfect, as h2-h4-h5 comes and an attack is a real possibility. Additionally the f1-bishop would then be like its opposite number on c8 (having no better square at its disposal), this is okay when White no longer has to castle kingside. Logic, then, is against the move selected by Karpov. Previous practise was not. Karpov chose to follow the statistics. As for Kasparov, he had to follow his own understanding of the position, based on logic and experience. I cannot help getting the feeling that Karpov did not have a fair chance...

9...a6!

The same move that is played against 9 0-0-0, and the idea is also still the same. White's structure needs to be attacked and the only real weakness is c4.

10 dxe5 ♘xe5

This is the natural move here. The knight is perfect on e5, whereas Black would seem somewhat cramped after 10...dxe5.

11 b3

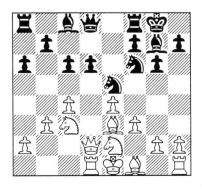

I dislike this move as it weakens the structure on the queenside and does absolutely nothing for the development of White's pieces. After 11 ♘g3 ♗e6 12 ♕xd6 ♕xd6 13 ♖xd6 ♘xc4 14 ♗xc4 ♗xc4 the position remains pleasant for Black, but it is time for White to realise that his idea has no value.

11...b5!

As White has a significant disadvantage in development Black will benefit from opening up the position. Note that this is at the cost of a pawn (d6), a familiar theme, perhaps, but nonetheless it can become quite complicated when put into practice.

12 cxb5

This also seems to be dangerous. Of course Black is fine after 12 ♕xd6 ♕xd6 13 ♖xd6 bxc4 but White is not particularly worse. Perhaps Kasparov had used a lot of time here figuring out how to meet Karpov's opening surprise, thus making Karpov optimistic.

12...axb5

Opening the a-file. As we shall see ...♖xa2 is very relevant indeed. Now Karpov receives his small gift – a pawn (all these advantages for only a pawn...).

13 ♕xd6 ♘fd7

No exchange of queens this time; not with the king in the centre. First you are going to sweat a little, Anatoly.

14 f4?!

This move is proof that Karpov is still too optimistic regarding the merits of his position – now the situation has changed from dangerous to terrible. Black now has time to attack before White gets close to completing development. Kasparov offers the following lines: 14 ♕d2 b4 15 ♘a4 ♖xa4 16 bxa4

♘c4 with compensation for the sacrificed material, and equally so after 14 a4 bxa4 15 ♘xa4 ♖xa4 16 bxa4 ♘c4. However, the game continuation is worse. Notice that 14 ♘g3 ♘xf3+ returns the sacrificed material and leaves White in an even more dangerous situation than before.

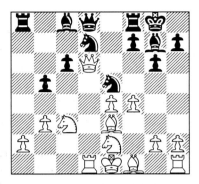

14...b4!

This is one of the great moves in this game, keeping the pressure at a maximum and trying to rid White of developed pieces. Karpov's next decision is terrible, but for some reason he has always had some kind of affection for placing his pieces on the back rank. Is this because they can be attacked only from one side?

15 ♘b1?

There is simply not time for this, and soon the a-pawn will be lost. In fact it is already so bad that the pawn does not matter, rather the activation of Black's rook. I personally do not understand how one of the greatest defensive players in history could make such a terrible move.

15 ♕xb4? Is not an alternative since 15...c5! 16 ♗xc5 ♘xc5 17 ♖xd8 ♘ed3+ wins material. 15 ♘a4 ♖xa4 16 bxa4

♘c4 also looks poor, but White should have tried 15 fxe5! bxc3 16 ♘xc3 ♗xe5. One possible continuation is 17 ♕xc6 ♗xc3+!? 18 ♕xc3 ♕h4+ and White is under considerable pressure, albeit in much less trouble than the game.

15...♘g4

As in the game with Shirov the advance of the f-pawn serves only to create weaknesses in the white camp. Black's knight has no problem exploiting the resulting weaknesses.

16 ♗d4 ♗xd4 17 ♕xd4

Forced. White would like to play 17 ♘xd4 but this is punished by 17...♖xa2 18 ♘xc6 ♕h4+ 19 g3 ♘xh2!!, finishing him off. This is an indication of how poor White's situation has become. I truly believe that, generally, a position must be very unhealthy when only unnatural moves at your disposal.

17...♖xa2 18 h3 c5!

Illustrating how awfully the queen is placed, even if it is centralised. A piece is, of course, not in a good position if it has nowhere to go. This counts for all pieces in most positions.

19 ♕g1

The alternative was 19 ♕d3 ♗a6 20 ♕f3 (20 ♕xd7 ♕h4+ 21 g3 ♖xe2+ 22 ♗xe2 ♕xg3+ wins for Black by checks...) 20...♘de5! 21 fxe5 ♘xe5 22 ♕e3 ♘d3+ 23 ♖xd3 ♕xd4 24 ♕xd3 ♗xd3 and the non-existent development of White's forces will be illustrated soon when they start to drop off the board (Nunn: 'Loose pieces drop off!'). Also ...c5-c4 is important since the b-pawn is a killer.

19...♘gf6 20 e5 ♘e4 21 h4?!

Another doubtful move. Karpov was obviously tired of looking at ...♕h4+, but it is nevertheless necessary to bring the queen back into the game with 21 ♕e3 ♗b7 22 ♘d2 ♖xd2 23 ♖xd2 ♘xd2 24 ♕xd2 ♘b6. Every black piece is superior to its white counterpart, and the weaknesses on b3 and g2 are terrible. However, either you resign or you try the best defence, and why should you ever resign?

21...c4 22 ♘c1

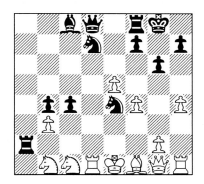

The following sacrifice is quite nice but Black surely has more than one route to victory. Look at White's pieces! Do you really need variations?

22...c3! 23 ♘xa2 c2 24 ♕d4

Okay — we can take a look at the winning lines anyway, just to avoid upsetting anyone. But you can see what I mean, can't you?

24 ♖c1 ♘xe5! 25 ♖xc2 (25 fxe5 cxb1♕ 26 ♖xb1 ♕d2 mate!) 25...♗g4 26 ♖d2 (26 ♗e2 ♘d3+ 27 ♗xd3 ♕xd3 does not help White) 26...♘xd2 27 ♘xd2 (27 fxe5 ♘e4 28 ♗e2 ♗xe2 29 ♔xe2 ♘g3+ 30 ♔f3 ♘xh1 31 ♕xh1 ♕d5+ and Black will help himself to the enemy pieces one by one...) 27...♖e8!! 28 fxe5 ♖xe5+ 29 ♔f2 ♕xd2+ 30 ♔g3 ♖e3+ 31 ♔h2 ♖h3 mate! A nice finish.

24...cxd1♕+ 25 ♔xd1

Black also wins after 25 ♕xd1 ♘g3 26 ♖h3 ♘xf1 27 ♔xf1 ♘c5 28 ♕xd8 ♖xd8 29 ♖e3 ♖d1+ 30 ♖e1 ♗a6+ 31 ♔f2 ♘d3+.

25...♘dc5 26 ♕xd8 ♖xd8+ 27 ♔c2 ♘f2 0-1

Here Karpov lost on time, but 28 ♖g1 ♗f5+ 29 ♔b2 ♘d1+ 30 ♔a1 ♘xb3 anyway leads to mate.

Kasparov's play surely looks impressive, but the reasoning behind the moves is not too complicated. The knight on a4 is as good as the rook on d1 and White's pawn structure is damaged — therefore Black is better. Black's bishop on g7 is enormous so the pawn does not matter, and with White's king trapped in the centre Black has more than enough compensation for the pawn. Such was the initial logic behind these three wins. Not complicated at all. However, Kasparov's play was indeed impressive. Yet the difficult part for him seemed not to be finding the key to the position — he knew this from experience and a strong sense of chess logic — rather the impressive part was the transformation of logic into strong tactics based on exact calculation.

If I claim that Kasparov does not calculate better than Shirov, then how can he then calculate so precisely? Well, the question has already been answered above — he knew what to look for. In the game against Shirov ...f7-f6 was the obvious idea because the g7-bishop is Black's major asset, and liberating this piece is therefore the natural strategy for Black. The rest is a question of implementation. Against Movsesian it was all about getting the pieces into play.

Basically, he simply developed and then opened the centre for his bishops. Not a difficult game for a top player. In the final game, against Karpov, the theme was brutality. Respect for pawns (little ones) would not blow White's position apart. A violent mind did. In my opinion 14...b4! is the really beautiful move in that regard, serving to put Karpov in serious trouble.

It is all a question of finding a way to prove your logic via calculation. Kasparov did so brilliantly.

Did you find this difficult? Are you impressed with the way Kasparov transformed simple ideas into brilliant moves? Or are you perplexed that top players like Shirov, Movsesian and even Karpov would show an ignorance of such ideas? I will try to provide some answers as to why.

I believe that Kasparov is much more aware of using logic in his games; he might often support his moves with many variations, but this seems to be more about actually proving his ideas. When Kasparov has an idea I think he works much harder at the board to find a way to put his logic to effective use in the form of concrete moves. He is very determined indeed to prove that he is right, and this is often the decisive force in his games.

As for Shirov, I find it difficult to believe that he works on a fully conscious level in terms of ideas, rather there is more feeling and less verbalisation. Playing through his games collection these ideas seem to be very bizarre indeed. I met him once on a train from Hamburg to Copenhagen and he told me that when he started out as a serious player he realised that computers would be very important, and this led him to create a style in which he has to produce something himself, where computers are of no help. Such an approach is by no means based on respect for material, being more a kind of chaos theory, if you like. As impressive as this style and his games are, there just has to be a price to pay somewhere, and I feel that it is facility to see pure logic that is somewhat weakened. Consequently Shirov could believe that he had an advantage in his game against Kasparov, above. For him variations are the key to almost any position, as they form the only logic left in the mess he tends to find himself in. His ideas are almost always based on twists and turns in the game rather than, for example, weak squares or strong bishops.

Karpov has a great feeling for positional play. We shall see below how he takes each and every possibility away from Kasparov in a game from their 1990 match. What the game above, the games in this match and several later games have shown is that Karpov cannot control Kasparov when the latter becomes really dynamic. Karpov has this unique style of prophylaxis, where he undermines or prevents the opponent's ideas as soon as he discovers them (relevant games on this subject can be found in the Dvoretsky books, where the annotations are terrific). During the period of their first encounters he was able to restrain Kasparov's aggression, but as the number of games between them grew Kasparov learned to include positional ideas in his attacks, and in the end Karpov was unable to maintain control. This is particularly the case in the 1990 match in New York and Lyon.

Movsesian is a player yet to reach the very top of the rankings, and he seems less determined than Kasparov, for example. While he is not world champion material he is nevertheless a great player who you should watch out for.

Which of these games did you find most difficult to understand? Well, I guess it is a matter of style, but for me it was the Akopian game, since I am a dynamic player. I find these little inaccuracies more difficult to notice than moves like 15 ♘b1? or allowing ...♖xc3.

When you play through the Karpov-Kasparov game, below, you will see that Kasparov could probably 'feel' the game, while for Karpov the game was more problematic. It is all a matter of strengths and weaknesses. I see Kramnik – whom we will also investigate below – as a development of the style of Karpov. He has a wonderful feel for the two bishops and a definition of drawn and lost positions. However, in terms of his match with Kasparov, he had had the opportunity to see his opponent in action and, more importantly, study and learn from his games for a decade before facing him over the board himself.

Enough talk – let's move on to another great game of logic.

Karpov–Kasparov
World Ch. New York/Lyon 1990
Grunfeld Defence

1 d4 ♘f6 2 c4 g6 3 ♘c3 d5 4 cxd5 ♘xd5 5 e4 ♘xc3 6 bxc3 ♗g7 7 ♗e3 c5 8 ♕d2 0-0 9 ♘f3 ♗g4

9...♕a5 (met by 10 ♖b1) is the main line these days.

10 ♘g5!?

This was a strong new idea at the time, addressing the fight for the centre, of course! Black wants to exchange the knight for his bishop since only the knight supports the centre, where all the action is on the dark squares. Since the second game in the Kramnik-Kasparov match the views concerning the centre in this opening are no longer the same, but that is another story.

10...cxd4

10...h6?! would be a careless weakening move, met effectively by 11 h3! ♗h5? 12 g4! hxg5 13 gxh5 gxh5 14 ♖g1 and Black's position is very weak around the king.

11 cxd4 ♘c6 12 h3 ♗d7!

The only available square for the bishop. The tricky lines with 12...♗xd4?! 13 ♗xd4 ♕xd4 14 ♕xd4 ♘xd4 15 hxg4 ♘c2+ 16 ♔d2 ♘xa1 17 ♗d3 and 12...♘xd4?! 13 hxg4 ♖c8 14 ♖d1! ♘c2+ (14...♖c2 15 ♕b4 ♘c6 has been suggested but after 16 ♖xd8 ♖xd8!? 17 ♘xf7! White seems to be winning material, e.g. 17...♖d7 18 ♘e5!) 15 ♔e2 ♕c7 16 ♔f3! ♖fd8 17 ♗d3 leave Black with insufficient compensation for the sacrificed material.

13 ♖b1

This might not be the strongest due to the reply found by Kasparov. Gurevich suggests the simple 13 ♗e2 as an improvement.

13...♖c8!

This is the move Black would most like to make so Kasparov, with his sense of logic and dynamics, finds a way to implement it.

14 ♘f3

14 ♖xb7? ♘xd4 15 ♗xd4 ♗xd4 16 ♕xd4 ♖c1+ 17 ♔d2 ♖d1+! 18 ♔xd1 ♗a4+ is the tactic behind Black's idea.

14...♘a5 15 ♗d3 ♗e6

This is the correct move as no other black piece needs to be improved as much as this bishop. 15...♘c4?! 16 ♗xc4 ♖xc4 17 0-0 (17 ♖xb7? would never have been considered by Karpov, who would have finished his development – his sense of danger is probably only weakened in home preparation, and not so much over the board) 17...♕c7 18 ♖fc1 is a shade better for White. There is no reason why the d7-bishop should be superior to the f3-knight.

16 0-0 ♗c4 17 ♖fd1

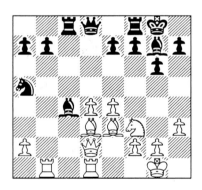

A practical move, after which the pieces protecting the d-pawn have the freedom to go elsewhere. This positional idea was first developed by Nimzowitsch, who called it hyper-prophylactics.

17...b5?

This move is an obvious mistake to some people. To me it is less so, but I understand the logic behind it. The move in itself achieves very little. Black already has control over c4 and need not reinforce it. And now the b-pawn is a weakness (as is the c5-square, by the way) and must later be protected by ...a7-a6, which is not an improvement for the a-pawn, either. Kasparov was never a master of these small moves. Is it a matter of patience? Could be – who knows? A better move is 17...b6, which blocks the b-file and creates only a slight weakness on c6. However, I would prefer White's position.

18 ♗g5!

Addressing 18...e6, which would be the natural follow-up for Black. The text is precisely the style of Karpov – Black wants to prevent d4-d5 but has no good place for his queen, so the prevention of ...e7-e6 makes life awkward for Black.

18...a6 19 ♖bc1! ♗xd3

Probably the only decent move. After 19...♖e8 20 ♗b1! Black is out of good squares for his pieces.

20 ♖xc8! ♕xc8 21 ♕xd3

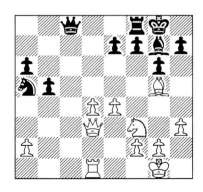

21...♖e8?

This surely shows that Kasparov finds it more difficult to manage logic when there are no real threats to consider. The move itself is passive and gives White time to occupy the c-file, with a tactic on the 26th move. Kasparov might have overlooked this, although this is no excuse...

Far superior is 21...♕b7, protecting numerous weak squares and preparing ...♖c8. The analysis goes 22 ♖c1!? (22 d5 ♘c4 23 ♖b1 ♖c8 24 ♘d4 ♘e5 and 22 ♕a3 ♘c4 23 ♕xe7 ♕xe7 24 ♗xe7 ♖e8 25 ♗c5 ♖xe4 26 d5 ♘b2 27 ♖d2 ♘c4 both seem okay for Black) 22...♘c4 23 a4 ♘b2 24 ♕a3 ♘xa4 25 ♕xe7 ♕xe7 26 ♗xe7 ♖e8 27 ♖c7 and White is better according to Gutman and Treppner, but they do not consider the dynamic 23...f5!, which appears to be just about the only move. The idea is, of course, to fight for the light squares, undermine the centre and perhaps create an outpost on d5 for the queen.

For once Kasparov's feeling for dynamics failed him. He should have seen that 21...♕b7 was the right move, and then made it work through calculations. Maybe the reason he did not do this is that his line of thought was not at its usual level, being influenced by the previous moves.

Gurevich claims that 21...♕d7 is equal, but 22 ♕a3! ♘c4 (22...♘c6 23 d5! and Black is in trouble, as 23...e6 24 ♕xa6 wins material) 23 ♕xa6 does not seem like a position Black should strive for.

22 ♖c1 ♕b7

Gurevich has suggested that 22...♕d7 23 ♕a3 ♘c4 24 ♕xa6 ♗xd4 25 ♘xd4 ♕xd4 26 ♕xb5 ♘d6 is equal but the position seems better for White after 27 ♕d5 ♕xe4 28 ♕xe4 ♘xe4 29 ♗e3,

when the a-pawn, combined with the superiority of rook and bishop over rook and knight, gives White the better chances, although Kasparov would find no problems in making the draw. But why should Karpov force this endgame? Black has no way to free himself anyway, as the game shows. Unforcing play – thank you. What happens in the game is that we see Black drift into worse and worse positions because he is not capable of playing these slow, positional improvements with the same accuracy. Perhaps 25 ♖b1 would be more natural, or even leaving out 23 ♕a3.

23 d5 ♘c4

It is too late to prevent the tactic at move 26, as can be seen from the following line: 23...h6 24 ♗f4 ♘c4 25 ♘d2 g5 26 ♗g3 ♘xd2 27 ♖c7! with a large advantage to White.

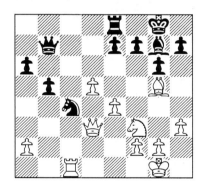

24 ♘d2!

Forcing Black to give up the blockade of the c-file. Black's play in this game is quite depressing, but I guess that is what happens when you succeed in putting the predator in a cage, or washing the blood from the boxer's face – it is a sad sight.

24...♘xd2

24...♘e5 25 ♕c2! underlines the lack of good squares for the knight and simultaneously prepares the invasion on c7.

25 ♗xd2!

A fine move. After 25 ♕xd2?! b4 26 ♖c6 a5 the pawns on the queenside provide Black with some counter-play. Now that idea is impossible since then White can play 27 ♕a6.

25...♖c8

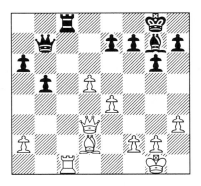

26 ♖c6!

This little tactic gives White time to take over the c-file and leaves Black in a poor position.

26...♗e5

Not a very convincing move, but 26...♖xc6 does not work due to 27 dxc6 ♕c7 (27...♕xc6 28 ♕d8+ ♗f8 29 ♗h6 is basic stuff) 28 ♕d7 ♗e5 29 ♗b4 e6 30 ♕e8+ ♔g7 31 ♕f8+ ♔f6 32 ♗e7+!! ♕xe7 33 ♕h8+ ♔g5 34 ♕xe5+ ♔h6 35 c7 and White will soon redirect his queen to d8.

27 ♗c3 ♗b8

Black cannot reduce the pressure with exchanges: 27...♗xc3 28 ♕xc3 ♖xc6 29 ♕xc6 ♕a7 30 e5 and the soon-to-be passed d-pawn will decide the game.

28 ♕d4

There is always time to force another weakness.

28...f6

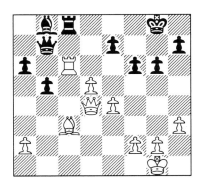

29 ♗a5!

Simply taking squares.

29...♗d6

Tactics fail, so Black has to wait: 29...♕d7 30 ♕c5 ♖xc6 31 ♕xc6 ♕d6 32 ♕e8+ ♔g7 33 ♗d8 ♕h2+ 34 ♔f1 ♕h1+ 35 ♔e2 ♗h2 36 ♕xe7+ ♔h6 37 ♗b6 and White wins (Ftacnik), or 29...♖xc6 30 dxc6 ♕xc6 31 ♕d8+ ♔f7 32 ♕xb8 ♕c1+ 33 ♔h2 and the queen conveniently occupies the b8-h2 diagonal, preventing a perpetual check.

30 ♕c3 ♖e8 31 a3

Ruling out any kind (actual or potential) of counterplay. Such is the style of Anatoly Karpov.

31...♔g7 32 g3

Again taking his time. According to Ftacnik 32 ♗c7! is even stronger, but I cannot see that Black has any way out of this mess the way that Karpov (so very safely) handles it. However, Ftacnik is probably correct.

32...♗e5 33 ♕c5 h5?

33...♗d6 is the only move, not allowing the queen to occupy the brilliant spot at c5. Instead Kasparov's attempt is a weakening move which has no chance of offering him counterplay. Had the colours been reversed, there might have been a slight chance that Karpov could have defended the Black position but, as it is, Kasparov might have already resigned himself to defeat.

34 ♗c7!

Now it comes, and with even greater impact.

34...♗a1

This piece just has a bad day...

35 ♗f4 ♕d7 36 ♖c7 ♕d8

Again a tactic proves what is obvious: that Black cannot take on h3 – 36...♕xh3 37 ♖xe7+ ♖xe7 38 ♕xe7+ ♔g8 39 ♗h6 f5 40 e5 with mate coming.

37 d6!

Promoting the patient candidate.

37...g5 38 d7! ♖f8 39 ♗d2 ♗e5 40 ♖b7 1-0

Enough of Kasparov for now. I believe I have given a good indication of how he makes use of logic in his games. Despite the fact that they are highly complex and feature much wild tactics they are still founded on a basic understanding of where the pieces should be placed. We saw above that Karpov used similar knowledge to focus on his opponent's pieces and subsequently thwart plans and ideas. This is the style that made him world champion in his day but, like Tal's style, I believe it needs refinement in order to survive the rigours of modern day chess. We saw how Kasparov finally succeeded in blowing him away, and similar games have since been played between the two.

Anyway, there are players ready to follow the heritage of Karpov. One of them is Kramnik, another is Anand. Both are players with a great feeling for the 'right' move, and both are represented with an example below.

In my opinion Vladimir Kramnik is the player whose understanding of chess is the deepest at the moment. Kasparov's problems in their match, whenever the game slid into a technical position, were indicative of this. And this happened often. I did not believe Kramnik would win the match because he never seemed as determined as Kasparov, but in the run up to the match he changed his way of living, gave up drinking, smoking and sleeping late. For a man in his early twenties this can be seen as something of an achievement!

I am not sure of whether Kramnik understands attacking chess in the way that Kasparov does. For example I believe that, had he not read it somewhere, he might not be aware that the number of pieces is almost the only thing that counts when you have a position with attacks on both sides. This kind of more subtle insight belongs to the old master. Kramnik, rather, has a great insight into how the pieces should co-ordinate and combine with different pawn structures, as the following game shows.

Ljubojevic–Kramnik
Amber Blindfold, Monaco 2000
Nimzo-Indian Defence

1 d4 ♘f6 2 c4 e6 3 ♘c3 ♗b4 4 ♕c2 0-0 5 a3 ♗xc3+ 6 ♕xc3 b6 7 ♗g5

d6!?

This is quite an interesting move. Black will decide whether to play ...♗b7 or ...♗a6 later, depending on what White plays. I had thought that this strategy was dubious due to the approach selected by Ljubojevic here, but after seeing how easily Kramnik gets a good position I have changed my opinion.

8 f3

White opts for a large centre.

8...♘bd7 9 e4 c5 10 dxc5 bxc5!

Black is preparing for ...e6-e5 and occupation of the d4 square. None of his knights can get there fast, but perhaps Kramnik has so much experience in such positions (he used to play them with White) that he knows that there will always be time.

11 ♘h3 h6 12 ♗xf6

This exchange is, sadly, forced, and White can no longer hope for an advantage. 12 ♗h4 d5! seems to be very dangerous for White's king. Note that 13 e5? d4 merely drops a pawn.

12...♘xf6 13 0-0-0?

In my experience you cannot castle queenside when the b-file is open and you have no open files on the kingside. This game in no way contradicts this observation.

13...e5!

Now is the right time. Otherwise White might play e4-e5 himself.

14 g4

White cannot allow ...♗xh3, after which his bishop is as poor as can be. One line is 14 ♕d2 ♗xh3 15 gxh3 ♘e8!, when Black will play ...♖a8-b8-b6 and the knight will be free to go wherever it wants.

14...♖b8

Here I want you to notice how Kramnik, with great ease, places all his pieces on the right squares. They almost float there.

15 ♘f2 ♖b6 16 ♖d2

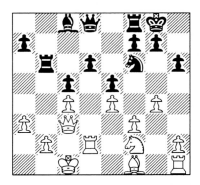

16...♕e7!

Preparing ♖f8-b8. Strangely, a lot of people would not consider lining up the major pieces on the b-file, but once you have seen it and once you begin to think appropriately, then it is impossible not to notice the power of the pressure on the b-file.

17 ♘d1 ♗e6

Ready to take care of a knight on d5.

18 ♗d3 ♖fb8 19 ♗c2 ♕b7 20 ♖e1 ♘h7

The knight is going to d4. Black already has a huge advantage as none of White's pieces seems well placed.

21 ♖e3 ♕a6 22 ♗d3 ♗d7

There is no way for the knight to get to d5 now so why not bring his own knight to d4?

23 ♗f1 ♘g5 24 ♖ed3 ♘e6 25 ♘e3 ♘d4 26 ♘d5

A blunder, of course, but White has already been outplayed.

26...♖b3 0-1

Kramnik's first appearance after his title match with Kasparov was a rapid-play match against Peter Leko in Budapest. About the first game it was said that the win was a proof of Kramnik's fantastic opening preparation for Kasparov. In response Kramnik said that he wished his preparation was so great but he had not yet come as far as analysing moves such as 14...♘e5. With this he can mean only that such a move is not investigated. We should analyse only good moves, poor moves can be refuted at the board. His opinion regarding 14...♘e5 was obvious.

Kramnik–Leko
Budapest match (1st game) 2001
Grünfeld Defence

1 d4 ♘f6 2 c4 g6 3 ♘c3 d5 4 ♘f3 ♗g7 5 cxd5 ♘xd5 6 e4 ♘xc3 7 bxc3 c5 8 ♗e3 ♕a5 9 ♕d2 ♘c6 10 ♖c1 cxd4 11 cxd4 ♕xd2+ 12 ♔xd2 0-0 13 d5 ♖d8 14 ♔e1

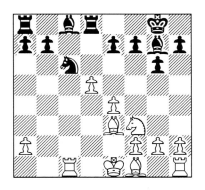

14...♘e5 15 ♘xe5 ♗xe5 16 f4 ♗d6 17 ♔f2 e5 18 ♗c5 ♗xc5+ 19 ♖xc5 exf4 20 ♔f3 ♗d7 21 ♗d3 ♖ac8 22 ♖hc1 g5 23 ♖c7 ♖xc7 24 ♖xc7 ♗a4 25 ♔g4 h6 26 ♖xb7 ♖d7 27 ♖b4

♗d1+ 28 ♔f5 ♔g7 29 h4 f6 30 hxg5 hxg5 31 e5 fxe5 32 ♔xe5 f3 33 gxf3 ♗xf3 34 d6 ♖d8 35 ♗f5 ♗c6 36 d7 ♖f8 37 ♖d4 1-0

In the following game we see how Kramnik's positional understanding is occasionally used to begin an attack. Although Kramnik is not a 'gunslinger' like Kasparov or Shirov his play with Black has at times proven his abilities as an attacking player. He has won memorable games against Topalov and Kasparov, including powerful mating attacks. The following game is a good illustration of the combination of positional considerations and attacking logic.

Gelfand–Kramnik
Berlin 1996
Semi-Slav Defence

1 d4 d5 2 c4 c6 3 ♘c3 ♘f6 4 ♘f3 e6 5 e3 ♘bd7 6 ♕c2 ♗d6

Some players are so afraid of the Shabalov variation (7 g4) that they play 6...b6 in this position. So far no one has proved anything wrong with this move. Incidentally in the 1990s Kramnik did a lot of work on the Meran and the Noteboom with his seconds and friends, and brought these lines back into fashion, this game being a good example.

7 g4 ♗b4!?

I really like this move, which reminds me of the Nimzo-Indian. Black cannot prevent g4-g5 and needs to know what to do with the knight. The logical square is e4 but, currently, this is not possible, so the bishop moves again.

Now it is time to consider whether g2-g4 has indeed strengthened White's position. The debate is still ongoing.

8 ♗d2 ♕e7 9 a3?!

Nobody fully understands this move. It probably has something to do with the possible ...e6-e5, but now Black is clearly fine. Other suggestions are 9 g5 and 9 ♖g1.

9...♗xc3 10 ♗xc3

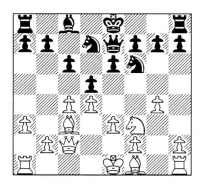

10...b6!

This is another example of great logic. The only minor piece with development problems is the bishop, so let's get going!

11 ♗d3

Kramnik believes 11 cxd5 exd5 is equal. I have the feeling that Black is already slightly better, as White finds no pleasure in the two bishops and is still to find a genuine justification for the weakness of his kingside.

11...♗a6

Black's strategy is simple. With White's pawns on dark squares the exchange of the light-squared bishop is strategically desirable for Black.

12 ♕a4 dxc4!

Based purely on tactics. 12...♗xc4 13 ♗xc4 dxc4 14 ♕xc6 is terrible for

Black, not only because of the pawn he will soon lose, but also thanks to 14...0-0 15 ♗b4 with further material loss.

13 ♕xa6

13 ♕xc6 ♖c8 14 ♕a4 ♗b7 15 ♗e2 a5 secures Black a very strong position according to Kramnik. The total domination of the centre is a very good illustration of Black's strategy. 13 ♗xc4 ♗xc4 14 ♕xc4 ♕d6 also poses Black no real problems, although it should be considered a decent alternative to the game.

13...cxd3 14 ♕xd3?!

Another slight error. White is positionally worse so he should not opt for simple moves because this tends not to help. Instead he should try to use the fact that none of the players has finished his development. Kramnik gives the following variation: 14 ♕b7 0-0 15 ♘e5! ♕e8 16 ♘xd3 ♖c8 17 ♕xa7 ♘xg4 with only a slight edge for Black.

14...0-0

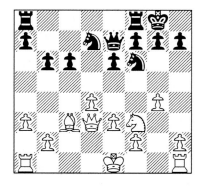

I quote Petursson: 'White's problem here is that he has weakened his kingside without obtaining any attacking chances.' How true. If there is no obvious defensive weakness a kingside attack usually requires more than two or three pieces to have a chance of success. Here, as Black has not moved any of the pawns in front of his king, his kingside has no real weaknesses. The c3-bishop might indirectly attack g7, but it is quite alone in doing so. And at the same time White has weakened both flanks, so he will find no safe haven for his king.

15 g5 ♘d5 16 ♗d2?

No other commentator has criticised this move, but I do not like it at all, especially in view of the strong response. I believe 16 e4!? to be a far better try. Then after 16...♘xc3 17 ♕xc3 White has numerous weaknesses but, with fewer minor pieces, and with more life in the centre, he might have a chance to survive.

same colour complex. Consequently Black should keep these pawns on dark squares for as long as possible. Note that 17 gxf6 ♕xf6 sees Black win material.

17 0-0-0

Another error, perhaps. This is something I will discuss in Chapter 4. White is worse and 'routine' play leads to his destruction, so he should try something (anything) to steer the game away from its natural course. *Fritz* suggests the weird 17 g6!, but Black should stay on top after the cool 17...h6, not allowing the opening of the g-file.

17...c5

Of course. If the king's position is weak it should be attacked.

18 ♔b1

16...f5!

After this advance commentators give Black a clear advantage, but perhaps 'positionally winning' is a more appropriate evaluation.

The text is indeed a beautiful implementation of logic. The knight on d5 is strong so e3-e4 should be prevented, while now the d2-bishop suffers from having all seven(!) of its pawns on the

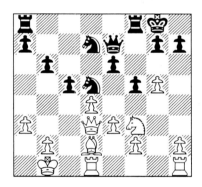

18...b5!

A natural sacrifice, which I am sure Kramnik found easy to play. An open file for the doubling of rooks is clearly worth a pawn. Notice the ease and simple logic behind every move in this very well orchestrated attack.

19 ♕xb5

Gelfand is becoming a spectator at his own game around this point, lacking options. Declining the pawn invites

...c5-c4 followed by ...a7-a5 and ...b5-b4.

19...♖ab8 20 ♕a5 ♖b3

An excellent outpost for the rook, which attacks many squares around White's king and cannot be driven away because the d2-bishop has nowhere to go in order to make room for ♘d2.

21 ♔a2?!

Giving Black a tempo later on. Black will double rooks anyway and there is no reason to force him to do so immediately. 21 ♔a1! is a better defensive try.

21...♖fb8 22 ♖b1 e5!

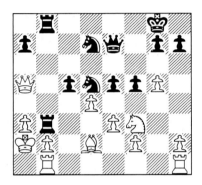

The final breakthrough comes in the centre. For the attack to succeed the queen will have to join in, and it does so on the a2-g8 diagonal.

23 ♖hc1

A last attempt to bring the forces into play. Need I say that by now it is far too late? 23 dxe5 ♘xe5 24 ♘xe5 ♕xe5 25 ♗c3 ♘xc3+ 26 bxc3 ♕e4! wins for Black, as pointed out by Petursson.

23...♕e6 24 ♔a1 exd4

Simple Chess. Why not take the pawn?

25 ♖xc5

White is, understandably, becoming desperate. 25 exd4 ♖xf3 is the price White has to pay for his early advance on the kingside – particularly for not finding an appropriate way of supporting it.

25...♘xc5 26 ♕xc5

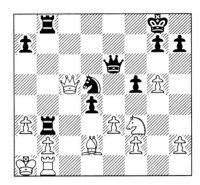

And now it is time for a truly great finish.

26...♘c3!! 27 ♘xd4

Of course this response was anticipated. Black only has one way to win this position!

27...♖xb2! 28 ♖xb2

28 ♕f8+ ♖xf8!.

28...♕a2+! 0-1

A beautiful game that illustrates the close connection between positional play and attacking chess. It is not only frustrating the opponent's plans – as Karpov tries to do – but also playing natural moves in the style of Kramnik that should be considered positional chess. As Kramnik does not seek to attack like Shirov or Kasparov (but will do so if and when appropriate) his style is positional. However, his chess is often very ambitious.

As I mentioned earlier another great player of the modern day is Anand. We can take a look at an example – similar to

Movsesian–Kasparov, above – in which Anand simply has a superior understanding than his opponent. Don't be fooled by the simplicity of this game – it was played in the strongest tournament of 2001!

Anand-Van Wely
Wijk aan Zee 2001
Sicilian Defence

1 e4 c5 2 ♘f3 d6 3 d4 cxd4 4 ♘xd4 ♘f6 5 ♘c3 a6 6 ♗e3 e5

This move is quite normal here, of course, but it does require something from Black since the d5-square is potentially weak. Occasionally we see games between amateurs where White emerges with a knight on d5 while Black has a bishop on d8, but rarely does this happen with top players. In fact I remember a game between Judith Polgar and Anand, where Anand did find himself in such a mess. In this game a 2700 player loses in similar fashion. I believe that Van Wely is simply not a 'Real' player but a hard fighter and a very innovative individual. A great player, but not a 'real' one...

7 ♘b3 ♗e6 8 ♕d2 ♗e7 9 f3 0-0 10 0-0-0 ♕c7 11 g4 ♖c8?!

With an indirect attack on c2. The idea is to push with ...d6-d5 and gain some freedom in the centre. Actually I find Black's idea altogether slow and dubious, and I believe 11...b5 to be a stronger move.

12 ♔b1?!

According to Chessbase the moves arrived in this order, but I have the feeling that Anand might have played 12 ♕f2! ♘bd7 13 ♔b1, after which we

have the same position as in the game but without the possibility given in the note to Black's next move. Of course I have personally examined 12 h4?! d5 13 g5 d4 14 ♘xd4 exd4 15 ♗xd4 ♘e8 16 f4, which is not to be recommended.

12...♘bd7?

If this really is the correct order of moves then Black has 12...d5 13 ♘xd5 ♘xd5 14 exd5 ♗xd5 15 ♕f2 (15 ♕xd5?? ♖d8 is the point) 15...♗e6 16 ♗d3 with an interesting position. At least Black does not have the space problems experienced in the game.

13 ♕f2 b5 14 g5 ♘h5 15 h4 b4 16 ♘d5 ♗xd5 17 ♖xd5 a5 18 ♗h3

Here we see the simple problems for Black. The h3-c8 diagonal is weak and the e7-bishop is worthless. Normally in these lines Black can play ...f7-f5 at some point, and the opening of the f-file after gxf6 brings life to Black's forces. However, with the rook on c8 instead of f8 this is not the case. I feel that any 'real' chess player would have avoided ending up in such a poor situation so soon but, of course, I could be wrong.

18...a4 19 ♘c1

At first I found it hard to believe that

this was a new idea. Anand's play is so simple and so obviously appropriate. 19 ♗xd7 might also lead to an advantage but the game leaves Black in dire straits.

19...♖cb8 20 ♗g4!

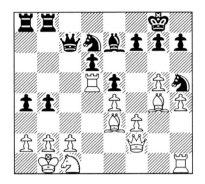

20...♘f4?

20...g6 is absolutely forced, although Black is in a terrible state after 21 ♗xh5 gxh5 22 ♘e2 with the idea of ♘e2-g3xh5 (at least Black's pieces have a chance to do some good here). After the text the position is hopeless.

21 ♗xf4 exf4 22 ♗xd7!

Obviously. Good knight, bad bishop. Textbook material.

22...♕xd7 23 ♕d2 ♖b5 24 ♘e2 ♖c8 25 ♘xf4 b3 26 cxb3 axb3 27 a3 ♖c2

One of the differences between the two players might be that Anand never feared this move, while Van Wely might have thought that it would provide him with counterplay. In fact White effectively has an extra piece, so Black will never be able to create any worthwhile attack against White's king.

28 ♕d3 ♖b8 29 ♖d4 ♗f8 30 ♘d5

The knight arrives on the best square. We could be forgiven for believing that this game was played in a simultaneous exhibition.

30...♖f2 31 ♕e3 ♖g2 32 ♖d2 ♖g3 33 ♕f2 ♖h3 34 ♖hd1 1-0

If nothing else, then 35 ♘f4 is a good move.

I hope I have succeeded in clarifying what is meant by a Real chess player, and what separates one from ordinary chess superstars. It is not a matter of calculation or home preparation but another, more basic quality, based on an understanding of where the pieces belong. The best example is probably the Ljubo-Kramnik game, where Kramnik's pieces just gravitated to the best squares. And this in a blindfold game!

In the next chapter I will discuss the background for this quality, which seems to be fully controlled by only a very few. And never really fully.

CHAPTER THREE

No Rules?

'A knight on the rim is dim, never take the b-pawn with your queen, queen and knight are better than queen and bishop and never ever invite a vampire into your house.' – Jonathan Rowson, *The Seven Deadly Chess Sins*

It is quite popular these days to say that there are no valid rules in chess. People claim that the game is rule independent, that the only rule is that there are no rules (Suba). Rowson's words offer a funny argument in favour of this view. When I read the passage I felt quite shocked – did Jonathan really believe that there are no truths in chess? I thought about it much over several months and came to the conclusion: no.

I understand the argument: if a knight on the rim is dim, then what about a position such as the following:

see following diagram

The position is from the game Rowson-Franklin, England 1995. Black won after 28...♘xh3+ 29 gxh3 ♘f3+ 30 ♔h1 e4 31 ♖e6 ♖f6 32 ♕xe4 ♖g6 33 ♖xg6

♕xe4 34 ♖e6 ♕f5 35 ♖eb6 ♕e5 White resigns.

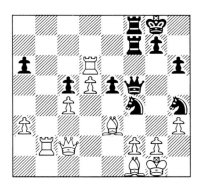

Black to move

Never mind that White could have defended better. I could have used other examples where there was no defence, where knights on the rim win the game, but I simply could not resist the temptation of using a Rowson game.

But now, does this mean that knights on the rim are not dim at all, or that they are dim only sometimes? Well, let me tell you a little story to help explain what I think about the importance of such examples:

The police were chasing a burglar, who went to hide at a friend's house. The police arrived at the friend's house and asked:

'Are are you hiding Mr. Burglar in there?'

The friend replied:

'No, I am alone.'

'But,' said the policeman, 'I see your table is set for two.'

'So? My alarm clock is set for four. That doesn't prove anything.'

I feel the same way about the game above and Rowson's funny comparison with horror comics. In my opinion knights on the rim are dim, as they lose a lot of their mobility compared to when they are in the middle of the board. No example will change this, only a change in the rules of the game could do so. But what about the example above? Is that what is called the exception that proves the rule? No. First I must say that I dislike this expression (all swans cannot be white if there is a black swan).

Secondly, remember the story of David and Goliath, how a giant was taken down by a boy. Or let us take a more recent example, the movie *The Fugitive*, where Harrison Ford has several encounters with a one-armed man. This man is still dangerous despite his reduced powers, and the same goes for the knights, above.

We will delve deeper into knights on the rim in the coming pages, but first I will do Rowson some justice. What he really wants to say is not that chess does not have an inherent mathematical logic. Rather he writes: 'Another way of looking at the matter is to acknowledge that the purpose of rules in general is to make sense of 'complex systems', such as chess. However, rules cannot be formulated mathematically, they must be stated in natural language and since language is essentially simple (easily understood), and chess is essentially complex, the rules are not going to 'fit' in any sort of exact way. It doesn't mean that rules are useless, but that we cannot rely on them exclusively to lead us to the correct decisions.' *The Seven Deadly Chess Sins,* page 47.

This is relatively close to my views, although I think that rules can do a lot more for us than Jonathan expresses here. But where Jonathan really makes me wonder is earlier on the same page, where he writes: 'Although there are useful guidelines in chess, it seems that there are almost no rules other than those which constitute the basic instructions. Watson does an excellent job of explaining this concept in *Secrets of Modern Chess Strategy* and calls the phenomenon 'Rule Independence'.'

This is in conflict with my views. I will use a lot of space below in countering this notion of rule independence, arguing why thinking about rules does do you some good. Having said this, I must warn you that the following twenty-something pages should not be taken as absolute truth. Rather these are thoughts based on logic and experience. Incidentally it must be said that I am not strictly interested in the truth of chess on a generic level, but in knowing how to win more games. To me chess is a competitive game, and that's it. I have written this chapter in the same way I have used these ideas in training my pupils over the years. But before we turn to my views on rules in chess I want to have a brief look at the most important recent book that argues against them.

Chess and its Rules

John Watson received much acclaim for his extremely interesting and thought provoking book on modern positional play, *Secrets of modern Chess Strategy – Advances since Nimzowitsch*. In this book he advocates the view of failure of rules in chess. By now it will not be a surprise to anyone that I disagree with him, no matter how trendy and well written his book seems to be. I do not want to account for his views and arguments in detail because that would be too boring (because it is a more theoretical discussion – not because Watson or his views themselves are boring!). Those especially interested in this debate should read his book and make up their own mind. John is a good writer, one of the best in the business, and reading his stuff is always interesting. Besides, he might be right and I might be wrong, although I have my doubts.

Here I will try to give a brief introduction to the debate, as it is important for my reasoning when I come to ways to improve your understanding later in this chapter. The following quotes are from his book and I use them here mainly to illustrate how I would attack the idea of rule independence. I will start at a familiar place. Of the game between Shirov and Kasparov that we discussed in Chapter 2, Watson writes

the following:

'It is important to note that from move 15 onward, Black's conception depended upon a remarkable string of difficult tactics, since White has critical options on every move; see Kasparov's own notes in *Informator 54* for the details. This is so very typical of the concrete analytical approach Kasparov advocates. In most top-flight contemporary games, one cannot expect the game to be decided by one side achieving static, obvious advantages and then driving them home with good technique. Rather, one has to be able to anticipate correctly that, of the conflicting possibilities for both sides, the opponent's will fade and one's own will triumph. This is a matter of intuition to some extent, but more so, a matter of good preparation and superior over-the-board analysis.' (Page 125).

I will begin by finding some common ground between my own view and that of Watson. Chess *is* a matter of intuition, preparation and calculation all blended together.

Opening preparation is an important asset in modern high level competition, but a look at the games shows that superior preparation offers only so much. When it is not backed up by a strong understanding of the opening very little can be achieved, even if you are better at calculation. A classical example of this is the return match between Tal and Botvinnik. In the first match Tal played some open systems against Botvinnik's Caro-Kann defence with good results, while in the second he used the closed system 1 e4 c6 2 d4 d5 3 e5. He had a number of new ideas and helped advance the system, but the positions were better suited for the slow positional style of Botvinnik, and Tal had no advantage of having the white pieces in terms of results.

The reason preparation is so important for top players is obvious. With little time to decide complicated issues over the board, the extra time gained by knowing a position from home, and knowing how to deal with the opponent's moves, is very important. But if the opponent finds a decent path that leads away from preparation, and you are lost, then it makes very little sense.

Calculation. I have argued before in this book that calculation is important, but knowing what to achieve is perhaps even more important. And this comes from understanding, or as Watson says, 'intuition to some extent'. Only his 'some extent' is wrong, as I see it.

His reference to Kasparov is dubious as well. In Chapter 2 we looked at a few of Kasparov's games, and although he does calculate well, and does like to analyse his games at home, the indication in the annotations are the opposite of what Watson said, above. Having a great understanding of dynamics is not the same as being reliable on tactics alone. Bareev said about Kasparov, after playing him the first time, that 'When you play Kasparov, the pieces start to move differently.' Bareev was joking, but there is still some truth to the claim. Kasparov does have an ability to make the most of his pieces in complicated positions. This does not come from an ability to calculate like a computer, but rather a deep understanding of how the

qualities of the pieces are used to their maximum. Kasparov does calculate very well but, like everyone else, he is limited by being a mere human.

The reference to *Informant 54* is highly unfortunate for Watson. I am sure that he must have been unaware of the annotations in *New In Chess* magazine, since this would otherwise not have happened. The point is, of course, that *Informant* has a universal format that uses no words. Consequently Kasparov simply cannot write about ideas there. It is my impression from reading Kasparov's annotations that he does frequently analyse many positions. But my conclusions are different from Watson's on this point. Even if Kasparov does like to prove/investigate the correctness of his play, and has no other method to do so than through analysis, it does not mean that he uses calculation only when he is sitting at the board. Also – and this is important – if you want to become a world class player you need to find your own understanding of chess. No trainer or book alone can take you all the way to the top. You will have to find your own understanding of the game, your own style. I do not think this can be done without extensive analysis. It is just like learning to do anything else. There is no better training than practising what you are going to do at competitions. A *Tour de France* cyclist will cycle, as well as use fitness and mental training. Professional football players run around with the ball for hours each day between matches, as well as simply running and weightlifting. In any field, simulating what you will have to do at the tournament is an important part of the training. If you want to understand chess and acquire a deep feeling for the game there is no avoiding the expenditure of considerable time solving exercises and analysing all kinds of positions. It is a shame that Watson seems unaware of the annotations in *NIC*. How would they relate to his view? Perhaps the future will tell.

One must also remember that the variations seen in *Chess Informant* and others are just as much an argument for more principal decisions during the game as they are related to what the players actually saw during the game. I know many people believe in the myth about the enormous abilities of calculation among the top players, but I am less convinced. They calculate better but not more. The brain can only make decisions in 480 milliseconds, as proved by German neurologist Ernst Pöbel, and this requires a level of concentration that cannot be sustained for a very long period of time. So the answer to the matter of seeing more over the board lies in more accurately seeing the variations and, later, analysing the games at home in order to investigate one's thoughts.

Another place where I disagree with Watson and feel that his argument is rather weak is on page 136. Here he presents another Kasparov game:

Kasparov-Kamsky
Linares 1993
Sicilian Defence

1 e4 c5 2 ♘f3 e6 3 d4 cxd4 4 ♘xd4 ♘f6 5 ♘c3 d6 6 ♗e3 a6 7 f3 ♘bd7 8

g4 h6 9 ♖g1 ♕b6 10 a3 ♘e5 11 ♗f2!

Watson writes: 'Moving this piece twice achieves the goal of driving away Black's queen; this takes priority over development.' We will return to this below.

11...♕c7 12 f4 ♘c4 13 ♗xc4 ♕xc4 14 ♕f3 e5 15 ♘f5 ♗xf5 16 gxf5 d5 17 fxe5 ♘xe4 18 ♖g4

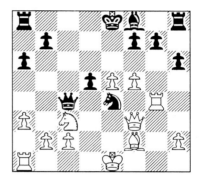

Watson: 'With a clear advantage for White. In this example, it almost seemed as though White forgot that he was supposed to get his pieces out; and yet in the end, his development was superior.'

I completely disagree with Watson on this one. Out of the first eight moves Black made six pawn moves. He followed this by moving his queen, moving a knight for the second time, then his queen again, then the knight yet again, followed by the queen! Of course some of these were forced by White, while others were forcing moves themselves.

The way Watson is arguing here, he makes it sound like relating to rules means ignoring what the opponent is doing. Presented like this it is obviously easy to prove that following rules is pure nonsense.

However, it is just as easy to argue in favour of rules with this game, which I now give with alternative annotations:

1 e4

This is the best move from a theoretical point of view because it offers the most number of possibilities on the second move. It is superior to 1 e3 (which also leaves twenty possible moves) for two reasons, since it takes control of two key squares in Black's half of the board (d5 and f5) and, secondly, one of the twenty possible moves after 1 e3 is pushing the pawn to the square where it is after 1 e4. Clearly this kind of thinking is for computer programmers. For us it is more important to look at possible structures. 1 e4 creates a more open game, more tactical and with greater emphasis on speed. So it is a matter of taste.

1...c5

Taking control over the d4-square without exposing the pawn to attack, as is the case after 1...e5 2 ♘f3 ♘c6 3 ♗b5, where White develops fast and Black defends himself with tactics after 3...a6!.

2 ♘f3

White regains control over d4 immediately. Notice that, although other moves are played here, only 2 c3, with similar ideas, is considered a main option.

2...e6

Preparing development.

3 d4 cxd4 4 ♘xd4 ♘f6 5 ♘c3

This both develops and protects. 5 e5 ♕a5+ violates a well known rule. Do not lose your pieces and pawns for no reason.

5...d6

This move is actually quite rare these days, as 6 g4!, gaining space and winning tempi, produces excellent results.

6 ♗e3 a6

Black has thus far concentrated on structure. Before developing he has engineered a structure to resist any kind of attack from White. The Sicilians with ...a7-a6 and ...b7-b5 are often characterised by Black making some pawn moves to chase the White pieces to inferior squares. So when Black prepares himself to defend against an assault it is logical for White to attack with his pawns. And Black's Achilles heel here is in the form of the light squares around the king. These are damaged mostly by pushing a pawn to g6 or f5. Therefore 7 f4!? and strategies involving g2-g4 are logical. Additionally, the f6-knight is quite well placed and White can gain a tempo by attacking it with the g-pawn. Actually, the two main moves these days here are 7 f3, as in the game, and 7 g4!?. The latter is met with 7...e5, beginning a cascade of tactics.

7 f3 ♘bd7 8 g4 h6

Black has no reasonable square for the knight so he makes a long-term weakening of the kingside, in return obtaining the short-term advantage of time in which to develop. In most cases, then, he will not be able to castle kingside because it is too dangerous, although special cases can occur. Those arguing against any form of rules in chess will find it difficult to counter this: Pawn moves in front of the castled king create structural weaknesses and make life easier for the attackers.

9 罝g1!?

This move is actually slightly strange. The idea is to play 10 h4 and 11 g5 to attack the kingside immediately with g4-g5-g6.

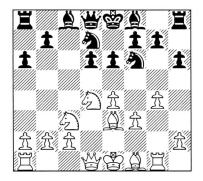

9...曾b6?

This seems to be an obvious mistake. Black is behind in development and has no safe spot for his king. What does he do? He develops his queen, setting up immediate threats. Unfortunately these are quite easily parried. Note that White is still ahead in development at this point, and that Black does nothing to alter that fact.

9...g5! is probably what should be played, the situation being all about structure. After 8...h6 Black can no longer seriously consider kingside castling, so only e6 and f7 are real targets for White. By pushing the g-pawn Black puts a stop to the pawn advance in the centre for the time being and thus wins time to complete development. Also, the stronghold on e5 is very important in these considerations. Note that after 9 罝g1 Black should be less afraid of h2-h4, the normal threat to his structure.

10 a3!

Protecting the b2-pawn, and also the c3-knight (against ...b7-b5-b4). Since Black's queen is soon making a lot of moves, the text is more or less for free.

10...包e5

This does little good since after White's next Black is forced to move his queen. Thereafter f3-f4 will force the knight to move again.

11 奧f2!!

Simple and logical. Now all White's pieces are protected again. Notice that White wanted to protect this bishop so that he could drive Black's queen away, and 11 曾d2 曾xb2 is the wrong way to do this. It is also important that White is still leading in development, while Black has done nothing at all in this regard.

11...曾c7

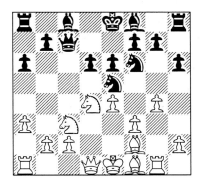

12 f4!

Forcing the knight away from the centre and beginning a serious attack on the kingside.

12...包c4 13 奧xc4

White exchanges an undeveloped piece for one that has made three moves already, thus emphasising the development lead, although this consideration has more weight early in the opening than the arrival of the middlegame, where all the pieces have been developed.

13...♛xc4 14 ♕f3 e5?

Opening up the position and leading to the end of the game. Black does succeed in exchanging the f5-knight in similar fashion to White's trade on c4, but while the queen is doing nothing special on c4 the open g-file is a significant asset for White.

15 ♘f5

Threatening ♘f5-e3-d5 with complete control.

15...♝xf5 16 gxf5 d5 17 fxe5 ♘xe4 18 ♖g4

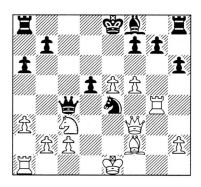

Now only the a1-rook needs to join in the attack, after which White is fully developed. Black, on the other hand, has spent time with his queen and the now absent knight. Not surprisingly Black is lost.

The game concluded as follows:

18...h5 19 ♖h4 ♝c5 20 0-0-0 ♝xf2 21 ♘xe4 dxe4 22 ♕xf2 ♖c8 23 ♔b1 ♖d8 24 ♖xd8+ ♔xd8 25 ♖h3 ♕d5 26 ♖c3 ♔d7 27 ♕b6 ♖d8 28 ♖c5 ♕d1+ 29 ♔a2 ♔e8 30 ♕xb7 ♕g4 31 e6 fxe6 32 ♖e5 ♕g5 33 h4 ♕xh4 34 ♖xe6+ ♔f8 35 f6 1-0

In these Sicilian Scheveningen posi-

tions Black starts by setting up his pawn formation before completing his development, a policy that runs the risk of leading to an early defeat (generally not the case). It is mainly because Black's pawn formation is so solid (on the third rank) that White cannot force a way through before the second player has completed his development. Therefore in order to attack White needs to push pawns on the kingside or in the centre, affording Black sufficient time in which to develop. If Black fails to do so he is often punished, as in the game above. I am sure that some people who doubt the validity of the notion of rules in chess would claim that this is not at all supported by rules, that Black is neglecting his development and not being duly punished. But the logic above does very much relate to the need for development. It is just a bit more complex than following dogmatic rules.

In his words, above, Watson does what all great politicians do – he takes the arguments presented by his counterpart (the old chess school – Watson himself draws the line at 1935, which he acknowledges is rather arbitrary) and simplifies it. And, like all simple arguments, it fails. He argues that in the game White neglects development, as if what Black is doing has nothing to do with White's choices. I think this greatly underestimates the intellect of the old masters, who speculated about such things as rules. In the game White was always leading in development, and Black's failure to develop contributed fully to his defeat.

A simple rule – do not move the same piece more than once in the opening – is among Watson's references. But obviously this is under the pretext: 'All things being equal.' The gain of 11 ♗f2 is so obvious that saying the piece moves twice is besides the point in terms of the interactive nature of chess. It is simply not fair to Tarrasch and friends.

In the game White moves a piece twice in the opening as early as the fourth move, but this move does not get any kind of comment from Watson, even though no other pieces have been developed and this fits in with the simplified universal logic he wants to attribute to the idea of rules. It would be interesting to consider this move from a theoretical point but here it is not relevant.

At this point I want to return to the question of the knight on the edge. Like Rowson, Watson is not in much doubt about the famous dictum: 'A knight on the rim is grim' (dim being used by Rowson, grim by Watson). We have already seen that this is not always the case, and that in extreme circumstances two knights on the edge of the board can be deadly. Watson provokes slightly by beginning the chapter entitled The Contemporary Knight (page 151) with the line 'They live on the edge.' Watson writes that this rule has its main validity in the endgame, when there are fewer pieces left on the board (referring to Grandmaster Jonathan Tisdall), and that it is less obvious in the opening and middlegame. He is right but this does only underline the validity of the rule. The fewer pieces there are on the board, the more importance these indi-

vidual pieces are accorded. Therefore if knights cannot be on the edge in the endgame, when only a few pieces remain, then this illustrates how little they contribute when out there. Again, a knight on the rim should not be understood in simplistic terms. In the King's Indian the queen's knight often goes to a6 and the other to h5, with ideas of going to c5 and f4 (the best squares for the knights). Using the rim as a transition point is clearly possible and often advisable. After 1 d4 ♘f6 2 c4 g6 3 ♘c3 ♗g7 4 e4 d6 5 ♘f3 0-0 6 ♗e2 e5 7 d5 Black's main development plan for the queen's knight is a6-c5. In the old days it used to be developed via d7, but this restricts the queen's bishop.

Watson considers a very interesting example:

Stohl-Kindermann
Bundesliga 1996/1997
King's Indian Defence

1 ♘f3 ♘f6 2 c4 g6 3 g3 ♗g7 4 ♗g2 0-0 5 d4 d6 6 ♘c3 ♘c6 7 0-0 a6 8 d5 ♘a5 9 ♘d2 c5 10 ♕c2 ♖b8 11 b3 b5 12 ♗b2 ♗h6

Here Watson takes a break (he looks at the position after 12...bxc4 13 bxc4 ♘a5, which seems logical to me) in order to explain the rather amusing paradox that although this line has done well for Black for decades the relevant games are used in middlegame books to help illustrate the weakness of the knight on the rim! Obviously these examples are from games where Black has failed in proving the validity of his position and consequently emerged with a poor position, with the knight a weakness on a5.

I have found that many people find it difficult to accept that a knight can be objectively poorly placed while the position remains acceptable, that the knight can contribute positively and still be a positional weakness.

Watson also notes that the weakness of c4 is the reason why the knight has a decent position on the edge of the board, and he is absolutely right. The amount of activity Black is forced to use here in order to justify his set-up does tell us something about this knight. It is poorly placed and at the same time an important element of the position. Again, translating this into a verdict on the position serves only to over-evaluate the rule itself, which says that the knight on the rim is dim – *not* the knight on the rim is responsible for the breakdown of the Roman empire!

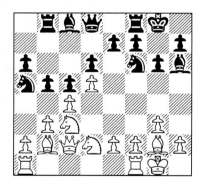

13 f4 bxc4 14 bxc4 e5 15 dxe6 ♗xe6 16 ♘d5 ♖xb2!

Practise has broken down the reliable possibilities here to include only this positional sacrifice. The compensation consists mainly of time and a superiority on the dark squares in the centre.

17 ♕xb2 ♗g7 18 ♕c1 ♗xd5 19

♗xd5!

A nice move. As everything is on dark squares it is logical for White not to allow 19 cxd5 ♘g4! with a dark square invasion. Now White's king has more breathing space (g2) and Black should exchange the bishop on d5, as it might otherwise prove to be a very powerful piece later in the game.

19...♘xd5 20 cxd5 ♕e7!?

Black is not so keen on taking back the exchange, although this could be done with 20...♗d4+ 21 ♔h1 ♕a8 22 e4 ♗xa1 23 ♕xa1 f5 with fine counterplay for Black. The move played by Kindermann gives control over the centre higher priority than pure material logic.

21 ♖b1 ♕xe2 22 ♕d1 ♕e3+ 23 ♔h1

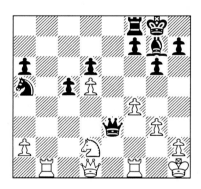

Here something goes wrong for Watson as he calls this game a draw. What has happened to his database I do not know, but such accidents are always possible. He bases the draw offer and its acceptance on an idea which Black did not actually choose in the game, which itself continued for many moves.

In fact it is his idea that I would like to discuss.

23...c4

Watson writes: '23...♘c4! Then after

24 ♘xc4 (24 ♕b3 ♕xd2 25 ♕xc4 ♖e8 is no better) 24...♕e4+ 25 ♕f3 ♕xc4 Black has two pawns for the exchange. White's weak pawns on d5 and a2, along with the somewhat exposed king, make for a dynamically balanced game, which will likely be drawn.'

I am not sure that I completely agree with Watson's evaluation. I have a feeling that too many pieces have been exchanged and the superiority of the rook over the bishop is enough to guarantee White slightly better chances. Having said that, this is difficult for any of us to evaluate properly. When I showed this position to some friends of mine they were actually more in agreement with Watson...

But this is not so important. What is important is that Watson, who argues for the strength of knights on the rim in this line, thinks that Black's best option is to exchange it for the rather ineffectual knight on d2 – even when this means increasing the difference between the rook and the bishop (with fewer minor pieces on the board the power of the rook increases, alongside the number of available squares) and not exploiting the momentum to get a valuable passed pawn on the third rank.

I am sure that Watson reasons that the knight on a5 no longer makes sense as the point of attack – the c4-pawn – has moved on. But would he agree with my general conclusion? According to his book I am doubtful. I would conclude that the knight on the rim is grim (just look at it!) and that it is a limited asset now that can best be used by the exchange with the knight on d2. Earlier the target on c4 held more importance

than the knight's general 'grimness' and justified its position. Now the justification is gone and the knight has become rather dubiously placed.

My conclusion on such reasoning is simple. The knight was always poorly placed from a general viewpoint, or, as was said earlier: 'All things being equal – the knight on the rim is dim.' If things are not equal, however, other properties in the position come into play rather than the knight's general grimness on the rim.

So, was the knight grim in this game? Certainly. It was so all along, only it also had some advantages out there. The rule 'winning pawns is a good idea' is more important than the 'knight on the rim is dim' – until now, that is. The same goes for the example at the beginning of the chapter. The knights are still dim, they do not control a lot of squares. But there the rule 'mate wins the game' seemed to be more important due to the weakness of White's king.

My claim is that chess can be viewed as a large collection of rules that constantly interact, with some of them having greater importance in this or that specific position. Below I will discuss what this knowledge should be used for generally, but here I want to say that both players are always aware that the knight is fragile on the edge, and that this might prove serious if other elements in the position should change. I believe this is why Kindermann chose the aggressive approach rather than Watson's more positional choice. As for which is better, the question remains...

The game concluded:

24 ♖e1 ♕a3 25 ♘e4 ♖c8 26 ♖b6 c3

27 ♕d3 ♕xa2 28 ♕xa6 ♖f8 29 ♖b5 c2 30 ♖xa5 ♕b1 31 ♕f1 ♖b8 32 ♖a8 ♖xa8 33 ♖xb1 cxb1♕ 34 ♕xb1 ♖a1 35 ♕xa1 ♗xa1 36 ♘xd6 ♔f8 37 ♔g2 ♔e7 38 ♘c4 f5 39 ♔f3 ♗d4 40 h3 ♔f6 41 g4 h6 42 ♘e3 ♗c5 43 h4 fxg4+ 44 ♘xg4+ ♔g7 45 ♘e5 ♗e7 46 ♘c6 ♗d6 47 ♔e4 ♔f6 48 ♘e5 h5 49 ♘d7+ ♔e7 50 ♘b6 ♗c5 51 ♘c4 ♔f6 52 ♘e5 ♗d6 53 ♘f3 ♗c5 54 ♘d4 ♗b4 55 f5 gxf5+ 56 ♘xf5 ♗e1 57 ♔f4 ♗d2+ 58 ♔e4 ♗e1 59 d6 ♔e6 60 ♘g7+ ½-½

As I said earlier I see chess not as one game only, but as a multitude of games decided by pawn structure. As Watson writes, modern chess has included a vast number of new opening ideas, which has led to new structures emerging. This should, logically, increase the diversity in the rules and options in chess, and it does. But Watson does not include this in his considerations on pages 108-110, where he discusses the old rule 'in the opening, develop you knights before your bishops' – something which he notes 'Lasker was very fond of.' He proves the limitation of this rule through different lines, the most distinct being 1 e4 g6 2 d4 ♗g7 3 ♘c3 c6 4 f4 d5 5 e5 h5 6 ♘f3 ♗g4. Here Black will soon finish the structure with ...e7-e6, which mainly benefits the dark-squared bishop. His idea is to exchange the other bishop and use c6 and f5 as knight outposts. The bishop drops back to f8 and interacts on the queenside and in the centre.

I think if people played like this in Lasker's day he would not have supported this view. But they did not. As Watson writes, 1 e4 e5 and 1 d4 d5 are played in the vast majority of games. If we look at these openings, then 2 ♘f3 after 1 e4 e5 is still the only move which enjoys great popularity among top players (Federov loses game after game with 2 f4, which Shirov has even given a '?!'). Meanwhile, after 1 d4 d5 2 c4 e6 White normally continues 3 ♘f3 or 3 ♘c3, as is the case after 2...c6.

So Lasker's fondness of this rule is still worth something in the openings he associated it with. I believe this is how we should approach the rules as presented by the old masters before we cynically judge them as false: *If all things are equal.* With knights before bishops this means that only the same openings that Lasker could be expected to refer to should be included in his rule. Otherwise all things are no longer equal. When Watson uses a lot of new opening ideas to invalidate a wise old observation, he is not doing it in the service of research, but purely to promote his own argument. I would probably have approached the examples differently because they are very interesting indeed. I would rather ask myself: why does this observation meet limitations when we move away from these symmetrical structures? This way I could learn something about the true nature of chess.

I really love Watson's book, but for different reasons than the one he intended. I see it mainly as a multitude of great examples of modern positional play, a kind of 'greatest hits' of the last ten years' best books. He is good at observing many changes in what is possible in positional chess, but I find that he draws the wrong conclusion. I would look for the logic behind the examples – instead of presenting logic applied to other structures – and illustrate their insufficiency.

It is true that the rules of the masters from around the year 1900 are limited and need to be revisited, but discharged for a notion of rule independence is not the way to do so. Chess is not simple, it is the interaction of sixteen pieces on sixty-four squares in an incomprehensible number of possible positions. But that does not mean that similar interactions between these pieces do not occur again and again – they do. And similar interactions often require similar reactions in order to achieve the desired effect, which is always the same.

We know this from cooking rice (and almost anything else in life), when it should boil for eight minutes in most situations. But just as we should not follow this rule if there are explosives in the pot, there is no rule in chess that counts in all positions. Only 'mate wins the game' seems to have that universal strength. It is always a matter of a great number of rules existing at the same time, trying to manoeuvre among them in order to make them work for ourselves and not the opponent. With these words I will move on to my personal way of viewing the chess rules, and how these should be used in practical play.

Elements and Concepts

I believe elements and concepts are a very good way to help understand positions. There are not lonely pieces on a large board, or two full armies encountering each other. Rather we have col-

lections of elements and concepts (in a mathematical sense), and these can be grasped and understood by everyone.

Let us begin with the following example:

Fischer–Petrosian
Curacao 1962

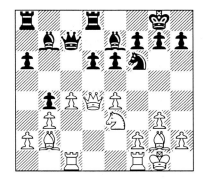

White to move

I normally start with the basics by simply comparing pieces, an idea I will return to later in this chapter. But first let's look at the simple idea of concepts.

The idea is based on an observation many chess thinkers have made individually: a strong player does not see a position as a collection of pieces but as a chunk where the pieces in some way weld together to form a single unit. Why do strong players do so? Because no piece is an army. The strength of a piece lies in its ability to co-operate with other pieces. This particularly counts for pawns, which alone are so enormously fragile.

One of the things we learn quickly is the importance of pawn structure. The pieces depend on each other, of course, but the role of the pawn structure is of paramount importance. In the position above Black's knight longs for c5, while its counterpart on e3 lacks a good square. This is one of the most important concepts in the position. Another is the x-ray pressure White's rook generates on the c-file, which we will touch upon later. For now we will look at different concepts and elements.

An element is something concrete, like a good square for a knight on c5, a focal point on g7 (a focal point is a square where a mate can be delivered) or a bishop on b7 attacking an e4-pawn with protection from a queen and bishop on d4 and g2 respectively. Elements are closely connected to the here and now, so basic that you often do not see them but just realise they are there, just as we tend to see only a word rather than the letters it comprises.

A concept is closely related to the elements. Here it is the knight going to d7 and c5, it is ...e6-e5 as a counter to f2-f4 (with the idea of e4-e5 as a possibility) in order to attack the e4-pawn, or f2-f4 followed by g3-g4-g5 with a kingside attack. A very important aspect of concepts is that they are independent of current realities. For example when the knight travels to c5 via d7 we ignore the threat of mate for the time being, and when we consider where White's knight should go (it is clearly the piece that most requires improvement) we take liberties when we choose – for now our three favourites are c4, d5 and f5. None are really possible at the moment, but the idea of going to all of these three squares exists nonetheless. That is what a concept is all about: the mere possibility/idea.

Chess is very often a matter of transforming concepts into elements, as in the position above. White has a problem with his knight and he is not at all interested in Black transferring his to c5. For now there is a mate, but a move like ...e6-e5 could change that. Naturally White would then gain f5 for the knight, but what else is there? These are logical thoughts to have during the game. We cannot always see these things instantly, we need to look for them. Here White's b2-bishop is suddenly thwarted by ....e6-e5; only the manoeuvre ♗b2-c1-e3x♘c5 makes any sense, but it does take a lot of time. It becomes more and more apparent that White needs to act.

Experience is helpful, of course. A normal positional procedure is sacrificing a pawn in order to vacate a square for a piece. I know that some people will find this idea rather alien, but look at a position such as the following:

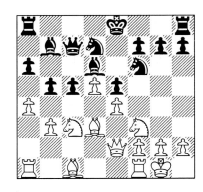

Black to move

This is a proto-typical position from the Meran variation of the Queen's Gambit Declined, although it is not normally played in this fashion these days. However, it illustrates perfectly what I am trying to say. Black could play 14...b4 and White would then respond with 15 ♘b1! followed by ♘b1-d2-c4. Obviously this is not tempting for Black, so instead he can try another approach.

14...c4!? 15 bxc4 b4!

In return for the sacrifice Black has a strong passed pawn on the b-file and a brilliant square for his pieces on c5. Let us not forget that the price is a pawn, so the position is fairly balanced. White should probably play...

16 ♘d1!

...going for the f5-square.

Anyway, back to Fischer-Petrosian. With the elements and concepts mentioned it is now time to look for a way for White to realise his plans.

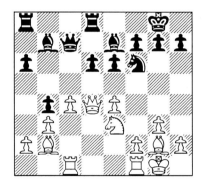

He wants a good square for his knight, he wants to prevent Black's from being planted on c5 and he is quite aware of the idea of sacrificing a pawn for a square. Consequently White will begin to investigate 16 c5, with unsurprising results.

16 c5!

Gaining a square (c4) for the knight and simultaneously preventing Black from using c5. Of course a pawn might seem too big a price to pay for this, but the c-file is a key factor.

16...dxc5 17 ♛xb4!

Another of the concepts mentioned above comes into play: the x-ray created by the rook on c1 on Black's unprotected queen. Now White simply has a clear edge, as Black is left with a weak pawn on c5, no good square for his knight and with no chance of keeping White's knight out of c4. Black is forced to accept damage to his structure, since after 17...cxb4 18 ♖xc7 ♖d7 19 ♖xb7 ♖xb7 20 e5 ♘d5 21 ♘xd5 exd5 22 ♗xd5 he will be a pawn down.

Primary Concepts

I believe that the idea of elements is easier to grasp than that of concepts. Elements are the actual interactions between pieces, while concepts are the possible interactions, and thus more abstract. Often, when you sit at the board, searching for ideas, you limit yourself to looking at the elements (come on, don't deny it – I know you do), rather like a man running down a street who answers 'I don't know' when asked where he is running to. This is often called calculation, where people lose their way because, since they have not decided what they want to do with their position, they look at every possible variation.

I am convinced that true calculation cannot take place before you have decided what you are looking for. The reason is simple, calculation is aimed at reaching a result. If you are not aiming for a result, but randomly checking out variations, then you might be a treasure hunter, an adventurer, but you are not a Real chess player, trying to find good squares for the pieces and making them work together.

Okay, so you look for concepts and you see as many as you do variations. You are just as lost as before, so where, you ask, is the improvement? Good question and, as for all good questions, there seems to be a good answer. Returning to Fischer-Petrosian, the *primary concept* in the position was Black's potential manoeuvre ...♘f6-d7-c5, not that this would decide the game, rather it would offer Black's forces harmony and in turn good chances. By preventing this and securing his worst placed piece a very nice square White tipped the balance and earned a large advantage. This was done by tactics, and is precisely what tactics do: they implement positional ideas and take advantage of the concepts. Elements do not depend on tactics as they are 'real', but with concepts we are concerned only with manoeuvring and tactics. Concepts are not immediate and therefore require some kind of transformation in a position.

Let us look at another example. Here Bobby Fischer, aged thirteen, gives us a lesson and demonstrates remarkable understanding. The reasoning in this kind of position is simple: in order to exert maximum pressure on the opponent White will have to attack weaknesses. If these don't exist, then the first step is to create them.

First we should define *weakness*, since for some players this seems not so simple. A weakness is a weak point that can be attacked. If this is not possible there

is no reason to call it a weakness. Take the f7-pawn as an example – it is not protected by any pawns and might eventually fall to a heavy invasion on the seventh rank, but this is highly unlikely. Right now there is no reason for White to speculate on attacking this point because he has no chance of success! So the only genuine weaknesses to consider are the pawns on d4 and b7. Note that a piece can be dominated and poorly placed but, as such, it is not a weakness since it is not fixed to a square.

Fischer-Popel
US Open 1956

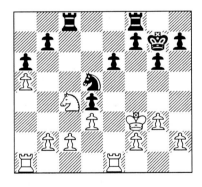

Let us briefly discuss these key features in the diagram position. The d4-pawn can be attacked but is quite easily protected. Black will most likely play ...♘d5-b4-c6, and in this way keep the pawn under control. White cannot seriously consider ♘c4-e5 as c2 would then become a target for attack down the c-file. Then there is the b7-pawn. This cannot be protected by the knight from any convenient square and the king is currently far away, so the rooks could suddenly find themselves in an uncomfortable position, tied to the protection of the pawn. No prizes for guessing what Fischer does!

22 ♖a3! ♖fd8 23 ♖b3 ♖c7 24 ♔e2!

The king is going to protect the c-pawn, thus liberating the c4-knight.

24...♘e7?!

This might be a mistake. The knight does look a bit silly on d5, but it keeps an eye on b6, a square which soon proves useful for White.

25 ♔d2 ♘c6 26 ♖b6! ♖d5 27 ♖a1 ♔f8 28 ♖a3 ♔e7 29 ♖ab3

Black is passive, although the game is far from decided. However, White's manoeuvring helps to illustrate the point of the most important concept. Here it was attack against b7, and Fischer then discovered how to carry this out.

Normally during training sessions I tell my pupils to look for concepts, then ask, for example, where they want a bishop to be placed. I have experienced that it takes quite a while before they reach the desired state of freedom of thought. Recently I have turned to the metaphor of Christmas. When you sit at the board wishing for this or that to happen, use the term Christmas to ask yourself what you would like to do. This can help free your mind. In the Fischer-Petrosian example Fischer wanted to occupy c4 with his knight, but my pupils have generally found this difficult to see because there is a pawn on that square. That is why I want them to think of Christmas, I want them to wish for just about anything. Forget about defended or occupied squares. I have found that this method helps in seeing

positions as more like a vast collection of concepts rather than elements, and this is very good for the tournament player.

The following example is rather complicated but a 2100 pupil solved it in ten minutes using this line of thinking.

Najer–Bocharov
Elista 2000
Sicilian Defence

1 e4 c5 2 ♘c3 e6 3 ♘f3 ♘c6 4 d4 cxd4 5 ♘xd4 ♕c7 6 ♗e2 a6 7 0-0 ♘f6 8 ♗e3 ♗e7 9 f4 d6 10 a4 0-0 11 ♔h1 ♖e8 12 a5!?

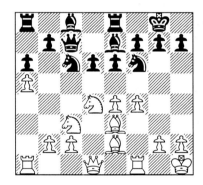

This is the latest fashion, and the idea is quite Christmas-like, in fact. White would love to have control over b6 and to open the f-file. This move threatens the first (13 ♘b3!) and thus undermines Black's control over the centre. The price, however, is a pawn, and the conclusion regarding this idea is yet to surface.

12...♘xa5!

The logical reaction. After something like 12...♗d7 13 ♘b3 White is better.

13 e5 dxe5

Forced. 13...♘d7? 14 exd6 ♗xd6 15 ♘db5! gives White an overwhelming advantage.

14 fxe5 ♘d7?!

I am a bit sceptical about this move, which seems to abandon the kingside. And with the knight misplaced on a5 White has a potential majority of pieces on the kingside, as we shall see in the game. 14...♕xe5 is probably the correct move, although matters remain undecided after 15 ♗f4 ♕c5 16 ♘a4 ♕a7 17 ♗c7, which has been played in some games.

15 ♗f4!

The logical move again, and a theoretical novelty. The e5-pawn is strong asset for White, contributing to the occupation of important squares on the kingside and supporting an attack. Eventually the pawn should fall but in the meantime Black has development problems, which he tries to solve with his next move.

15...b6?

Black decides that his queen's bishop needs attention, but there are more important aspects of the position to address. At the cost of a pawn White has gained a lead in development and a potential attack on the kingside. Key weaknesses in Black's position are e6 and f7, which is why the bishop does not belong on b7 (Black would find it hard to develop any real threats of his own here). Furthermore White's superiority in the centre needs testing. The important transit squares d3, d4, d5, e3, e4 and e5 and f3, f4 and f5 are all under White's control. This is the position I show my pupils. It does not take a long time for them to realise that White

should attack f7, but it is more difficult for them to realise that it should be with something that will attack e8 and g8 simultaneously, like a queen, bishop or pawn.

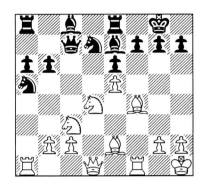

Attack f7!

16 ♘d5!!

To me this move is simple and logical, but I am an attacking player, so these things come quite naturally. To my pupils who, at the moment, at least, are more positionally oriented, this move is very difficult to find. I am sure it would be easier to see if a pawn stood on d5. Anyway, Black is practically forced to capture the knight, after which White's pawn can proceed to e6 with gain of tempo.

16...exd5

16...♕d8 17 ♖xa5! exd5 18 e6 ♘f6 19 ♘c6 wins the queen. 16...♕c5 is the only genuine alternative, but after 17 b4 ♕xd5 18 ♗f3 ♕c4 19 bxa5! (do not give up your lead in development for the sake of a simple exchange!) 19...♖b8 20 ♘c6 White wins sufficient material to think of victory.

17 e6 ♕b7

The only square as dark squares leave

the queen subject to a discovered check in the event of ♗f4.

18 exf7+ ♔xf7

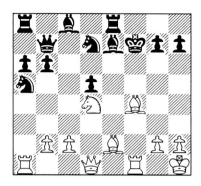

Now White has an attack but he needs to bring his pieces to the kingside as quickly as possible. The first move to be considered should be 19 ♗h5+, but after 19...g6 the problem is how White should continue the attack. Note that White's dark-squared bishop is already active, so it is more important to focus on including the three pieces that do not yet contribute to the attack, namely the other bishop, the queen's rook and the queen. If we think of Christmas, then it is not difficult to come up with ♕h5+, which seems to be much more dangerous for Black than the bishop check. Therefore...

19 ♗xa6!

The gain of tempo is crucial because in response to something like 19 ♗d3 Black has 19...♘f6!, shoring up the kingside defence considerably.

19...♖xa6 20 ♕h5+ ♔g8

It does not take long to realise that this is the only option, even if it is undesirable. The alternatives all look grim. 20...g6 21 ♕xh7+ ♔f6 22 ♗d6+ ♔g5 23 ♘e6+ and 20...♔f6 both invite mate,

while 20...♔f8 21 ♘e6+ ♔g8 22 ♕xe8+ ♘f8 23 ♘xf8 ♗xf8 24 ♗d6 wins for White.

21 ♕xe8+ ♘f8

21...♗f8 loses immediately to 22 ♗d6. Again we are concerned with finding the weakest point in the opponent's position and, subsequently, a way to attack. Black can delay defeat here with 22...h6 but White will be ahead in material and continue the attack. Now White needs to find a way to get the maximum from his pieces. The queen's rook needs to join the attack, and at the moment the f4-bishop lacks an active role.

22 ♗g5!

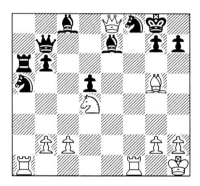

The best approach, and easiest found by calculation and imagination. The right way to explain this through primary elements/concepts is the terrible weakness of f8. White could develop his rook with tempo after 22 ♖ae1 but the big question will then be: what is the rook doing on the e-file apart from attacking the bishop? Nothing, really. After 22...♗c5 Black has a chance to fight since the bishop is no longer unprotected, thus reducing Black's problems by one, at least.

The text opens the f-file with tempo by attacking f8 in the only way this piece can. Again we have White's remaining pieces attacking and undermining the weakest point in Black's position. It is all pure logic.

22...♗c5 23 ♖xf8+!

The f-file is where the action is. This is the rule mentioned in Chapter 2 being put into practise: *the number of pieces in an attack on the king is more important than their independent value.* Here White effectively exchanges his queen's rook for a knight and a tempo, and Black is unable to respond as his pieces are stuck on the opposite flank.

23...♗xf8 24 ♖f1 1-0

Black resigned as mate will follow.

There were some global rules that hint at the way in which White should act around the fifteenth or sixteenth move. These mainly have to do with the development lead and the majority of pieces on the kingside. Perhaps this sounds quite vague – below I will explain why.

Global and Local Rules

Chess is still a mystery for us. As mathematics it is a deep combinatory exercise but, mathematically, not too complicated, although it is not possible to calculate it to the end at the moment. It is the same with the rules in chess, which are approximate. Our knowledge is limited in many ways and will probably always be. For the same reason we cannot have ultimate rules, but we can have rules that are more reliable than others, and those that are so reliable that it would be difficult to imagine them not being true. However, they are not mathematically exact. The only rule that would be 100% exact is one defined by numbers and calculations – not by understanding.

But humans cannot calculate to that degree. We cannot calculate 1% of 1% of 1% of anything in chess. Therefore we need to get nearer to the model that can work in practice, when we interact with the pieces and try to make them perform as we want them to. This is where the idea of rules originates.

In my thoughts about truth and chess, with the idea of improving first my own play and then the play of my pupils, I have come across two kinds of rules. First there are global rules that are the same all over the board, and these often have a generic structure. It can be something like 'In rook endings the rook should always be active' (Dvoretsky), 'Bring all your pieces into the attack' or 'The bishop is better than the knight in an open position.' There are plenty of these and, as I cannot bring justice to all of them here I have chosen to limit myself to three – two are considered elsewhere in this book and the third we look at below.

Note that they should not be understood as truths but near truths. They are good guidelines if you understand what they contain and do not use them dogmatically.

Let us investigate two examples of bishop against knight in an open position. Both are taken from a book by an excellent chess writer, Edmar Mednis, called *From the Middlegame into the Endgame.* (His books are generally highly recommended).

Geller–Dorfman
Lvov Zonal 1978

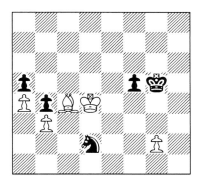

Here the bishop is stronger than the knight for several reasons. The bishop can protect the important b3-pawn, while the knight cannot do anything to prevent the enemy king from hunting down the a5-pawn. This is due to the difference in the general nature of bishop and knight. A bishop can operate from afar whereas a knight can work only at close quarters. This is why open positions generally favour the bishop and closed positions generally favour the knight, since in closed positions the knight's ability to jump over pieces is crucial but the bishop's long-range advantage is negated by the presence of blockading pawns.

In the diagram position the knight is inferior to the bishop, lacking a much needed stronghold. Moreover, if the bishop needs to move away from a threat (as is the case here) it can continue its work from somewhere else on the diagonal, while the knight cannot move to another square and continue exerting pressure on b3 (more than one move is required to do so).

41 ♗g8!

A good square from which to operate.

41...♚f4 42 ♚d3!

A nice move. The knight is very well placed on d2 but must now go to an inferior square. White does not lose any time, as d4-c5-b5xa5 is no faster than d3-c4-b5xa5. Mednis' analysis shows the need for this logical move: 42 ♚c5 ♚e3 43 ♚b5 ♚d4 44 ♚xa5 ♚c3 45 ♚b6 ♘xb3 46 a5 ♘xa5! 47 ♚xa5 b3 48 ♚b5 b2 49 ♗a2 ♚d2! with a draw in view.

42...♘f1 43 ♚c4 ♘e3+ 44 ♚b5 ♘xg2

Black secures himself a passed pawn. This is his only chance of a successful defence.

45 ♚xa5 ♚e5

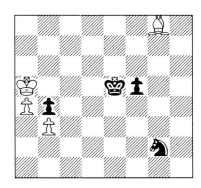

46 ♚xb4

This move is logical as White now has two connected passed pawns on the kingside. Combined support from king and bishop will probably win the game. Otherwise a reasonable alternative is 46 ♚b6!? ♘e3 (46...f4 47 ♗c4 ♘e3 48 ♗b5 seems to be a winning plan for White) 47 a5 f4 48 a6 f3 49 a7 f2 50 a8♕ f1♕ 51 ♕a5+ followed by the capture ♕xb4, with excellent winning chances.

46...♔d6 47 ♔b5?

The wrong plan. Better is 47 a5! ♘e3 48 ♔c3 followed by b3-b4 and moving the king to the kingside. Whether this is enough to win I am not completely sure, although Mednis seems quite confident that it is.

47...f4 48 ♗c4 f3 49 ♔b6

These king moves do cut off Black's king but they do not push the pawns forward, so, suddenly, Black already has a well advanced passed pawn, while the white pawns still have to take their first step forward.

49...♘e3 50 ♗d3 ♘d5+ 51 ♔b7 ♔c5! 52 a5 f2 53 ♗f1

53 a6 ♘b4 54 ♗f1 ♘xa6 55 ♔xa6 ♔b4 draws.

53...♘b4

54 ♗c4??

White is still trying to win the game, but he is suddenly very close to losing. The correct route is 54 a6, which is the same as before.

54...♘c6! 55 a6??

55 ♗f1 ♘xa5+ 56 ♔c7 ♘xb3 57 ♔d7 and White will probably be able to hold the draw, but only just. Now Black wins easily.

55...♘a5+ 56 ♔b8 ♘xc4 57 bxc4 f1♕

58 a7 ♕f8+ 59 ♔b7 ♕e7+ 60 ♔b8 ♔b6! 0-1

White is mated in four moves, hence the resignation.

This might seem like a strange example to include for the bishop's superiority over knight, but I feel that clear-cut examples can sometimes be misleading. Here it was obvious that White had a commanding position due to the better minor piece, but it was not enough to automatically win the game. If you treat your bishop with disrespect, then it is no better than the knight. And in the endgame there is another rule: *Passed pawns should be pushed unless they become weak in doing so.* White failed to appreciate this, instead preparing the advance of the pawns for way too long, ultimately doing nothing about it.

So, here we are: Bishops are better than knights in open positions, but the rule is not 'Bishops against knights win the game' – only mate has that kind of strength! The rule describes a general comparison of the two pieces and their abilities. In the position above the superiority of the bishop was somewhat limited by not being able to help in the attack of the opponent's pawns, but it was still far stronger than the knight, which had trouble being on both flanks at the same time. Incidentally this is another famous difference between knights and bishops – long-range bishops are best when there are pawns on both sides, while the knights are at their strongest when the action is on one flank only. Again this is quite natural, as the knight has potential influence on all squares while the bishop can go from one side of the board to the other in just one move.

The diagram below illustrates an example where the difference between bishop and knight is seen at its maximum:

It was a position such as this that my old coach, the legendary Grandmaster Henrik Danielsen, once showed me. I was not sure whether or not Black was winning. Actually, Black is winning very easily. White can do nothing to attack the a4-pawn, so Black is effectively a piece up on the kingside, where the game will be decided. I believe I was confused by the fact that the bishop is protecting the pawn. I got the feeling that Black should try to win on the queenside instead of simply letting the pawn and knight comfort each other while White's kingside is taken apart.

In the next example from the Mednis book the bishop is not better than the knight. The position is less open than the previous two examples, the pawn structure is uneven and the black pawns on the bishop's own colour limit the range of the bishop and provide the knight with excellent squares.

Bronstein-Yusupov
Lucerne Olympiad 1982

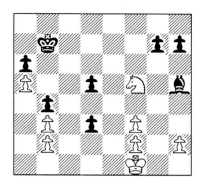

Incidentally, as far as I am aware this is the Argentine Luis Bronstein, and not the famous David Bronstein. White is better due to Black's weaknesses and the possibility of creating a passed pawn on the kingside. The only weaknesses in White's camp are the two doubled pawns on f3 and b3, as all the other pawns are on dark squares; the a5-pawn, being out on the flank, is by no means convenient to attack.

33 ♘d4?

Passive. It is true that the knight is well placed here and that the position still favours White, but it is more logical to play 33 ♘xg7 ♗xf3 34 ♔e1, after which Black will have a hard time defending his pawns and keeping an eye on the potentially dangerous passed pawn on the f-file. It is often impossible to play for a win with passive moves. We can also conclude that, by simple comparison, this exchange is favourable for White, since the f3-pawn is not as important as the g7-pawn.

33...g5!

Monitoring White's kingside pawns. Yusupov knows that he is losing and that he can do nothing about it, so he wisely chooses to gradually improve his position. It is not for nothing that he has been a top player for twenty years. Note that if White could not find the correct plan once then there is a chance that he might fail to do so again, so it makes sense to persevere.

34 ♔e1 h6 35 ♔d2

35 ♘f5!? is suggested by Mednis as an improvement. I have my doubts concerning this since it takes time – not that the move is poor, I simply do not believe that it is superior than the game continuation.

35...♗g6 36 f4!

Now White has to act before the structural advantages disappear and all he has got left is a passive position.

36...gxf4 37 ♘e6 f3

38 ♘d4?

This is a bad mistake. White must have been in time trouble here, otherwise it is surprising that he should decide that f3 was the pawn to remove. It probably has something to do with White not realising the importance of the weak moves he has made. He is still better, but not as much as before. This question is considered in Chapter 9.

38 ♘f4! ♗e4 39 ♘xd3 ♔c6 40 ♔e3 ♔b5 41 ♘e5 ♔xa5 42 ♘xf3 offers White excellent winning chances. Now he underestimates (fatally) the strength of the passed d-pawn.

38...♗e4 39 ♔e3 ♔c7 40 ♘xf3??

Losing immediately, but the position is no longer easy to play when trying to win. After 40 ♘e6+ ♔d6 41 ♘f4 White has the advantage as 41...♔e5 42 ♘xd3+ ♗xd3 43 ♔xd3 results in a winning pawn ending.

40...♗xf3! 0-1

After 41 ♔xf3 d4! 42 h4 h5 White is in zugzwang.

The knight was superior to the bishop in this example despite the fact that the position should be characterised as open in nature. However, the pawn formation in the centre severely limited the scope of the bishop, and the poorly placed king also presented problems.

What does this tells us about the rule 'The bishop is better than the knight in open positions'? Well, quite a lot, actually. It helps to explain why it is so, and to understand when it is not so. This is not because the rule has exceptions – it is still valid. The bishop is better than the knight in open positions, but more important in the game above was the rule regarding 'good' and 'bad' bishops. A bishop is not good if it is restricted by its own pawns, or by the opponent's pawns. In our example Black's bishop had trouble operating properly since it was restricted by its own pawns, and that was more important than the position being open. Nevertheless we could see that this alone did not win the game.

A knight is only better than a bishop in such a position if used well – merely moving around will lead to trouble.

This is the reasoning behind rules in chess. A bishop is not better than a knight in an open position just because I say so. There are some exact properties for these pieces that create the rule, and if these properties are obscured for this or that reason, then the rule becomes less important. Again the key condition is *all things being equal.* Some would claim that this falls in 'exceptions' to the rule but, in my opinion, that is silly. Bishops and knights retain the properties that created the rule even when other elements of the position are more important. For example a hitherto dormant bishop can suddenly be transformed into a powerful piece. It is more of a concept in the position than an element.

This is where the discussion ends. I understand chess as a combination of elements and concepts. I cannot understand it as a combinational mathematical exercise. At least it does not make any sense for me as a player wanting to win games over the board. Therefore I must accept that my cognitive system will need to find another way to deal with truth in chess, as described above.

Comparing Pieces

This is a technique I have used for some years in my training and, although it seems stupidly simple, it has served to improve my pupils' understanding of positions immediately.

What we do is very simple. We compare the white pieces with the black pieces, one by one, selecting them for comparison by simply deciding which will most likely be exchanged with each other. I have discovered that in this way it is possible to get a good overview of the position. We also discuss and consider pawn structure, but in most positions the pieces will reflect the pawn structure in a way that makes this less important. The pawn structure is hardly ever advantageous for one player if it does not help his pieces.

The following example illustrates how I would use this method to reason in a complex position. The position has occurred in more than one game and is somewhat interesting from a theoretical point of view. For me the story behind the position is an interesting one. In 1998 I wrote a book about the Panov-Botvinnik Attack (Caro-Kann Defence) and I somehow failed to consider an option for Black (17th move), despite the fact that it had been played in a tournament in Hungary while I was resident in Budapest! I guess that the information age is only really beginning these days as far as chess is concerned. My database is currently growing faster than the number of new games played throughout the world, thanks to old games suddenly surfacing.

Anyway, I met Swedish soon-to-be Grandmaster and team-mate Stellan Brynell on a train in Germany. He had been playing in the Bundesliga and presented with over the board problems which he felt he had not solved successfully. As always the guy who wrote the book some years previously is held accountable for everything, especially the moves he did not include in the book (Brynell had earlier brought my attention to a giant hole in my book – I had not included 5...♗e6!?, which is not a major line but nonetheless merits a place). Brynell showed me the position before White's 19th move and the problems he was facing. It did not take me long to decide that I felt White should be better. From there it was easy to pick out the right continuation from the principles I have tried to promote in this book.

Acs–Ruck

Hungary 1996
Caro-Kann Defence

1 e4 c6 2 d4 d5 3 exd5 cxd5 4 c4 ♘f6 5 ♘c3 ♘c6 6 ♘f3 ♗g4 7 cxd5 ♘xd5 8 ♕b3 ♗xf3 9 gxf3 ♘b6

Black avoids the endgame that arises after 9...e6 10 ♕xb7 ♘xd4 11 ♗b5+ ♘xb5 12 ♕c6+ ♔e7 13 ♕xb5 ♕d7 14 ♗g5+ f6 15 ♘xd5+ ♕xd5 16 ♕xd5 exd5 17 ♗e3 ♔e6 18 0-0-0 ♗b4 19 ♔b1!, which I am certain favours White. I know that Kasparov wrote that Black had excellent drawing chances, but one month doing nothing but studying the fine details of this endgame in 1997 led me to a different conclusion. I am sure that Kasparov's 6 ♗g5 has more to do with stylistic preferences than an actual evaluation of the position.

10 ♗e3 e6 11 0-0-0 ♗e7 12 d5 exd5 13 ♘xd5 ♘xd5 14 ♖xd5 ♕c7 15 ♔b1 0-0 16 f4 ♘b4 17 ♖d4

In my book I considered this position and suggested only 17...♘c6 and 17...a5!?, but another move is occasionally tried...

17...♕c6?

I truly dislike this move because it serves only to force White's rook to the best open file, in turn setting up ♗g2.

18 ♖g1 ♖ad8

Okay – here we go!

Let us start with comparing the pieces. The kings seem to be more or less equal. White has some pressure on the g-file and Black has potential pressure on the e4-b1 diagonal. Actually, Black threatens ...♖xd4 followed by ...♕e4+. This was what made Brynell play the awful 19 ♖c4? and end up in a poor position that he won in thirty moves. It is hard to see a difference between the kings, but there is one when we come to the queens. White's queen is posted on practically the best square, monitoring the key squares d5, b7 and f7 and assisting the attack on Black's knight. The black queen is also well placed, but not permanently since it can be easily challenged by ♗g2 at any moment. In fact it is not easy to see where the queen should find a long-term resting place, so this is a positional problem for Black. The rooks on d4 and d8 appear to be of equal strength; I like the pressure White's exerts on b4, but I also like the potential pressure on the d-file. As for the other rooks, White's is aggressively posted on the g-file and is clearly superior to Black's, which does nothing on f8 and is yet to find a decent role. The dark-squared bishops are evenly matched, and it is a case of which will occupy the long diagonal first (at the moment it looks like Black, but nothing is decided yet). I prefer White's light-squared bishop to the knight (despite the fact that it is not well placed at the moment) in view of the respective long-term prospects of the pieces. Both b7 and f7 are major weaknesses (see the paragraph on missing bishops, below) and Black cannot find a safe spot for the knight in this open centre. Actually this is a powerful example of a bishop being superior to a knight in an open position. The bishop can move freely and the knight has nowhere safe to go.

Had Brynell carried out this brief exercise (he was busy worrying about Black's threat) he would probably have been more optimistic, although I know Brynell would have been careful nonetheless. It is my conclusion that White stands better and thus should play aggressively. The best way to put pressure on the opponent before you strike is to improve your worst placed piece, and we already know that this is the light-squared bishop. So we ask ourselves: at Christmas where would we want the bishop? The answers are e4 or d5, central squares from where the bishop can concentrate on different weaknesses in the enemy camp. But how do we engineer this? Brynell wanted to play 19 ♗g2 but noticed the seemingly deadly

check 19...♕g6+, after which 20 ♗e4 loses to 20...♕xg1+. Note that 19 ♗d3 allows an exchange of a great bishop for what we have already discovered is Black's worst piece. Thus Black's threat and 19 ♗g2 ♕g6+ prompted Brynell to opt for 19 ♖c4?, but this is the wrong attitude. We can see that 19 ♗g2 is the correct move from our logical assumptions, so we should try harder to make it work – as do the best players. So, I quickly came up with...

19 ♗g2!! ♕g6+

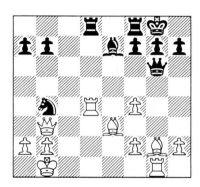

20 f5!

This is not so difficult to find but, alas, was overlooked by Brynell. In fact this is Brynell's great weakness. He is a very careful player who dislikes sacrificing material without immediate gain and is not too fond of lengthy calculations. Consequently a tactic such as the text might be lost on him. I guess that is why he will not become world champion.

20...♕xf5+ 21 ♗e4

One of the ideal squares for the bishop.

21...♕a5

Played because the knight was 'suddenly' hanging – 'bad' pieces have this tendency, unless they are on the back rank, as the knight will be in a few moves.

22 a3 ♘c6

22...♘a6!? might be better.

23 ♖xd8

White is now ready to cash in on b7. Note that White is not giving up any advantages for this, and nor should he.

23...♘xd8?!

23...♗xd8 24 ♕xb7 ♘e5 25 ♕xa7 gives White a clear advantage so Black tries to maintain his material lead. However, this is too passive. When we arrived at this position it was not difficult for me to sense that White should have some kind of attack. All four pieces are engaged in an attack on Black's queen, while none of Black's pieces is able to defend properly.

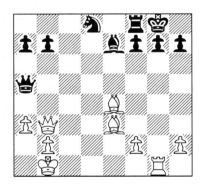

24 ♗d4

Adding extra pressure to g7.

24...♗g5

No other move would have saved Black. Winning for White are 24...g6 25 ♗xg6 hxg6 26 ♖xg6+ ♔h7 27 ♖g7+ ♔h6 28 ♕h3+ ♕h5 29 ♖h7+ and 24...♘e6 25 ♕xe6 fxe6 26 ♖xg7+ ♔h8 27 ♖xe7+ e5 28 ♗xe5+ ♖f6 29 ♗xf6+ ♔g8 30 ♗xh7+ ♔f8 31 ♗g6. Less

straightforward is 24...g5, which still loses in a multitude of ways, one of them being 25 ♕d3 f5 26 ♗c3 ♕c5 27 ♗d5+ ♘f7 28 ♗b4 ♕c7 29 ♕e3!! ♖d8 30 ♖c1 ♕d7 31 ♗e6 ♕e8 32 ♖c7, when White wins material.

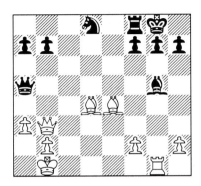

I cannot believe that Black really escaped this position with a draw against a player as strong as Peter Acs. How does White win? What is the weakness in Black's position?

25 ♕h3?

The primary weakness is the pin on the g-file. Black's g-pawn was a problem, hence the rather desperate ...♗g5, with the idea of dropping back to h6. But at the moment the bishop is protected only by the queen. This leads us to 25 ♗c3!, forcing 25...♕c5, after which White wins with the simple 26 ♗b4. Then after 26...♕e5 White should not capture on f8 because the e4-bishop is hanging, but instead there is the elegant 27 ♗xh7+!, earning a full exchange with no trace of compensation.

After White's error the game was soon drawn:

25...g6 26 ♕f3 ♘e6 27 ♗c3 ♕b6 28 ♗xb7 ♗h6 29 ♗d5 ♗g7 30 ♗xg7 ½-½

Talk Exercises

These are exercises I use a lot with my pupils in order to increase their positional understanding. Basically the idea is that two people talk about a position in more generic terms and thus find the right course of action. Normally it is I who talks to pupils, asking questions to help them organise their thoughts. We usually start by comparing pieces and then we proceed to discussing different elements and concepts in the position. We use the concept of Christmas as much as we can.

Only after we have discussed plans, ideal squares for the pieces, which piece needs the most attention (this is the answer to the riddle: 'Why are Russians such strong chess players?' – they talk to their pieces... where do you want to go my little friend...) and whatever else comes into our minds, do we move on to discussing concrete action.

The aim of this exercise is to improve the verbal aspect of thinking. I am convinced that every time we make spoken, verbal conclusions, these are stored in our cognitive framework for future processing. In other words, they form the foundation of our intuition. The reason why it is very useful to speak these conclusions out loud is that we listen to ourselves about 99% of the time. And inputs from around us have a greater impact on our future way of thinking than if we keep words internal.

In his arsenal of training methods Dvoretsky has a similar exercise that is concerned with formulating thoughts about different positions. For example if you speak to yourself about them and then return to the subject some months later you will find that you no longer have the same kind of views. You have improved.

I have included a chapter about Talk Exercises at the end of the book in order to provide some examples.

Looking over the Shoulder Exercises

This is a simple exercise that my good friend FM John Richardson once showed me. Actually, he did not show it to me – we just did it. He took a game from the newspaper and we played through it, trying to guess the next move. We talked about what was the best move (and why) and often our conclusions seemed to be superior to the players' themselves, unless their names were Kasparov, Karpov or Basman.

The best way to do this exercise is to use a facility in ChessBase – this program has so many useful facilities that I forgive its existence for being primarily based on searching for your opponents' games and for concrete theoretical positions. Anyway, when you have the game on the screen you set it on Training. The program then hides the moves so that all you have on the screen is the position and the latest moves – simply take it from there. Again I strongly recommend that two people carry out this exercise because the subsequent discussion proves useful. Therefore – unless you find it normal to talk to yourself – find a training partner of similar strength. It is advisable that you use annotated games, as these make more sense. Remember to believe in yourself just as much as the annotator, and ask questions.

Missing Bishops

I have already discussed the properties of the pieces, and generically, it is easy to understand what I am talking about. We all know how the pieces move. But what is the practical impact on pawn structures and the rules of chess? Too many to name here, obviously. However, I would like to look at an example (also from Watson's book) of how bishops can effect pawn structure. Watson uses the example to illustrate rule independence in the opening, but I want to show it as a basic example of the exchange of bishop for knight, and how this can affect a position.

Shliperman-Yermolinsky
Philadelphia 1997
Bogo-Indian Defence

1 d4 ♘f6 2 c4 e6 3 ♘f3 ♗b4+ 4 ♘bd2

This is probably the best move in the position if you are of equal strength to your opponent but, as mentioned in Chapter 7, it is often in the stronger player's interest to exchange bishop for knight, or knight for bishop. There are pros and cons for both the text and 4 ♗d2, and I guess it is a matter of taste and personality.

4...d6!?

This is quite an interesting move. I have the feeling that Yermolinsky, with his great experience in this kind of position, already had the basic idea of the pawn sacrifice in his head, if only as a general idea. Perhaps his thinking was along the lines of – if I do not move the b-pawn too early I will save a tempo when I sacrifice it later. The standard continuations here are 4...0-0 5 a3 ♗e7

6 e4 d5 and 4...b6 5 a3 ♗xd2+.

5 a3 ♗xd2+ 6 ♕xd2

A standard decision. White can also recapture with 6 ♗xd2; the decision is based on where White wants to develop his dark-squared bishop.

6...♘bd7!

Precise play. Black wants to be able to act on the queenside immediately and thus delays castling. White should probably play the calm 7 e3 now in order to address kingside development and concentrate on the light squares, where his influence is already lessened by placing his pawns on the opposite colour complex. In fact White's failure to develop his light-squared bishop gives Black good chances to try for an initiative on the light squares.

7 b4?! a5!

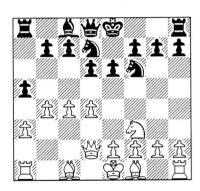

White has no decent response to this thrust. After 8 ♖b1 axb4 9 axb4 Black takes over the a-file without any effort, while the game continuation leaves the bishop misplaced and also presents Black with a tempo, which he uses to increase his domination on the light squares.

8 ♗b2 axb4 9 axb4 ♖xa1+ 10 ♗xa1

Now, let us start by comparing the

pieces. Black's king is the safer of the two because there is more open air to the left of White's. The queens seem to be evenly matched – Black's needs to find a good base while c2 is probably the best for its opposite number. Black's rook is closer to being developed, a factor that will prove significant when its route into the game is cleared by the other pieces. The c8-bishop is no better or worse than White's on f1, while the knights on f3 and d7 both control dark squares in the centre, although this is not where the battle will be fought. Finally Black's remaining knight is more useful than the a1-bishop *for the time being*, since the bishop has the potential to be very harmful for Black. With a structure that could quite easily see black pawns on c7, d6 and e5 Black might well have trouble containing this piece. And herein lies one of the consequences of the exchange of bishops – in the long-term Black will end up with structural problems, so before this happens he will have to generate counterplay or some kind of structural advantage in order to compensate. However, in the short term the knight is the bishop's superior, having available a strong outpost on the e4-square and the facility to help create threats in enemy territory.

We can conclude, then, that Black is leading in development despite appearances to the contrary. The pieces needing most attention from Black are the bishop and queen, although he should not forget about the rook and king. But now we are approaching the core of the position. Black has structural problems due to the now absent bishop, and to compensate this he has an extra minor piece monitoring the light squares. He needs to act as his advantages are based on time, especially the better king's position. The appropriate policy fully exploits these advantages.

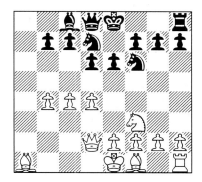

10...b5!

Taking control of the light squares in the centre. White is unable to keep a hold on d5 and must also respond to the challenge from the b-pawn, after which Black will soon gain a further tempo with ...♕a8. Nevertheless, White should be able to defend a whole lot better than he does in the game.

11 c5?!

This seems to do nothing to help White. As he is lacking in development the future threat of ♗xb5 appears hollow because this opens further lines on the queenside, where White is poorly represented. The other advantage of the text, the prevention of ...♘d7-b6, also seems to be of minor importance, as the knight will be able to use f6 as a transition square anyway, only the d5-square being of real interest to the knight.

I prefer 11 cxb5, which makes more sense. Black will probably spend some time regaining the pawn and in the meantime White will be able to complete development and perhaps even generate some pressure on the only weak spot in Black's position, the c7-pawn. Yermolinsky's suggested line goes 11...♗b7 12 e3 ♕a8 13 ♕c3 (why he did not consider 13 ♗b2 I do not know, but it has little relevance here), aiming at c7. Then Yermolinsky prefers 13...♘d5!? 14 ♕b2 ♘xb4 15 ♗e2 ♘c2+ 16 ♔d2! ♘xa1 17 ♖xa1 ♕b8, which he assesses as equal, over the less clear 13...♗xf3 14 gxf3 ♕xf3 15 ♖g1 0-0 16 ♕xc7 ♖a8 17 ♗b2 ♖a2 (I tend to prefer Black but, then again, I like to attack).

11...♗b7 12 e3 ♕a8 13 ♕b2?

The kind of move that makes me ill just looking at it. Obviously White wants to both protect the bishop and get away from ...♘e4, but he has done this the wrong way – or, as someone who talks with his pieces would say: the bishop is very angry!

13 ♗b2!? is Yermolinsky's suggestion, when after 13...♕a4 14 ♗d3 ♘e4 15 ♗xe4 ♗xe4 16 0-0 ♕a8 17 ♖a1 ♕b7 18 ♘e1 White prepares f2-f3 and later e3-e4 with a dynamically balanced position. However, I think he has underestimated 13...♗xf3! 14 gxf3 ♕xf3 15 ♖g1 0-0 (15...dxc5? 16 dxc5 0-0 17 ♕xd7!!), when I believe Black has a safe extra pawn, e.g. 16 ♗xb5 ♖b8 17 ♗xd7 (a sad move to make, but even the more natural 17 ♗e2 ♕h3 does not really improve White's situation as far as I can see, while 17...♕d5 is also strong) 17...♘xd7

see following diagram

Black is structurally better. Notice how Black carried out exchanges on the light squares and now has the clearly superior minor piece.

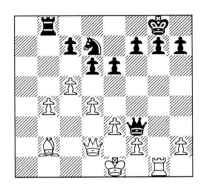

Analysis Diagram

Returning to the position after 12...♕a8, the best defence available to White seems to be 13 ♕d1! 0-0 14 ♗e2 ♕a3 15 ♕b1.

13...♗xf3 14 gxf3 ♕xf3 15 ♖g1 0-0!

Black is fully developed and well coordinated, which certainly cannot be said of White, whose next opens up the queenside for only a pawn, and in this way helps Black. White should accept the pawn deficit and do something for his bishops.

16 ♗xb5? ♖a8 17 ♗f1

17 ♗xd7 ♘xd7 leaves White with little prospect of recovery. The bishop is one of the worst minor pieces I have seen.

17...♘e4

Hitting f2.

18 ♖g2 ♘df6 19 cxd6 cxd6 20 b5 ♘d5 21 b6 ♘b4! 0-1

White resigned in view of 22 b7 ♖xa1!.

Human thinking!

When we first learn to read we begin by learning the letters, and then move on to how they combine to form simple words. Later these words will be so natural that they fade into the background, with more complicated issues – usually the meaning conveyed by the words – taking the foreground. We then build level upon level of understanding...

The same happens when learning chess. We begin by learning how the pieces move, their start position and so on. Then come captures and an understanding of the basics concerning the different natures of the pieces. The next stage concerns tactics and strategy, followed by pawn structure and how to change the nature of the game. We expand our understanding of the opening, our deeper appreciation of pawn structures and tactical abilities.

When people doubt the idea of rules in chess they usually say that real improvement comes when we begin to realise the limitations of these rules. I disagree. At some point a player will inevitably learn new, exciting things about strategy and tactics, and he will try to use such new knowledge as much as possible. These rules are more complex and less global when improvement helps take a player past beginner level, whether it be the nature of pawn structures, pieces etc. As the aspects of the laws of chess become more complex, instruction books are no longer enough.

You will notice that as you begin to see complex interactions over the board you will forget about the elements from which they are created. When players stop looking at these things so regularly they quite naturally have blind spots. I remember an old game where Alekhine, one of the greatest tactical masters of all time, simply 'forgot' about – and lost – a bishop on b5 because it was too basic a consideration to be calculated.

What I have tried to illustrate above is how positional understanding can be trained, and how we can get closer to the rules governing chess. It is obvious that we cannot use all our limited time at the board comparing pieces and thinking about elements; we also need to calculate tactical variations. I believe that the Real chess players are so well trained in the positional elements of chess that they can simply *feel* where the pieces need to go. They are like boxers with longer arms.

Every player has a different experience of sitting at the board, and every human thinks in a different way. What I have tried to do in this chapter is to illustrate a good training method for expanding the learning of positional chess. This has been mainly with young people in mind, although in my time as a coach I have seen that adults can also achieve remarkable improvement in their understanding of positional concepts.

When we sit at the table to play we often find that our thoughts drift and become less structured. Often this is not good, but things should not be too structured, as the following example illustrates.

I do not know from where this position originates. I saw it on the front page of a chess club magazine, indicating no names, year or place. The combination is quite difficult but still possible, so let us begin!

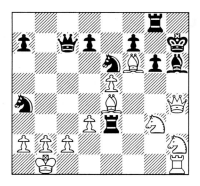 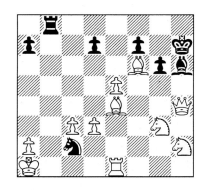

Your time could not be better spent
than solving this... Black wins!

First we realise that White has a very strong attack, the threat of 2 ♕xh6+!! Being devastating. Consequently we think of 1...♖e1+ in order to distract White's rook from the h-file, and then, after 2 ♖xe1 ♖b8, we have threats of over own. For example after 3 b3 ♕c3 it seems that White has no defence. But no – then we notice that 3 ♕xh6+! works just as well, and that Black will be mated. Therefore something immediate is required and the best way to do this is with a checking sequence. We investigate 1...♕xc2+ 2 ♔xc2 ♘d4+ and find that there is a mate after 3 ♔b1 ♘c3+ 4 bxc3 ♖b8+ 5 ♔a1 ♘c2 mate. But soon we fail to find a good way to continue after 3 ♔d1! ♘xb2+ 4 ♔c1 ♖e1+ 5 ♔xb2 ♖b8+ 6 ♔a3 ♘b5+ 7 ♔b4. This is where we start to lose our good sense of humour – or at least I do – but this is also where the cognitive system in our brain will present us with the solution, the brilliant...

1...♖e1+!! 2 ♖xe1 ♕xc2+! 3 ♔xc2 ♘d4+ 4 ♔b1 ♘c3+! 5 bxc3 ♖b8+ 6 ♔a1 ♘c2 mate.

What fascinated me about this example was not the pretty combination itself, but the way I solved it. The combination of ...♖e1+ and ...♕xc2+ was not a product of logic or deep calculation. No method could teach me to do what I did (that is if I follow the method at the board). What happened was that my brain combined available ideas and the solution just popped up. And this is actually the state we are looking for – structured ideas that affect each other. The question of analysis is considered in Chapter 9, so here I want to remain focused on the question of elements. Human thinking, when it works, is a perfect interaction between calculation and understanding.

But how do you get there? How do you feel what is the right move if you do not have the talent of Karpov, Capablanca, Adams and Tal? If you are a mere mortal and have to work hard for every inch you gain in this life?

For the positional part I would recommend the exercises (and the type of exercises) shown above. Work with logic and words. Talk to yourself – or even better – talk to a friend or a trainer. As far as tactical chess is concerned, nothing beats pattern recognition. Look at the following example:

Nunn–Portisch
Reykjavik World Cup 1988

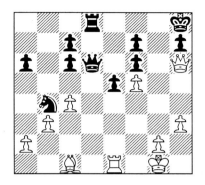

We join the game after 31 h3, when White has a serious threat.
31...c5?
Now Nunn executes a pretty simple combination.
32 ♖e4 ♖g8 33 ♕xh7+! 1-0
Mate soon follows.

Nunn had obviously intended this combination. It is no coincidence that in his Best Games Collection he writes that, as a child, he had solved every combination (999 in all!) in a book and this very same theme had featured. If Portisch had solved the same exercises in his childhood he might have seen the threat but, as it was, only Nunn had the necessary patterns installed in his brain. As has been said elsewhere there is no alternative to actually studying chess if you want to become a stronger player. Other factors are important, too, such as physical and emotional shape, but the merits of studying the game cannot be underestimated.

Alexander Yermolinsky describes in his excellent book how he improved mainly through the study of his own games. This is something I recommend. By finding your weaknesses you will know in which area the greatest need for improvement is required and, consequently, you will be better placed to find exercises that will help you the most. I also recommend working with a trainer. You will often have blind spots in your understanding and, of course, you will not be able to notice all your mistakes.

Another very important issue when working on your own games is never to believe in bad luck, or to put a reverse down to the unfortunate fact that you played well but overlooked something. Try to find the pattern in your mistakes by describing them in more generic terms. When I was an active player I made tournament reports at the end of each event I played in, listing all my mistakes and subsequently explaining them. I found that I made only four to five different types of mistakes in these games. I have the feeling that you will make similar discoveries in your own games. However, I am sorry to say that when you fix these mistakes by improving your understanding of these weaker points, you will then find new weaknesses, only this time at a higher level. The process will never stop, but your tournament results will improve.

I would like to finish this chapter with a recent game played by a pupil of mine (Black). It illustrates how this way of thinking can be implemented in practical play. I think the game is quite impressive when we consider that the winner has an Elo rating of below 2100, and I feel that he could be considerably stronger (at the moment he does not demonstrate such strength in every game he plays).

I must say that I am proud of this game because my pupil illustrates all the principles we had discussed in training, winning a brilliant positional game in which he seems far stronger than his opponent. We shall investigate the reasoning behind the moves in order to have a sense of how the idea of logic is implemented in practice.

Poulsen–Nøhr
Copenhagen 2001
Vienna Game

1 e4 e5 2 ♘c3 ♘f6 3 f4 d5 4 fxe5 ♘xe4 5 ♘f3 ♗c5

Opening theory thus far. My pupil is not a tactical beast (unlike his trainer) and chooses to play the more quiet lines such as the Petroff and the Ruy Lopez. Here his opponent has chosen the Vienna.

6 ♕e2 ♗f2+ 7 ♔d1 ♘xc3+ 8 bxc3

It is hard to criticise this move but standard theory prefers 8 dxc3, easing development.

8...♗h4!

This is cold reasoning. After 8...♗b6 9 ♗a3 my pupil preferred his opponent's bishop, but now he plans to redeploy on e7, which makes much more sense. Note that after 9 ♘xh4 ♕xh4 White will have to use an extra tempo to prevent ...♗g4, although this is just as feasible as the text.

9 d4 ♗e7 10 ♖b1

Here – and particularly with his next move – White shows a disregard for the development of his minor pieces, and this gives Black a chance to open the position to his advantage.

10...0-0 11 h4?!

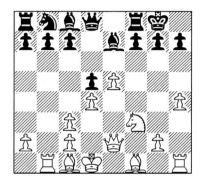

How this helps White I do not know.

11...f6!

I like my pupil's logic here. He wanted to play ...c7-c5 followed by ...♘c6 to put pressure on the centre, but felt that it was not really possible to exert any pressure of significance. Whether this is true, or if ...♕a5 is a potential threat, is not clear. I for one believe him, for if Black does go to a5 White will soon be able to develop an attack on the kingside, with good chances of success in view of Black's lack of defensive forces there.

If White now captures on f6 Black's play against the centre will have more impact after 12...♗xf6 because the bishop also eyes d4. For these reasons, and due to his exposed king position, White chooses to keep the position closed.

12 e6 ♕d6!

Again Black is doing well. He noticed that White will quickly play g2-g3 and

♗h3 if given the opportunity, when the e6-pawn is a problem for Black. Consequently he decides to trade it for the b-pawn, even if this means exchanging queens and thus forgetting about punishing White for having his king in the centre – a factor that might anyway prove difficult to exploit with the centre closed.

13 g3 ♕xe6

13...♗xe6 14 ♖xb7 followed by ♗f4 is awkward for Black, with White's pieces on decent squares and Black's less comfortable. There is pressure down the e-file, the weakness of c7 and the question of where the queen should be placed. Perhaps Black has nothing better than 14...♕c6.

14 ♕xe6+ ♗xe6 15 ♖xb7 ♗d6!

Provoking a weakness in White's pawn structure. After 16 ♖g1 (avoiding the weakness and perhaps a better move than the text) White has no good square available for his queen's bishop.

16 ♗f4 ♗xf4 17 gxf4 ♗g4

Tying White down while improving the bishop.

18 ♗e2

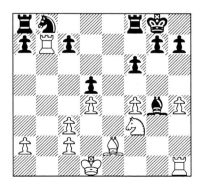

How should Black proceed?

18...♘c6!

This is a very logical pawn sacrifice. Black has decided that f5 is the best square for the knight and plans to go there via e7. He has also concluded that the b7-rook is White's only good piece, and that he would happily give away the c-pawn in return for its removal, which in turn provides Black with pressure on the c-file. I have no doubt that his decision was correct, and I was truly impressed when he explained his reasoning to me.

19 ♖xc7 ♖fc8 20 ♖xc8+ ♖xc8 21 ♖g1?!

White is being outplayed, although his extra pawn might lead to the false belief that he stands better. Black has no weaknesses that White can attack within reasonable time, while White has weaknesses on c3, f4 and h4, soon to be joined by a weakness on d4. The defence of all of these seems very difficult indeed, and the only reasonable plan for White is to address the potential knight outpost on f5. This could be done with 21 ♖f1 followed by ♔d2 and ♗d3, when Black would still have much pressure for the pawn, but whether this is enough for an advantage is less certain. Notice that the wrecked pawns and the semi-closed centre most favour Black's knight, since White's lacks a good square. Consequently Black is not interested in exchanging his knight for the bishop, with the knight being potentially the strongest piece once it reaches f5.

21...h5!

Structure. Black fights for his knight.

22 ♘d2?

This exchange is horrible. White now has no way of either challenging the knight on f5 or even protecting the c3-pawn.

22...♘e7!

Avoiding 22...♗xe2+ 23 ♔xe2 ♘e7 24 ♔d3 and White has achieved some kind of solidity.

23 ♗xg4 hxg4 24 ♖xg4

Equally terrible – if not worse – is 24 c4 dxc4 25 ♖xg4 ♘f5.

24...♖xc3

Black is still a pawn down but his strategy has not been fully understood by his opponent, and White will now have to sit and watch while Black tears his position apart. I have a feeling that this is where White realised he was much worse, thus leading to his truly awful moves.

25 ♖g2?

What is the rook doing here? 25 ♘b3 ♘f5 26 ♔d2 ♖h3 with a clear advantage to Black is preferable, although White's pieces still lack harmony.

25...♘f5 26 ♘b1?

And the knight here?

26...♖f3

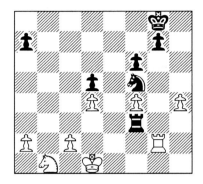

Black won this ending without a problem. I feel the right thing to do is to stop here, just before Black regains his material – with interest.

CHAPTER FOUR

Unforcing Play

I will begin this chapter by trying to define the nature of what I call *unforcing* play, moving on to suggestions as to how the understanding of it can be evolved. I have not seen anything about this subject anywhere else and will, not surprisingly, be walking on thin ice here, so please have a little patience while I try to outline my line of thought.

The principle of unforcing play was the first I came up with when I decided I wanted to write a book about general chess themes. Moreover I believe it is one of the most important topics in this book.

We have a tendency to force play (as opposed to searching for good moves), and the less we *feel the need to do so*, the freer we are to address the matter of finding the best move. The reason we employ forcing moves is obvious – forcing variations give us a sense of control, while less forcing play, in contrast, can leave us with a sense of floating in air and lacking control, which is not a naturally welcome feeling when anxious about the outcome of the game.

When I talk about unforcing play I am concerned with freeing yourself from the tendency to force the position. (It is important, of course, that you do not go to the extreme and take this advice too far, for refusing to adopt forcing play at all times creates another kind of problem – missed chances, for example).

Here are some examples of forcing and unforcing play that will help you better appreciate the subject. I have not yet developed a tried and tested method with which to work on unforcing play, but I am sure that a basic awareness of the phenomenon will take your far.

The first example is from the game Shirov-Kasparov, Linares 1993. After the moves **1 d4 ♘f6 2 c4 g6 3 g3 ♗g7 4 ♗g2 0-0 5 ♘c3 d6 6 ♘f3 ♘bd7 7 0-0 e5 8 h3 c6 9 e4 ♕b6 10 c5 dxc5 11 dxe5 ♘e8** Shirov decided to try a relative new idea with **12 e6!? fxe6 13 ♘g5 ♘e5 14 f4 ♘f7!**

Kasparov was once again caught in his opponent's home preparation, and had to use a great deal of time discovering the right defence.

15 ♘xf7

Shirov and his second had not spent much time studying 14...♘f7 because they did not see what Black should do after 15 ♘xf7 ♖xf7 16 e5, when Black's pieces lack activity. But Kasparov had another, rather simple idea.

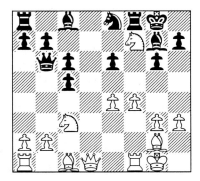

15...♗d4+!

This is it! By inserting the check Black's bishop will not be shut out of the game, and now the knight has a good square available on g7, from where it can defend against the dangerous pawn-push f4-f5 (supported by g3-g4). Shirov writes in his book, *Fire On Board*, that they had not considered this move during their analysis, but when we look at the diagram position it is apparent that no other move suffices for Black. So why did they not think of it?

The answers are many, but the most important one, which is our chief concern here, is that a recapture is the natural (to humans) way to meet a capture. Any other reason you can come up with (14...♘d3 was normally played, for instance) will always depend on this single fact. They did not worry about the recapture and just went on from there.

This is a simple case of unforcing play. Black will have to recapture the knight, but before that he improves the positioning of his bishop. I have long had the feeling that Real chess players are less inclined to force variations, perhaps because they do not have the same insecurity as the rest of us, where we always fear (don't lie to me, I know you do it too) that we are about to mess up our position.

This often has to do with tension, which I will define as follows: *for every reasonable capture in a position the tension rises.* If it is possible to capture material for free the tension further rises, of course. At some point the tension will be too much for the players, who will have to react in order to feel psychologically better. Eventually everyone can lose his way, and the placement of the pieces will appear to be random. But for some players this happens very late.

The greatest masters in unforcing play are almost always from East European or former Soviet countries. They are educated in a different way to Westerners, with a very rich chess culture. They are also the best players...

One of the great exponents of unforcing chess was Mikhail Tal. He once said that he did not mind having five pieces simultaneously hanging because the opponent can take only one at a time. We shall now play through one of his best games, where the tension in the position works to his advantage. It is not because the game itself seems too complicated and unforcing that I have selected it, rather for the interesting material available for discussion regarding the psychological reasons for Black's success.

Botvinnik-Tal

World Championship, Moscow 1960
King's Indian Defence

1 c4 ♘f6 2 ♘f3 g6 3 g3 ♗g7 4 ♗g2 0-0 5 d4 d6 6 ♘c3 ♘bd7 7 0-0 e5 8 e4 c6 9 h3 ♕b6 10 d5

As we saw earlier, 10 c5!? is a serious move here, and as far as I know it is currently the main line. 10 ♖e1 is also played. Botvinnik's choice is rarely seen these days.

10...cxd5 11 cxd5 ♘c5 12 ♘e1

White does not want to allow the knight to stay on c5. 12 ♖e1 seems like a reasonable alternative.

12...♗d7 13 ♘d3 ♘xd3 14 ♕xd3 ♖fc8 15 ♖b1?!

This move cannot lead to an advantage for White. Tal correctly points out that 15 ♕e2 is best, protecting b2 and countering the plan of ...♘f6-h5 followed by ...f7-f5, where exf5 would leave Black with no decent recapture. This is easy to understand after seeing the game.

15...♘h5 16 ♗e3 ♕b4!?

Optimistic play from Tal, who writes in his book that he had already considered the coming sacrifice at this stage.

17 ♕e2 ♖c4

This is the move Tal would blame if his combination can be refuted. I am not sure I would agree. By now this move looks so healthy and logical that I would feel more inclined to criticise 14...♖fc8, and even then it is all a matter of opening theory, and positional issues so deep that they are impossible to fully comprehend at the board.

18 ♖fc1 ♖ac8 19 ♔h2

Other moves might be better. Now Black has the chance to prove his idea.

19...f5 20 exf5 ♗xf5 21 ♖a1

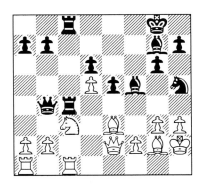

Tal writes the following in his book: 'Botvinnik probably thought that now Black's pieces, due to the threat of 22 g4, were forced to retreat and White would be able to occupy e4 at his own convenience, but there is a surprise waiting for him.' If we presume that Tal is right – not that it matters to me, it just makes it more convenient when trying to illustrate my point – then this is clearly a case of forcing logic in action. White is threatening g3-g4, so should Black, for this reason, let himself be pushed back up the board? Sometimes, perhaps, but not if he can avoid it!

Let us step out of Botvinnik's mind for a second and into Tal's, and pretend that he had not planned the coming sacrifice much earlier. Of course he is alarmed by the threat of 22 g4 (winning a piece) but he does not relish the prospect of being forced to retreat, either. The result is the next uncompromising move.

21...♘f4!

Tal's move has several advantages and only one disadvantage, this being it loses a piece. The text limits the freedom of White's forces and facilitates the liberation of the g7-bishop. On the whole this is a good trade for a knight. Botvinnik had probably failed to take this advance seriously. Remember that chess was different in the years leading up to this match. The idea of sacrificing material after completing development and then hoping for the best was more or less devised by Tal, or at least developed a great deal. Botvinnik was thinking along forced lines, despite this not being a truly forcing position. This is easy to explain from a psychological point of view – Botvinnik wanted to occupy the e4-square and thus analysed variations favouring his ambition. As no obvious move countered this, he assumed that everything would go his way. Tal, on the other hand, had no intention of letting himself be forced back, and had thus foreseen the necessity of this sacrifice much earlier. And if we look at moves 15-21 we realise that Black could hardly have played more natural moves, so there is really no logical foundation for assuming he should be worse if we presume that he was fine on the fifteenth move. So in many ways this move seems to be justified. What follows is also interesting and relevant to the discussion of forced play.

22 gxf4 exf4 23 ♗d2

23 a3 has been suggested as a winning move, but Tal shows in his excellent books that this is far from simple. However, I have a feeling that it is a better move than the text. The idea is

that 23 ♗xa7 is completely useless in view of 23...♕a5, but after 23 a3 ♕b3 24 ♗xa7 ♗e5 25 ♗f3 b6 Black still needs to prove his compensation.

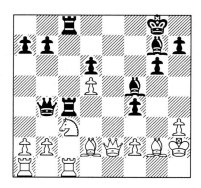

23...♕xb2?

Tal felt, correctly, that this is wrong. Natural is 23...♗e5!, suggested by Tal in his annotations. I do not understand why he had such doubts about this during the game since it is so obvious that White cannot improve his position while he is preventing 24...f3+. Meanwhile Black has gained considerably in activating the bishop and supporting the f-pawn.

Tal was afraid of 24 f3 ♕xb2 25 ♘d1 ♕d4 26 ♖xc4 ♖xc4 27 ♖c1 ♖xc1 28 ♗xc1 ♕xd5 29 ♗f1 and he felt that the position was slightly better for White. I am not sure that this is true. Black has three pawns, none of them is visibly weak, and White's minor pieces have a problem co-ordinating. The correct verdict is probably that the position is practically level. 24 ♔g1 does not work due to 24...♕xb2 25 ♖ab1 ♗xb1 26 ♖xb1 ♕c2 27 ♖c1 ♕f5 28 ♕f3 ♕h5 29 ♘e2 ♖c2, and it is clear that the rook is better than minor pieces here. Nor does 24 ♗f3 work, as 24...♕xb2 25 ♘d1

♕a3 26 ♖xc4 ♖xc4 27 ♕xc4 ♕xf3 gives Black an irresistible attack.

Nevertheless Tal chose a lesser move which he believed would lead to a forced draw, but if we look at it logically we cannot believe that 23...♕xb2 is better than 23...♗e5, which leads to a position in which White still needs to play precisely in order to maintain the balance. Therefore a move that does not achieve this improvement of the position, yet aims for the same complications, should logically be inferior. And surprise, surprise, it is!

24 ♖ab1 f3!

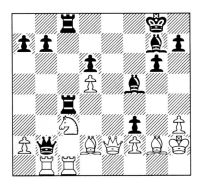

It was this move upon which Tal had pinned his hopes. The forcing move, of course, is 24...♗xb1. In this position Botvinnik makes a mistake which is quite difficult to understand when we remember that he was the world champion. Tal explains it as an oversight, but this is only half an explanation. How can Botvinnik overlook Tal's simple 26th move? There are two possible explanations and I do not want to guess which is the appropriate one. Botvinnik might have had a tendency to overlook his opponent's opportunities, as we saw with Black's 21st move. But it can also be because the

tension created by so many 'hanging' pieces unsettled Botvinnik.

25 ♖xb2?

Losing. Correct is 25 ♗xf3 ♗xb1 26 ♖xb1 ♕c2, when people believed that 27 ♖c1, with equality, was best until Grandmaster Flohr discovered 27 ♗e4! ♖xe4 28 ♘xe4! ♗e5+ 29 ♔g2 ♕xb1 30 ♘xd6 ♗xd6 31 ♕e6+ ♔g7 32 ♕d7+!, and White has good winning chances.

Botvinnik was originally afraid of 27 ♖c1 ♕f5!?, but Tal showed him 28 ♗g4 ♕e5+ 29 ♕xe5 ♗xe5+ 30 f4 ♖xc3 31 ♗xc8 (the move Botvinnik had overlooked).

After the text Black is simply winning.

25...fxe2 26 ♖b3 ♖d4 27 ♗e1 ♗e5+ 28 ♔g1 ♗f4

White now has nothing better than to return the piece with a lost endgame. However, after 28...♖xc3 29 ♖bxc3 ♖d1 30 ♖c7 ♗f4 White can resign.

29 ♘xe2 ♖xc1 30 ♘xd4 ♖xe1+ 31 ♗f1 ♗e4 32 ♘e2 ♗e5 33 f4 ♗f6 34 ♖xb7 ♗xd5 35 ♖c7 ♗xa2 36 ♖xa7 ♗c4 37 ♖a8+ ♔f7 38 ♖a7+ ♔e6 39 ♖a3 d5 40 ♔f2 ♗h4+ 41 ♔g2 ♔d6 42 ♘g3 ♗xg3 43 ♗xc4 dxc4 44 ♔xg3 ♔d5 45 ♖a7 c3 46 ♖c7 ♔d4 1-0

The truly interesting question in this classic is why Botvinnik made the mistake on his 25th move. Of course he overlooked a possibility at the end of a long line, but this cannot be the full explanation. I believe that the pressure of the hanging pieces influenced Botvinnik's feel for the position. Moreover I am in no doubt that the relief of exchanging queens was just as important a factor for Botvinnik's choice of continuation as the poor variation mentioned above.

This feeling of insecurity is very important. In the modern game the top players are less likely to feel uncomfortable because pieces are hanging. They are accustomed to this situation from working with computers. They are also more likely to see 'unnatural moves' and to grab pawns nobody would have captured twenty years ago. It is well known that defending is much more difficult than attacking because it is easier to be the player dictating the event than the one attempting to meet, and subsequently deal with, aggression. This is mainly because you have to foresee all the opponent's ideas in advance, whereas he has only to produce them as he goes along, but there is also the matter of being under stronger psychological pressure – another crucial symptom of too forcing play. The only way to eradicate this is to learn to feel confident in such positions.

It is often very difficult for us to know when we should try to force events and when we should keep things flowing. The following example is an illustration of how emotions can influence these choices in even very basic positions. It also demonstrates how often such mistakes are committed.

S.Pedersen–Aagaard
Drury Lane 1997

This game was played in a closed Grandmaster tournament in London, where I was close to achieving a Grandmaster-norm, shortly after receiving the International Master title. I had prepared very well and rehabilitated a line in the Nimzo-Indian that at the time had a poor reputation. I did not get the chance to prove my preparation directly, but I did use a similar idea. My opponent defended rather well after being under pressure, liquidating the position into this drawn rook ending. By now I had advanced about as far as I could, creating suitable, and I hoped for the best.

Thus far, then, both players have performed reasonably well, but now we both become victims of forcing play.

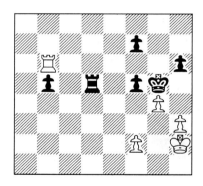

38 gxf5?

This is a rather simple mistake, albeit an understandable one. My opponent had arrived more than thirty minutes late for the game due to problems with the Northern Line (anyone acquainted with the London Tube knows how normal this is), and by now had used up most of his time.

The logical move is 38 ♔g3! but my opponent feared 38...♖d3+, yet after 39 ♔g2 it seems that Black has no better try than 39...♖b3, after which his rook is less well placed than on d5 (See why in Chapter 5). I think that Black would not be able to win this position without some help from his opponent, but, of course, I was ready to give him all the room he needed if this would help me achieve my aim.

38...f6 39 ♔g3 ♔xf5 40 f3 ♔e5 41 h4 h5 42 ♖b8

42 ♔f2 f5 43 ♔e3 f4+ 44 ♔e2 ♔d4 45 ♖f6 b4 46 ♖xf4+ ♔c3 seems to be a winning line for Black.

In this position I was losing my way. I had a pawn more and suddenly I had something to lose (a draw would not help me in the tournament standings). I did not have the confidence and understanding of the endgame that I have now (and often confidence and ability go hand in hand), so I was relying on my abilities to calculate. My next move is logically wrong since my rook is ideally placed on d5, so instead I should improve my king.

42...♖c5?!

A silly waiting move. 42...♔d4 43 ♖b6 ♖f5 is ideal, Black's rook keeping an eye on the pawns and the king now able to help the b-pawn advance. No direct line is necessary to see that this is winning – that is if you are aware of what you are doing. I, as it soon emerges, was not.

43 ♖d8!

This is the natural move. I do not remember if I was counting on this but, probably, I was not counting on anything. Now I decided that I should force a win and so I started calculating. I decided to sacrifice the h-pawn, using the extra tempo to promote my own little guy. Unfortunately I miscalculated the position and consequently threw away the win.

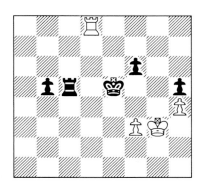

43...b4??

43...♖d5 44 ♖b8 ♔d4 still makes a lot of sense.

44 ♖b8 ♖c4 45 ♖b5+ ♔d4 46 ♖xh5 b3 47 ♖b5 ♔c3 48 h5 b2 49 h6

Here I was relying on 48...♖b4, but it is easy to see now that White has sufficient time to promote his own pawn.

49...♔c2 50 h7 ♖c8 51 ♔g4 ♖h8 52 ♔f5 ♖xh7 53 ♔xf6 ♖h3 54 ♖xb2+!

I would love to say that this is the move I had overlooked, but because I have already told you the truth that would be silly. 54 f4 is obviously wrong in view of 54...♖b3.

54...♔xb2 55 f4

This endgame is drawn. It is even very easily drawn – as long as things such as emotions are not involved. But after almost six hours of hard fighting easy moves, for some reason, become difficult, and simple logic becomes terribly complex.

55...♔c3 56 f5 ♖e3!

This move deserves an exclamation mark due to psychological reasons. It was played with a relaxed hand and without any plan, the idea being simply that my opponent should be allowed to do something stupid without my help.

For I knew that if I forced the position, it would just be drawn. So the text is designed to irritate the king by preventing 57 ♔e6, which would be the most logical move.

57 ♔g7 ♖g3+ 58 ♔f7 ♔d4

59 ♔e6?!

This is already a slight indication that things are not going well for White. As soon as the passed pawn can be pushed it should be. My opponent wishes to avoid the line 59 f6 ♔e5 60 ♔e7 ♖a3 61 f7 ♖a7+ 62 ♔e8 ♔e6 63 f8♘+ as this still involves an accurate move or two. But this, of course, is not something an International Master should fear. I guess that he – like I – did not have the confidence he should have had.

59...♖e3+ 60 ♔d6 ♖f3 61 ♔e6 ♖e3+ 62 ♔d6 ♖a3

Avoiding three move repetition. Notice that there is nothing in Black's moves that indicates he is playing for a win, rather he is playing for the delay of the end of the game. This should not have any effect at all, but see what happens!

63 f6

Forced this time, but this is actually an advantage for Black, since it means that White does not advance his pawn with the intention of promoting it, but only because he has to. This will soon become significant.

63...♖a7!

This weird move also makes sense. Again White has only one move, so he is not thinking, but at the same time the draw is not happening. Had we played three hours and not six, were this the first and not the eighth round and had my opponent not had problems with the train earlier that day, I am sure the following would not have happened. But it did and that is the nature of tournament chess.

The text is also logical from a psychological perspective. White's next is forced, but not in the same way as if I had played 63...♖a6+. Checks and threats of capturing pawns just seem more real!

64 ♔e6 ♖a6+

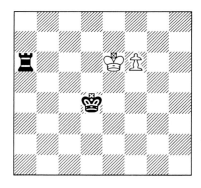

Again not really leaving White with a choice, but there is still the feeling of possibilities. Compared to the check a move earlier this is less forcing in practical play.

So, we are moving the pieces around and White suddenly becomes a little nervous. Okay, the position is obviously drawn, and soon he will promote to a knight, and then after another ten or fifteen moves a draw will be agreed. But then the madness struck him like a bolt from the blue. I am sure that he had a feeling of uneasiness that now had a disastrous impact on his power of judgement. He got the feeling that he could force a draw with his next move, which actually just loses the game immediately...

65 ♔f5??

In the rear view mirror it is possible to understand the nature of this mistake, but at the moment I was deeply in shock. I had tried to confuse him a little bit with my weird rook moves, and by playing them casually, with only one ambition: not to force anything, as the draw would then move much closer. Now the draw was not happening at all!

White wants to avoid underpromotion and, to do so, he needs to bring the king to the other side of the pawn. Unfortunately this is a simple mistake. The reason why the pawn can draw against the rook in this kind of endgames is because the defending king shifts between threatening to help the pawn to the 8th rank and keeping the enemy king at bay.

65 ♔e7 ♔e5 66 f7 ♖a7+ 67 ♔e8 ♔e6 68 f8♘+ is a theoretical draw. Just to annoy my opponent further I would probably have played 65...♖a7+!? here.

65...♔d5!

Now Black has the opposition and his king will join forces with the rook in stopping the pawn.

66 f7 ♖a8 1-0

White resigned in view of 67 ♔f6

♔d6 68 ♔g7 ♔e7 etc.

I have noticed as a trainer that weaker players calculate more opportunities and variations, including forced variations, but they often miss intermediate moves, the idea of delaying a recapture and all other kinds of unforcing play.

This is illustrated in the following simple exercises, in which you need to find the best move:

Exercise 1
White to move

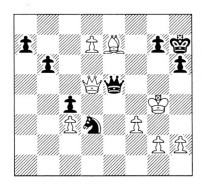

Exercise 2
White to move

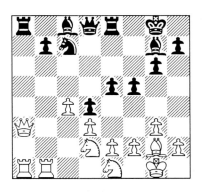

Before we look at the solutions I want

to show you another example of how most players think in forced lines. White is a student of mine rated 2100, his opponent somewhat weaker at 1850. I think the game is very instructive and I could have placed it anywhere in this book. I chose to put it here because it illustrates very well how inexperienced players prefer to force moves on the opponent, even if this does not lead him anywhere.

Nøhr-T.Nielsen
Copenhagen 2000
Caro-Kann Defence

1 e4 c6 2 d4 d5 3 exd5 cxd5 4 c4 ♘f6 5 ♘c3 e6 6 ♘f3 ♗e7 7 cxd5 ♘xd5 8 ♗d3 0-0 9 0-0 ♘c6 10 ♖e1

Thus far we have a standard position. Black has a number of possible moves here, 10...♘f6 being the main line. There are many subtleties in these positions and we shall see White present a few of them over the next few moves.

10...♘cb4?

This is poor. Generally knights are less effective when they are protecting each other, and this game is no exception. The text move also leaves White with full control over his most important asset, the e5-square.

11 ♗b1 ♘f6 12 a3 ♘bd5 13 ♕d3 b6 14 ♗g5

White develops naturally, while Black has no respect for the weakness of his light squares around the king.

14...g6 15 ♗a2!

A standard move. The bishop is no longer doing any good on the b1–h7 diagonal, so it helps in putting pressure on d5 and e6 (and f7) instead. White has

a clear advantage, and if Black does nothing special he will have to face all kinds of threats.

15...♗b7 16 ♘e5 ♖c8

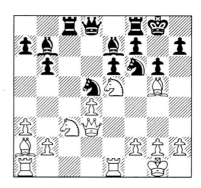

17 ♗h6

This is the first time I am unsatisfied with my pupil's play. The text forces a strong position, whereas my suggestion (see below) does nothing of the sort, although I am in no doubt concerning the superiority of my choice. The need for playing forcing moves is a result of insecurity regarding simple chess logic, and this is also the reason why it is more common among weaker players.

17 ♖ad1! is the correct move. The rook is not playing on a1 and it is perfect on d1, protecting d4 and introducing the possibility of the break d4-d5. However, after the text White has a fantastic advantage.

17...♖e8 18 ♕h3

Again White is forcing Black to make specific moves and, although this is not wrong here, the psychology is not perfect. Why should White want to force Black to get his bishop to g7? This is the overall achievement from this sequence and it does not seem right.

18...♗f8 19 ♗g5 ♗g7 20 ♘e4

Setting up an annoying pin, which Black feels himself forced to escape.

20...♕c7

What should White do now? After the game we analysed for a long time and did not find anything conclusive, although it is quite simple. My proposal was 21 ♗xd5 ♘xd5 22 ♖ac1 ♕b8 23 ♘d7 ♕a8 24 ♘ef6+ ♗xf6 25 ♘xf6+ ♗xf6 26 ♗xf6, which I felt was very dangerous for Black. But after 26...♖xc1 27 ♖xc1 ♖c8 28 ♖e1 ♖c2 it is hard to believe that White should be better as his pieces have no activity with which they can exploit the holes around Black's king. Instead 21 ♗xf6! ♘xf6 22 ♘g5 is best, when Black is forced to play 22...♗d5 since he cannot protect f7: 22...♖f8 23 ♘xe6! fxe6 24 ♗xe6+ ♔h8 25 ♘xg6 mate.

21 ♖ac1?

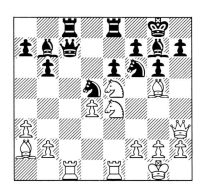

The line of thought behind this move is obvious. White sees no square for Black's queen other than b8 and therefore expects this retreat, after which he has planned the winning sequence 21...♕b8 22 ♖xc8! ♖xc8 (22...♗xc8 23 ♕f3!) 23 ♘xf6+ ♘xf6 24 ♗xe6! ♖c7 25 ♗xf7+ and White wins.

21...♘xe4!!

Missed by White. Now Black comes out on top.

22 ♖xc7 ♘xg5 23 ♖xb7

23 ♕g3 also fails: 23...♘xc7! (23...♖xc7? 24 ♘d3! gives White a new chance) 24 ♕xg5 f6 and Black stays ahead in material.

23...♘xh3+ 24 gxh3 ♖c2

The game ended in a draw a few moves later because Black did not have the confidence to steer his completely winning position to victory. What we can learn from this game is obvious. White forced events from the thirteenth move onwards, but not always to his own advantage. He did not develop his rook in time and he did not play the winning move when he had the chance. Rather he looked only at forced variations and did not see the move Black had at his disposal when the forcing lines just seemed to win. Instead of calculating White should have stopped and thought: 'I wonder why he is allowing this forced winning line? Can it be that my opponent is not completely stupid, and that he has an idea about what he is doing?' Had he asked himself such a question he would easily have seen Black's idea and, consequently, avoided it. He did not, however, and was lucky to get a draw.

Now let us return to the exercises.

Solution 1
Smyslov-Petrosian
Zurich Candidates Tournament 1953

The game continued 47 ♕xd3+? cxd3 48 d8♕ with a draw in view of the line 48...♕e2 49 ♔h3 d2 50 ♕d7 d1♕ 51

♕f5+ and White delivers perpetual check.

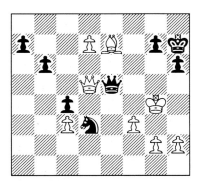

However, returning to the diagram position, Smyslov could have won immediately with the sneaky **47 ♕d6!!**, which solves all his problems (...♘f2+ followed by ...♕xh2+ is ruled out, for example) and nets the full point. Note that this move has much in common with the 50 ♖h8 that I overlooked in my game against Stempinski in the opening chapter.

Solution 2
Larsen-Chandler
Hastings 1987/88

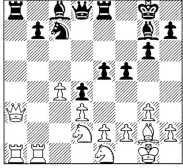

This is a less well known example, which I believe is much more difficult

than the previous exercise since it has more to do with confidence and knowledge. Most players will find a good option and present it as a suggestion, whereas only a few will present the correct move and feel truly confident about it. Larsen is one of the few, but he is famous for his confidence. His reasoning here was simple – he wanted to sacrifice the queen. The b-pawn is weak and the c-pawn is a strong future candidate. But then he realised he wanted to improve his position first – a big improvement indeed. I am convinced that this kind of understanding that this is exactly the right move, without feeling the need for any kind of evidence in the form of exact variations, is the feeling a Real chess player has.

18 ♗d5+!

The bishop is obviously immune and 18...♗e6 is also out of the question as b7 would then be impossible to defend. So, before the sacrifice White has succeeded in establishing an enormous piece in the middle of the board. The rest of the game is a true *tour de force* from Larsen, proving the strength of his logic.

18...♔h8 19 ♕xa8 ♘xa8 20 ♖xa8 ♗h6 21 ♘df3 ♕e7 22 ♗xb7! ♗d7 23 ♖xe8+ ♗xe8 24 ♗d5 ♕d6 25 ♖b7 g5 26 h4! gxh4 27 ♘xh4 ♗d7 28 ♘ef3 f4 29 ♗e4 fxg3 30 fxg3 ♗e3+ 31 ♔g2 ♗g4 32 ♖xh7+ ♔g8 33 ♖b7 ♕a6 34 ♘xe5 ♗e6 35 ♖e7 ♔f8 36 ♘hg6+ ♔g8 37 ♖xe6 ♕a2 38 ♖e8+ ♔g7 39 ♖e7+ ♔h6 40 ♘g4+ ♔h5 41 ♖e5+ ♗g5 42 ♘f4+ ♔xg4 43 ♗f3 mate.

Thus far this chapter has been one long line of assumptions based on the most forcing line/move, showing that these clearly were not the only moves to be considered. But what should one do then?

Well, a complete answer here features numerous levels. One of the problems illustrated here is the need for control that most players feel. If you can rid yourself of all insecurity then you are definitely on your way. Being able to keep an open mind when looking at a position is incredibly useful. Often, if you proceed slowly, you will see much more of these sneaky moves – even if you do not have the time to analyse these long variations you can show them to your friends after you have lost the game! And if you did not base your decisions so much on calculations but more on implementing logic and ideas, you would also feel less inclined to play forcing variations.

Playing through top level games, as suggested in the 'looking over the shoulder' exercises, is also a good idea. If you pay attention to how often the top players refrain from forcing events you will most likely improve your own overall understanding of chess.

Another good teacher in unforcing chess is *Fritz* (and other computer programs). Obviously such programs do not work with ideas, concepts and elements, but they also have no emotions. And it is my claim that our need for control has considerable influence on our tendency to force events.

Below are two brilliant examples in which *Fritz* found saving moves of incredible beauty and logic in positions where the forcing lines were unsuccessful.

Aagaard-Hummel
Oakham 2000

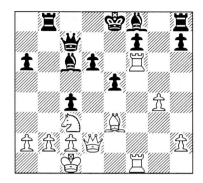

How can Black save this position?

23...♕d7?

After this move Black is already losing. It is well known that in mutual attacking positions it is rarely any use being passive, and this position is no exception. My opponent decided not to play the obvious 23...♕b7! due to my planned response 24 ♕f2!, but this is what he should have done. Black is in trouble if he plays the forcing 24...♕xb2+ 25 ♔d2, after which both 26 ♖xf7 and 26 ♖b1 are serious threats.

Fritz showed me what I should have figured out for myself. Black's only problem is the pressure in the f-file, and if this could be neutralised he should be fine. As f7 is very awkward to defend with any piece other than the queen another way must be found (of course these do not always exist). Here Black could have played the remarkable 24...♗g2!!, intending 25 ♖g1 ♗c6 (25...♕xb2!?) 26 ♖f1, repeating. But nor should White limit himself to seemingly forced moves. Stronger is 25 ♖xf7! ♗e7! (forced as 25...♕xb2 26 ♔d2

♗xf1 27 ♕f6!! mates quickly – 27...♖b7 28 ♗g5!) 26 ♖g1 (26 ♖xe7+!? ♔xe7 27 ♕f7+ ♔d8 28 ♗g5+ ♔c8 29 ♕xc4+ ♕c6 30 ♕e6+ ♕d7 31 ♕c4+ ♕c6 seems to be a draw by repetition and nothing more) 26...♗c6 27 ♕f5 ♖f8!, when White's attack has been stopped for now. White has regained the pawn he sacrificed in the opening and should not feel that his strategy has failed in any way, Black was just capable of finding the best line of defence, that's all. In the game he was not and I won easily.

Another possibility is 24...♗e7!? 25 ♖xf7 ♔d8 with a messy position. White has time to defend b2 but he no longer has any direct way of attacking Black's king. I still believe in White, but not in the same way as in the game.

24 ♕e2 ♖b7 25 ♕xc4 ♗b5 26 ♘xb5 axb5 27 ♕d5 ♖g8

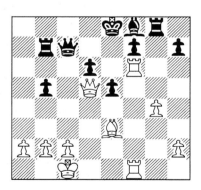

28 g5!

This, of course, gives Black the chance to defend with 28...♖g7, but this did not disturb me at all. All his pieces would then be inferior to mine, with nothing by way of compensation. So I chose to improve my position before I took the queen.

28...♖g6 29 ♖xf7 ♕xf7 30 ♖xf7 ♖xf7

31 ♕xb5+ ♖d7 32 a4 ♗e7 33 a5 ♗xg5 34 ♗xg5 ♖xg5 35 b4 1-0

Once again in these variations the strongest moves had practically nothing to do with the seemingly forced moves. Black never got to play ...♕xb2+ after threatening to do so, and White did not respect that threat, nor ...♗xf1. However, both these threats were of great importance to Black, and in the game, where he refrained from them, he lost without a chance.

In the next example White is in trouble but has a forced draw, only this does not consist of truly forcing moves, and involves what seems to be the loss of material.

Smejkal-Larsen
Leningrad Interzonal 1973

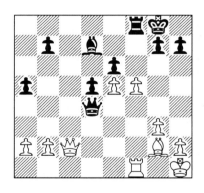

In this position White has a fantastic little sequence which in some respects is forcing and in others not. It is forcing on a purely chess level since Black has only one reply to each of White's moves, and White has no choice but to play these moves (in order not to be worse). Psychologically, though, it is a different case, as we shall see.

26 ♕c3?

After this Black is on top. 26 ♕c7!! is the natural forcing move, when in response to 26...♗c6 the most forcing is 27 f6 but, apparently, this just loses a pawn. However, White's idea is 27...gxf6 28 ♖f4!, when 28...gxf6 leaves Black highly vulnerable to the check on g4, so he has to play instead 28...♕d1+, buying time and defending g4. White, in turn, must play 29 ♖f1, which forces Black to keep an eye on f6 with 29...♕d4, after which 30 ♖f4 forces a repetition of moves.

Instead Black simply won: **26...♕xc3 27 bxc3 ♖c8 28 ♖d1 ♖c5 29 fxe6 ♗xe6 30 ♔g1 ♔f7 31 ♖d3 ♖b5 32 ♖d2 a4 33 a3 ♖b3 34 ♗xd5 ♖xa3 35 c4 ♖b3 36 ♔f2 a3 37 ♔e2 ♖b2 38 ♖xb2 axb2 39 ♗e4 ♗xc4+ 40 ♔d2 ♗a2 1-0**

International Master Thomas Hutters suggested to me that a reversal of the neural network could be a way to improve your chess once computers become even stronger. Computers will not be able to explain why a move is wrong, but if you have sufficient tests you will develop a feeling for right and wrong.

I think there is no reason to wait. When you play your tournament games, first analyse and annotate them yourself and only then check them with a computer. Try to understand the positional and logical reasons why you miss something at the board (or at home).

And when you do study your games, do it slowly. Do not play out the moves as if they were forced. Look carefully at each move to see whether there are options you did not originally consider. Dvoretsky told me that for a long time

he did not believe Petrosian could calculate, then it occurred to him that he did. In fact he calculated extremely well indeed, albeit no further than one move in advance, yet he did so with very few mistakes (he once overlooked his queen was threatened...). I think this is a very important lesson. When a world champion does not calculate beyond what he can immediately see, but is instead focused on long-term issues he would never be able to calculate, it tells you something about how important calculation is. If you are brilliant at it you can calculate long, complicated lines but, if you are not, you do not have to.

To be able to play like this you need to foresee your opponent's ideas a long time before he does, and when you succeed in this you prevent them. This is called prophylactic thinking. I would like to write a lot about it, but Mark Dvoretsky and Arthur Jusupov have already done so in the books *Training for the Tournament Player* and *Positional Play*. I can only recommend that you turn to these books for further knowledge. Nothing will ever do more for your chess than understanding prophylactics.

Unforcing play is not just a matter of intermediate moves and prophylactic thinking. Unforcing play is a state of mind, where you look for good moves instead of being a slave to captures and threats. It is about being open to more complicated ideas and more fluent possibilities. Be aware that we all have this tendency to force positions, but that this is often not the right thing to do. Only when we force a concession of some sort should we do so, and often this concession will come anyway.

The example below illustrates the idea of looking instead of calculating:

Kasparov–Chiburdanidze
Baku 1980
King's Indian Defence

1 d4 ♘f6 2 c4 g6 3 ♘c3 ♗g7 4 e4 d6 5 ♘f3 0-0 6 ♗e2 e5 7 ♗e3 ♕e7 8 d5 ♘g4 9 ♗g5 f6 10 ♗h4 h5 11 h3 ♘h6 12 ♘d2 c5 13 ♘f1 ♘f7 14 g4 hxg4 15 ♗xg4 g5 16 ♗xc8 ♖xc8

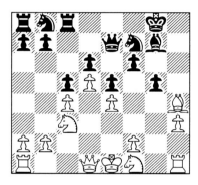

Don't think – Look!

Black's idea is to answer 17 ♗g3 with 17...f5!, after which the position is unclear. As the young Kasparov (age 17) illustrates here there is no reason to save the bishop.
17 ♘e3!
The knight cannot be removed from f5 and for this reason the extra piece is not so important. In fact White is probably winning. 17...♘h6!? seems best now, but Chiburdanidze chooses to go for material gain, after which there is little doubt about the result.
17...gxh4 18 ♘f5 ♕d8 19 ♕g4 ♘g5 20 ♘xh4 ♖c7 21 ♘f5 a6 22 h4 ♘h7 23 ♖g1 ♕f8 24 ♔e2 ♖a7 25 a4 b6 26 ♕h5

♔h8 27 ♖g6 ♖d7 28 ♖ag1 ♖ab7 29 ♕g4 ♖bc7 30 ♖g2 ♖b7 31 ♔f1 ♖a7 32 ♔g1 ♖f7 33 ♘e2 ♕c8 34 f4 b5 35 axb5 axb5 36 cxb5 ♖ab7 37 h5 ♘f8 38 ♕h3 ♘xg6 39 hxg6+ ♔g8 40 gxf7+ ♔f8 1-0

The next example shows how we should be careful not to let tactics rule over logic.

Yermolinsky-Smirin
Yerevan 1996

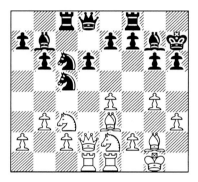

17...e5?
Black obviously had some idea based on 18 ♕xd6, which he had carefully calculated, but why should White go for this? Instead he plays a normal move and Black's position becomes critical thanks to the weakness on d6. So Black has achieved nothing at all, except the weakening of an important pawn in the centre.
18 f4! exf4
18...♘e6 19 ♘b5! is also bad for Black.
19 ♗xf4 ♖e8 20 ♕xd6
Now White cashes in. He did not force this, but waited until the most advantageous moment. Black is in big trouble.

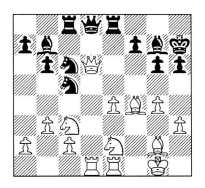

20...♕h4 21 ♗g3 ♕g5 22 ♕d2

♖cd8 23 ♕xg5 hxg5 24 ♖xd8 ♖xd8 25 ♘d5 ♖e8 26 c4 ♘xe4 27 ♘ec3 ♘d6 28 ♖f1 ♖d8 29 ♗xd6 ♖xd6 30 ♘e4 ♖d8 31 ♖xf7 ♗c8 32 ♖c7 ♘e5 33 ♘xg5+ ♔h6 34 ♘e4 g5 35 ♖xa7 b5 36 ♘xg5 bxc4 37 bxc4 ♖e8 38 ♖c7 ♗a6 39 ♖xg7 ♔xg7 40 ♘c7 ♖c8 41 ♘xa6 ♖xc4 42 ♘c5 ♖c2 43 a4 ♘c4 44 ♘ge6+ ♔f6 45 g5+ ♔e5 46 g6 **1-0**

What else can I say? Let the unforce be with you!

CHAPTER FIVE

Why Study the Endgame?

Someone told me during a recent tournament that he did not need to study the endgame because of his last twenty-two games only two had reached this stage. Later in the same tournament I saw him self-destruct in a position where he could have made it to a slightly worse endgame that offered drawing chances. I am sure that this is the usual pattern for him; he does not know the endgame very well and therefore he avoids endings at all costs. His reasoning comes afterwards. Obviously you can do this if you like, but why should you? Does the endgame bore you that much? Do you not think there is a chance that perhaps this is because you never properly understood it?

I am not sure at what age I started taking an interest in the endgame. I was always an inventive player, trying to mate my opponents with beautiful sacrifices. But such an approach does not always work, of course. However, unlike my friend, I did not dislike the endgame on principle. To be honest I was more interested in scoring points.

During the first ten years of my chess career I cried when I lost, now I just hit the pillow. I keep it to myself the best I can, but losing hurts. Winning, on the other hand, is great. It makes me euphoric and, no matter how weak the opponent, it makes it all worthwhile. So I go for the endgame when there is no other reasonable path to follow.

After turning my attention to the endgame I soon saw that this phase of the game is very important. It took me many years to actually begin studying it, but I knew very early that it was a good idea. I was also surprised to discover that I could have fun playing through annotated endgames from the Kasparov-Karpov matches, and with pleasant anticipation and high ambition I bought the first volume (of four) of Cheron's Rook endings manual. In an act of impressive discipline I made it to the fourteenth page, playing through endless variations of simple positions with no guidance other than 'draw' or 'White is winning'...

... It took years before I returned to

endgame study, and when I finally did so maturity had had an impact on me. I was no longer a loose cannon, as had been the case in my late teens, but an independent young man. Under the influence of Danish Grandmaster and cult hero Henrik Danielsen, I typed all the main lines from Averbakh's two volumes on rook endings into Chessbase, and played them through again and again. This is an interesting method that Danielsen has brought into chess. The idea is that unconscious pattern recognition should help you when you face theoretical endgames over the board. I believe the method works, and for the serious player – specifically the professional – I strongly recommend it, as long as it is not the only way you study the endgame.

For ambitious amateurs like myself I believe it is far more important to understand how the properties of pieces alter in the endgame than knowing five thousand limited piece positions. The book I found most beneficial was Shereshevsky's *Endgame Strategy*, which is based on a training concept developed by Dvoretsky, then further developed by the author. Dvoretsky himself has also published an excellent book on the endgame, *Technique for the Tournament Player*, which, unfortunately seems to be out of print, but not for long I suppose. When I spoke to Dvoretsky in the summer of 2000 he was writing a basic endgame manual. The idea was that there are a limited number of theoretical positions you should know, and then there are some endgame principles you need to understand. Should be interesting.

Getting Started

Whenever I get a new pupil I know I have to address a dislike of the endgame. People seem to play faster when the number of pieces decreases, and this happens despite the fact that intuitive decisions are now less important since it is not possible to 'feel' your way through an endgame. You need to reason logically what to do and, often, it helps to try to calculate variations to the end – and if not that far, then at least far enough to gain some insight into the resultant position.

I usually present a new pupil with the following position, which I find quite instructive even if it is relatively simple.

White moves and wins

In this endgame, with only four pieces on the board, White has only one route to victory. This involves a nice but basic trick that wins a tempo, and the correct king manoeuvre. Usually my pupils solve it in two attempts, making a mistake along the way. Sometimes they fail in the first part of the exercise, sometimes in the second part.

1 ♖c7+!

This intermediate check wins a very

important tempo. Black now has the simple choice of blocking his pawn or going to the d-file. The latter is the most testing.

1...⌘d3 2 ⌘b7!

Attacking the pawn and thereby forcing Black to go to c4. Had White played 2 ⌘d7 Black would be able to help the pawn from c3 instead of c4, and thus have one move less to reach the crucial c2-square.

2...⌘c4 3 ⌘c7!

This is, in fact, elementary, but many 2100 players have failed here. White's king needs to attack the b-pawn from the opposite side Black's king. The rest needs no comment.

3...b4 4 ⌘b6 b3 5 ⌘a5 ⌘c3 6 ⌘a4 b2 7 ⌘a3 0-1

This might look quite simple when you see the solution, but in practise many good players experience difficulty. Obviously, at International Master level (or perhaps 2300) most or all players will find the solution with ease (I showed these exercises to a friend rated 2550 and he could not properly focus on the first exercise but, having understood the theme, he immediately solved the far more difficult exercise below). Well did you solve it? You did, great, but what about the next one?

After the previous exercise I always give my pupils this one. So far no one (except for the Grandmaster) has managed to solve it!

Incidentally there are two funny stories connected to this exercise. One of my pupils failed to solve it after fifteen minutes, and took it home as an assignment. He called me two days later to verify the position because he believed he had written it down incorrectly. On learning this was not so he exclaimed: 'Then there is no solution!' – so confident and yet so wrong.

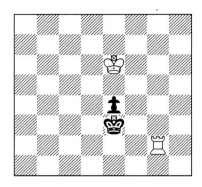

White to move and win

The other story features a player rated 2300 who was interested in some training sessions. He told me he had played through the Averbakh book I mentioned earlier. I presented him with the exercise and after two minutes he claimed he had a solution. He began with 1 ⌘e5 ⌘f3 2 ⌘a2 e3 and then became baffled, realising that Black is drawing easily. I then presented him with the solution, which he found amazing. However, I never heard from him again about training, and for some time it seemed as if he was avoiding me.

What I try to illustrate to my pupils with these two exercises can be verbalised in two ways. From an abstract perspective there are some basic rules governing the endgame and, once mastered, these will help you enormously. In concrete, actual terms the rook should be behind the passed pawn, and the king should be on the opposite side of the pawn. Elementary knowledge, right?

Well, if so, why do my pupils fail to solve the exercises? The explanation comes in two parts: they might not be aware of the universal rules of the endgame, and they might not have any experience in implementation. My training methods are aimed at helping with both.

Lecturing in Copenhagen, June 2000, Dvoretsky said about rook endgames: 'The most important thing .... is that the rook should be active.' I believe that he is correct. But we should not stop there; we should be even more basic in our considerations. What does it mean that a rook is active? What does it mean to be active at all? My answer can probably be questioned but is quite useful in practise. To be active is to attack, and to be passive is to defend. Note that defending does not necessarily mean protecting, and attacking does not necessarily exclude defending. If a rook is behind a passed pawn of its own the pawn can be the frontman in an attack.

We now turn to some basic positions in rook endings.

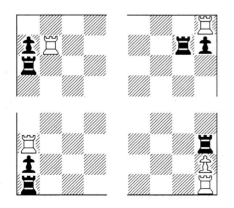

In the bottom left quarter (a1-d4) Black has a passed pawn but White's rook is active, attacking the pawn and therefore limiting the freedom of the enemy rook. Black's rook defends its own pawn, which in turn limits the movement of the rook. Therefore the rook is passive.

In the top left quarter (a8-d5) White's rook remains active, but less so than the a3-rook. White will need to follow the pawn once Black starts pushing it. Alas he does not have the same freedom for manoeuvre as is the case with the rook behind the pawn. Black's rook is still a passive defender, but if we compare it to the a1-rook, then at least it can move up and down the a-file, which is a clear improvement.

In the top right quarter (e5-h8) White remains active, his rook being behind the pawn, which cannot move at the moment. Here Black's rook is seemingly better off than the one on a6, but it is not quite so simple. White's rook also has potential for manoeuvring (e.g. ♖h8-f8) and, if Black then pushes the pawn, can return to h8. So the distant, closed spot on h8 is, perhaps, not as bad as it appears.

In the bottom right quarter (e4-h1) White's rook appears to be active. It is behind the passed pawn and therefore pushing the black rook backwards. If Black gives way the pawn will follow. On the other hand Black is also attacking the pawn and thus tying down White's rook. With the pawn on h5 White's rook would have more space to manoeuvre and thus be much more active and, being closer to promotion, the pawn would require more attention from Black's rook which, at the moment, might have to perform other duties before returning to the job of blockader.

It makes sense that which rook is the active one is constantly dependent on what else happens on the board. The rules concerning activity are *local rules*, as explained in Chapter 3, while Dvoretsky's claim that 'the rook must be active', is a *global rule* and, as such rules should be, is more abstract, being dependent on local rules.

Let us return to Exercise 2.

Actually the solution is the same as in Exercise 1, only a bit more difficult because it coincides with a standard intuitive notion. Normally we prefer to put our rooks on the edge of the board and we rarely consider other squares. This notion is so strongly implanted in our minds that we never think of it as a rule (similar to not speaking and eating simultaneously). It is a basic rule we learned while taking our first steps in chess, and which we never question. Anyway, here is the solution:

1 ♖g5!!

As in Exercise 1 White needs to win a tempo and activate his rook behind the pawn. Because White's king is in the

way 1 ♖g8? does not achieve this aim, as after 1...♔f3 2 ♖f8+ ♔g2 the pawn cannot be immediately attacked.

1...♔f3 2 ♖f5+ ♔g2 3 ♖e5

White has achieved the desired position for his rook with the sufficient gain of time.

3...♔f3 4 ♔d5 e3 5 ♔d4 e2 6 ♔d3 and White wins.

Studying the Endgame to Learn it

I would claim (when full of confidence) that this short lesson (45 minutes if you tried to solve the exercises) is just as useful to the tournament player as playing through all of Cheron's four volumes. Why? It explains what is going on instead of frustrating you with endless variations that you are not sure about trying to remember. An important thing when you try to improve your chess is to appreciate that you need to remember as little as possible, a decent understanding being far more useful. I remember Short saying something like 'I cannot remember a line where the moves are not logical.' In the endgame understanding is crucial. Occasionally you will find yourself in theoretical positions, but not often. Rather you will need to find your own way in foreign territory. Enhancing you understanding of the endgame will help you make good choices when you need them.

In this chapter we will have a look at some portraits of strong players. Some of them are famous for their superior endgame technique, others just for being great players. I will try to paint a realistic picture of how endgames are played at the highest level, and how I think they should be understood as a collection of ideas rather than variations.

I will start with an amazing player, ranked twentieth in the world at the time of writing. A chess giant and my superior in all aspects of the game, but not a great endgame player, however.

Grandmaster Kiril Georgiev

I will be somewhat presumptuous by connecting the two games I have chosen to present here. I will assume that Georgiev, after the first defeat, realised that he had little knowledge about rook endings and went home to study. Subsequently, in the second game he confused two different methods of defence. Unfortunately he did not seem to get to the core of the endgame, and never really understood anything substantial. This might seem like a strong accusation against one of the world's strongest players, but I have played through all the rook endgames I could find from his grandmaster period, and it seems to me that he rarely gains points in this phase. Of course he wins winning positions and draws drawing positions but, just as often, he does not. And he never seems to win drawn endgames against his peers.

Of course it is always slightly uncomfortable to write a negative portrait of anybody, but I have chosen to do so anyway for several reasons, one being that I was certain it would fit the purpose. Georgiev is also so much stronger than I, so if I am wrong in my theories it is not really that important. If I were writing about a local player I would, of course, feel different. Finally I must say that I have never met Georgiev in person, and have no reason to like or dislike him.

Okay, I have apologised enough now, so let us move on to the first game.

Kir.Georgiev- Yermolinsky
Groningen PCA qualifier 1993

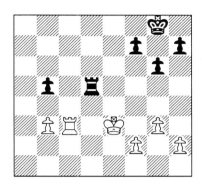

White to move

When I showed this position to a girlfriend of mine, who barely has an ELO rating, she said: 'Of course White is better after ♖d8+ and ♖b8 but I refuse to believe he can win it'. Well, I could not agree more. The rook would be active on b8, preparing b3-b4 with the idea of creating winning chances after ♖c8-c5. However, Black should comfortably draw with active play.

38 ♖d3?

A typical time-trouble move, I suppose — not necessarily one which has been played instantly (the check is more automatic), but one which follows ten seconds of confusion. The only real winning attempt in this position is 38 f3!? ♔f8 39 ♔e4 ♖d2 40 ♖c5 ♖xh2 41 ♖xb5, when White has gained a passed pawn, although Black will eventually create his own passed pawn on the kingside, and thereby make a draw.

38...♖c5!

Of course Black cannot exchange rooks and enter the pawn ending, so he slightly improves the position of his rook, staying active on the rank and eyeing the c2-square as a possible entry point.

39 ♔d4?

This is where White's problems begin. Instead of activating his rook he is activating his king. Unfortunately this is not a very good plan. Alright, 39 ♖d8+?! ♔g7 40 ♖b8? is out of the question due to 40...♖c3+, when a certain level of accuracy is required to draw (quite a task, I feel, if the rest of the game is anything to go by). Instead he should force a draw with 39 b4! with the idea of 40 ♖d5, practically forcing a repetition of moves with 39...♖c4 40 ♖d4 ♖c3+ 41 ♖d3 ♖c4.

39...♖c2!

The natural square for the rook, monitoring f2 (and h2) and cutting off White's king from Black's only potential weakness, the b5-pawn.

40 ♖f3

Forced. Georgiev must have felt somewhat uncomfortable here. His rook is obviously ridiculous while Black's dominates his king. However, the position is surely drawn, but the trend seems to be that White makes mistake after mistake and, slowly, the position is becoming difficult for him. For more on the concept of 'trends' I recommend you read Yermolinsky's own brilliant book, *The road to Chess Improvement*.

40...f5 41 ♔d3

Let us be nice and assume that White's bout of serious time-trouble has just ended, and only now can he stop moving and start thinking. Upon realising how he has misplaced his rook he should now be suffering from a severe headache, needing to do something about it.

41...♖c5

Black is forced to cut the king off or the b-pawn will soon be fatally exposed.

42 ♖e3

The rook returns to play from its hiding place.

42...♔f7

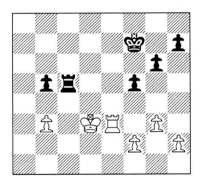

What should White do here?

43 f4?

This serves only to weaken White's kingside. I guess he was afraid that Black might advance his pawns and thus create some chances, but that is no justification for the damage to his pawn structure. The correct path is 43 ♖e2, when the most obvious idea is then ♖e2-a2 in order to generate activity via a6 or a7. But another plan is even more solid – White can come to c2 as the pawn ending is completely drawn: 43 ♖e2! b4! (43...♔f6 44 ♖c2! ♖xc2 45 ♔xc2 ♔e5 46 ♔c3 ♔d5 47 ♔b4 ♔c6

48 ♔a5 g5 49 b4 and White even wins)
44 ♖c2 ♖xc2 45 ♔xc2 ♔e6 46 ♔d3
♔d5 47 f4 etc.

43...b4!

Tying White down.

44 h4?

This is another mistake, presenting
Black with a new target on g3. The h2-
pawn was less of a weakness because it
would be difficult to attack for some
time (b3, on the other hand, is truly
weak). Now White has two weaknesses
and the position is close to – if not already – losing.

44...♖c7

An attractive idea. Black prepares
...♔g7-h6-h5-g4 without allowing White
time to get behind the b-pawn with a
check on e7. We can also clearly see the
negative effect of White's last move, as
his rook is obliged to stay on the third
rank.

45 ♔d4 ♔g7!

Black activates his king, which White
has in no way restricted.

46 h5

White needs to exchange the h-pawn
before it becomes a weakness once g3
falls, and capturing on h5 is undesirable
for Black.

46...♔h6 47 hxg6 hxg6 48 ♖e6

Here begins a new and interesting
phase of the game. Can White be saved?
Actually I do not believe that he is en-
tirely lost just yet, but it is a very difficult position. His only chance now is a
waiting strategy.

**48...♖c3 49 ♖e3 ♖c1 50 ♖e6 ♖g1 51
♖e3 ♖c1 52 ♖e6**

Threefold repetition? Just kidding.

52...♔h5

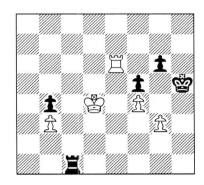

Can White survive?

53 ♖b6?

After this move the answer is definitely no. I guess Georgiev drifted into
time-trouble for a second time and did
not have time to properly calculate the
consequences of his move. Yermolinsky, on the other hand, does not
seem to have had any problems taking
stock of the position. White should be
able to make the draw with 53 ♖e3,
when Black has two possibilities.
53...♖g1 54 ♔c4 ♔g4 55 ♔xb4 ♖xg3
56 ♖xg3+ ♔xg3 57 ♔c5 ♔xf4 58 b4
♔g4 59 b5 f4 leads to a drawn queen
ending, although not without chances
for Black, while 53...♔g4 54 ♖e6 ♔xg3
55 ♖xg6+ ♔xf4 56 ♖b6 ♔g3 57 ♖xb4

f4 58 罝b8 罝d1+ 59 當e4 罝e1+ 60 當d4
f3 61 罝g8+ 當h2 62 罝f8 當g2 63 罝g8+
當f1 64 b4 is an easy draw.

**53...罝c3 54 罝xb4 罝xg3 55 當e5 罝e3+
56 當d4 罝f3 57 當e5 當g4 58 罝b6
罝e3+ 59 當d4 當xf4 60 罝xg6 罝xb3 0-1**

After a continuation such as 61 罝g8
罝b4+ 62 當d3 罝e4 White's king is cut
off and we have a theoretically winning
position.

Not an impressive game from White,
but it should be said that a lot of money
was at stake, and that this might have
influenced Georgiev's play.

As I mentioned earlier I will pretend
that I know for a fact that Georgiev was
a sensible player who, after losing this
game, went home to put a lot of hours
into studying the endgame. So, some
years later, in the world championship
knockout tournament in Las Vegas, he
felt comfortable about entering a rook
endgame a pawn down, as he knew for
a fact that it was drawn. Unfortunately,
he did not remember how to make the
draw, and he had no basic understanding of the endgame to guide him at a
time when he had to think for himself.

The endgame has been well known
for a long time, and has been drawn
many times. Averbakh has the following
version in his book:

---

see following diagram

1 a6 當f6 2 當f3

Note that 2 a7?! is an immediate draw
because Black has to do nothing other
keep an eye on the a-pawn. When
White's king approaches the pawn (in
order to free his rook) Black will begin a
series of annoying incredibly annoying
checks.

N. Kopajev 1958

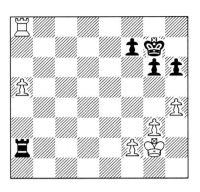

**2...h5 3 當e3 當f5 4 f3 罝a3+ 5 當d4
罝xf3 6 罝f8 罝a3 7 罝xf7+ 當g4 8 罝f6
當xg3 9 罝xg6+ 當xh4 10 當c5 h3 11
當b6 h4 12 罝g5 罝xa6+ 13 當xa6 當h3
14 當b5 h3 15 當c4 當h1 16 當d3 h2
17 當e2 Stalemate**

There is no reason to memorise this
example. It will suffice to learn the main
idea of Black's defence. While White
promotes the a-pawn Black attacks the
kingside, wins a pawn and, ultimately,
draws by a tempo or two. Now let us see
how Georgiev approached this situation.

Akopian-Kir.Georgiev
Las Vegas 1999

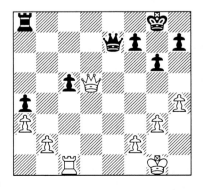

Black to move and force a draw?!

26...♖d8!

A nice pawn sacrifice, forcing a drawn ending.

27 ♕xc5 ♖d1+! 28 ♔h2

28 ♔g2? ♕e4+ is not advisable.

28...♕xc5 29 ♖xc5 ♖d2 30 ♔g2 ♖xb2 31 ♖c4

White wins a pawn but Black is about to achieve the desired position on both flanks. The pawns are placed optimally on the kingside and the rook will be perfect on a2. Meanwhile White's rook is less than perfect in front of its own pawn. In fact Black has a good version of the endgame we have just seen.

31...h5!

This is the optimal position for Black's kingside pawns. Experience has shown that if White gets time to play g3-g4 Black will find it more difficult to make a draw – this goes for all of these rook endgames, where the best defensive structure is f7-g6-h5 in 99% of cases.

32 ♖xa4 ♖a2 33 ♔f3 ♔g7 34 ♔e3 ♖a1

Compared to the Kopajev position, above, White has not even started advancing his passed pawn, so Black wisely waits.

35 ♖a6 ♖a2 36 ♖a4 ♖a1 37 ♖a6 ♖a2 38 a4

Now we are getting close to the Kopajev position and Black has to choose a plan.

38...♖a3+

This is one of the two possible strategies. It is basically very simple – with the check White is forced to leave his pawns, and Black can attack them immediately with the rook. The other plan is to play ...f7-f6 and ...g6-g5, leav-

ing White with a choice of either hxg5 fxg5, when Black will draw due to his new passed pawn on the h-file, or allowing ...gxh4 followed by ...♔g7-g6-f5-g4, creating a passed pawn on the h-file anyway. In the latter strategy the rook is well placed on a2, where it is behind the a-pawn and attacking f2 – Ultimate activity. Both plans should draw without any problems.

39 ♔d4 f6?

An unfortunate mix-up, but not yet the decisive mistake. In cognitive science this is known as a *conceptual blend*. The two plans from the previous note are blended together, producing elements from both. This is a very basic brain function and, presumably, the key to most new discoveries. Yet here it is not very convenient. Now White's king reaches the queenside quickly and therefore White has genuine winning chances. Incidentally, for anyone particularly interested in the notion of conceptual blending as a cognitive process I recommend G.Fauconnier's excellent *Mappings in thought and language* from 1997.

40 ♖a7+ ♔h6 41 a5 g5 42 ♔c5 gxh4 43 gxh4

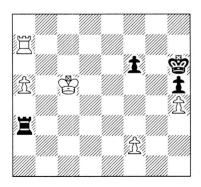

How Should Black continue?

We see here that White's king stands on c5 while Black's counterplay is yet to begin. Nonetheless the position is probably still drawn.

43...♖a4??

This is quite horrible. Black does not have time to actually take the h4-pawn so the text simply throws away a vital tempo. In fact this is the second tempo that Black loses, so now the position is hopeless. Whether Black can draw with 43...♔g6 or 43...♖a2 is not clear. Perhaps both these moves draw, but it is not important to investigate here in order to classify Georgiev's choice as a mistake. We are interested in ideas and concepts more than lengthy analysis. Moreover – and this is important – in order to improve our rook endgames, understanding ideas is more important than extensive analysis. We should try to find arguments and reasoning which *can improve the process of making decisions at the board*!

Try to make a comparison between 43...♔g6 and the game and you will see the difference clearly.

44 a6! ♖a2

Now it is obvious that Black has wasted a move. He must have overlooked 44...♖xh4 45 ♖a8! ♖a4 46 a7 ♔g7 47 ♔b6! with the idea of 48 ♖b8. Now we see that the rook is too close to White's king and thus cannot keep checking – an important concept! After 47...♖b4+ 48 ♔a5 ♖b1 49 ♖b8 White wins. Of course this variation would not have been possible with Black's rook on the second or third rank.

45 ♖a8 ♔g6 46 ♔b6 ♖b2+ 47 ♔a7 ♖xf2 48 ♖b8 ♖f4

48...♔f5 49 ♖b4! leaves Black in a hopeless situation.

49 ♖b5!

The comparison to 43...♔g6 is now apparent. Now the king is cut off and the game is lost.

49...♖xh4 50 ♔b6 ♖e4 51 a7 ♖e8 52 ♖a5 h4 53 a8♕ ♖xa8 54 ♖xa8 ♔g5 55 ♔c5 h3 56 ♖h8 ♔g4 57 ♔d4 ♔g3 58 ♔e3 ♔g2 59 ♔e2 h2 60 ♖g8+ ♔h3 61 ♔f2!

A well-known trick in this kind of endgame. Black is forced to into underpromotion, and knights are not too happy in the corner.

61...h1♘+ 62 ♔f3 ♔h2 63 ♖g2+ ♔h3 64 ♖g6 ♔h2 65 ♖xf6 ♔g1 66 ♖g6+ 1-0

The knight is lost after either 66...♔h2 67 ♖g8 or the alternative 66...♔f1 67 ♖g2.

When you have an advantage but cannot win the game, let the opponent draw it. It is not always that he does, as experience (and this game) shows us. Sometimes it is better to let the opponent be the one who works to make the game move forward.

Well, that is enough picking on poor Georgiev. What I wanted to illustrate was how a world class player can be lacking in technique in the endgame, and how this has been very expensive for him, eliminating him from two world championship cycles.

Before moving on to powerful endgame performances I would like to add one final example. Already famous despite being played only a year ago, it is from the final game in the Club Kasparov organised Internet Knockout tournament.

Piket-Kasparov

Club Kasparov Internet Match

English Opening

1 ♘f3 ♘f6 2 c4 c5 3 ♘c3 d5 4 cxd5 ♘xd5 5 g3 ♘c6 6 ♗g2 ♘c7 7 d3 e5 8 0-0 ♗e7 9 ♘d2 ♗d7 10 ♘c4 0-0 11 ♗xc6 ♗xc6 12 ♘xe5 ♗e8 13 ♕b3 ♗f6 14 ♘g4 ♗d4 15 e3 ♗xc3 16 ♕xc3 b6 17 f3 ♗b5 18 ♘f2 ♕d7 19 e4 ♘e6 20 ♗e3 a5 21 ♖ad1 ♖ad8 22 ♖d2 ♕c6 23 ♖c1 ♕b7 24 a3 ♘d4 25 ♔g2 ♖c8 26 ♖b1 ♖fd8 27 ♗xd4 ♖xd4 28 b4 axb4 29 axb4 ♕d7 30 bxc5 bxc5 31 ♖bb2 h6 32 ♖a2 ♔h7 33 ♖a5 ♖d8 34 ♕xc5 ♗xd3 35 ♖xd3 ♖xd3 36 ♘xd3 ♕xd3 37 ♖a2 ♕b3 38 ♕c2

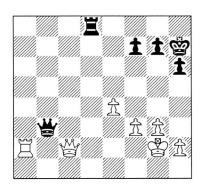

Exchange the queens?

Kasparov, in his usual style, sacrificed a pawn for active play. However, unlike twenty years ago when he first appeared on the chess scene, the top players now know how to defend better. This has never been Kasparov's strength, though; he seems a little too impatient to me.

Anyway, here he goes for a rook endgame which is known to be completely drawn. Indeed we get a very pro-

totypical version of this endgame. The only problem is that Kasparov does not know how to draw it.

38...♕xc2+ 39 ♖xc2 h5!

The defensive structure mentioned in the previous game.

40 f4 g6 41 e5 ♖d3 42 ♔h3 ♖e3 43 ♔h4 ♔g7

Here we find the first opportunity for Black to force a draw. After 43...♔h6! White has no way to make genuine progress as Black draws 44 ♖c7 ♖e2! 45 ♔h3 ♔g7, while 45 h3? ♖e4! is dangerous only for White!

44 ♔g5

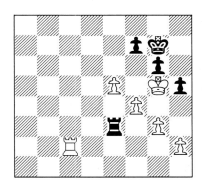

Still a draw!

44...♖e1?

Kasparov realises too late that this waiting policy leads to disaster. Black can draw easily with 44...♖a3 45 ♖c7 ♖a5!, preventing e5-e6. White can try 46 ♖e7 ♖b5 47 f5!? but after 47...gxf5 48 e6 (the point) Black has the simple defence 48...f4+ 49 ♔xf4 ♔f6 50 ♖xf7+ ♔xe6 and there is no way that White can win the h-pawn. This method has been known for a long time, and has been used with success. Jon–Karasjev, Leningrad 1983, is one example, the only difference being that Black's rook was on the b-file in that game.

45 ♖c7

Now the threat of e5-e6 is hanging in the air, and Black can no longer prevent what follows.

45...♖e2 46 ♖e7! ♖a2

The pawn ending after 46...♖e1 47 e6! ♖xe6 48 ♖xe6 fxe6 wins for White.

(Analysis Diagram)
A pawn ending – how lovely!

White wins as follows: 49 h3! ♔f7 (49...♔h7 50 ♔f6) 50 ♔h6 ♔f6 51 g4 h4 (51...hxg4 52 hxg4 ♔f7 53 g5 wins for White) 52 g5+ (52 ♔h7? g5! 53 ♔h6 gxf4 54 g5+ ♔e5! and Black is back in the game, this time with winning chances) 52...♔f5 53 ♔g7 ♔xf4 54 ♔xg6 e5 55 ♔f6 e4 56 g6 e3 57 g7 e2 58 g8♕ e1♕ 59 ♕g4+ ♔e3 60 ♕e6+ ♔f2 61 ♕xe1+ ♔xe1 62 ♔g5 ♔f2 63 ♔xh4 ♔f3 64 ♔g5 etc.

47 f5!

Closing the fifth rank and winning the game.

47...gxf5 48 e6 h4 49 ♖xf7+ ♔g8 50 ♔f6 1-0

White threatens both ♖b7-b8+ and the immediate ♖g7+, both winning.

Now, how could Garry Kasparov, the best player of all time, lose such an elementary rook endgame? In abstract terms we could say that he did not have the right feeling for the endgame to begin with. Kasparov is, of course, a great technical player, but not on the level of Kramnik, Karpov and other living legends. With a more concrete approach we could say that he was not aware of the pawn sacrifice (e5-e6) in advance and, when he finally saw it, it was too late. Had he had the feeling for the endgame he would have seen and prevented this but, as it happens, he became nervous and did not focus enough on his opponent's possibilities. In the end this was what proved fatal.

Schematic Thinking!

I play for a team in the Swedish league, of which I am very fond. My team-mates are strong amateurs, like me, and weak professionals. I remember after one match some of my team mates were telling me about the game between grandmasters Jonny Hector (our guy) and Ulf Andersson. Jonny had played a very good game, winning the exchange, but eventually failed to win. Actually, he came close to losing control near the end, and had to force a spectacular draw. After the game he was analysing with Andersson, who repeatedly illustrated different fortresses and ideas for fortresses. Only the one played in the game had actual relevance, and my team mates found it very amusing. Jonny, who would never laugh or say anything bad about anyone, kept telling Ulf: 'Yes, but this is not the game'. Ulf answered by showing a new fortress idea.

I laughed when they told me about it, but not for the same reason. They believed, or so it seemed, that Ulf got all excited because of his great love for the endgame. This might be true. They also believed that the lines he was showing had no relevance to the game. This is simply not true, and if you think about it for a few seconds I am sure you will come to the same conclusion. Ulf Andersson, one of the greatest masters of the endgame, thinking about a lot of irrelevant things yet still almost winning a very difficult endgame? It sounds suspicious to me. I have found over the years that you should give people the benefit of the doubt. Most people are highly aware of what they are doing, they just think in a different direction. In the case of Ulf Andersson we should try to understand his way of thinking, and see what this can bring us in terms of insights.

I would like to apologise to my friends for using this example, but I needed it to make a point. I do not want you to think that I believe myself to be superior to my friends when I actually learn a lot from them every time I have the chance to play for the team. As I said, I was not present at the analysis of this game, so instead I will use another example with which one of my teammates in Germany impressed us.

Zharm-Zieher
Germany 2001

A pupil of mine with an ELO of 2300 actually played 1 ♖g7? here because he could not sufficiently calculate the consequences of winning the bishop. This is

in fact a very interesting question.

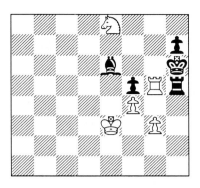

Try to analyse this position.
Can you win with White?

When should we believe in our intuition and when should we believe in our abilities to calculate? I believe the answer must be to play through many exercises and our own games, which should lead to strong intuition. Then all we need to do is to learn to listen to this intuition. Here it should not take long to compare the two variations and decide that only winning the piece grants White genuine winning chances.

1 ♖xh5+ ♔xh5 2 ♘g7+ ♔g4 3 ♘xe6 ♔xg3

This was Black's plan when he chose to sacrifice the piece (if indeed it was a sacrifice). Now Harm sank into deep thought. Together with three teammates I was analysing the endgame and, fifteen minutes later, the conclusion was that Black would make a draw. We never made it to the seventh move of the game because the idea never occurred to us. Harm, on the other hand, used a different kind of thinking. He asked himself 'Where does my knight want to be' (after having assured himself that wasting two tempi going to e5 with the king was pointless). Then he just looked and found the surprising answer: h6! Once he had discovered this his calculation improved considerably since he knew what he wanted to achieve. With five minutes remaining on the clock he executed all the moves with great confidence, and in fifteen minutes had achieved far more than boards one, two, three and seven together. This is simply because he knew where he was going. He used his abilities as a human and not as a calculator. Very impressive indeed.

4 ♘g7!

The only winning line, it seems. 4 ♔d4? h5 5 ♔e5 h4 6 ♘g7 (6 ♘g5? manages to lose: 6...♔g4 7 ♔f6 ♔xf4 8 ♘h3+ ♔g3 9 ♘g5 f4 10 ♘e4+ ♔g2 11 ♔f5 h3 and the pawn promotes) 6...h3 7 ♘xf5+ draws after either 7...♔f2 8 ♘h6 ♔g3 or 7...♔g2 8 ♘e3+ ♔f3 9 ♘f1 ♔g2.

4...♔g4 5 ♘e8!

Prevents ...h7-h5 for the time being.

5...h6 6 ♘f6+ ♔g3

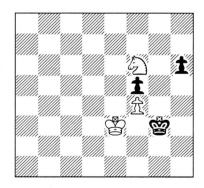

7 ♘g8!!

The conclusion of a beautiful manoeuvre.

7...h5 8 ♘h6

Finally the desired square is reached, and the game is over.

8...h4 9 ♘xf5+ ♔g4 10 ♘xh4 ♔xh4 11 ♔e4 1-0

This example of clear human logic is more powerful than trying to calculate like *Fritz*. It is true that *Fritz* did beat me using only one minute from the start position, but I am sure Ulf Andersson would also come close. Yet some strong players to whom I have shown this position have had great problems finding the solution.

If we consider the Piket-Kasparov game again, Black lost because he failed to anticipate (in time) what White was intending. One of the greatest calculating players in the world did not make a draw in that rather elementary endgame because he did not have the necessary understanding of the position. Schematic thinking could have saved him.

Now we turn to the first positive portrait.

Ulf Andersson

The Swedish grandmaster Ulf Andersson has been around for a long time. When he was a junior he competed with Timman, Adorjan and Karpov for the World Junior Championship and, later, after Karpov had been announced world champion when Fischer decided not to defend the title, Andersson was the first player to beat the new king (and with Black). When he was in his late twenties, in 1979, Bent Larsen wrote about him in his book about the Clarin tournament in Buenos Aires: 'Why do young players always want to play endgames with Ulf?' In the 1980s he played many of the strongest tournaments and generally kept a world ranking of around 10th-20th. He was never really a candidate for the world championship but many regard him as a technical player who might have met his match only in Anatoly Karpov.

Andersson's style is very dry indeed, and he seems mainly to be interested in avoiding defeat. He once answered the question 'Are you afraid of losing?' with the cunning reply 'I hate to lose, but I am not afraid of winning!' and he also once said: 'When you do not play, you do not lose ELO-points!'

Certainly this attitude has been restrictive, but we all need to find the path in life which suits us best. Ulf Andersson was never that ambitious, rather he just loves chess. In his forties he took up correspondence chess and became − as far as I know − the first double Grandmaster. In that connection he said: 'I cannot understand how anyone can lose a correspondence game.' It turned out that when given the time to make sure that he was not taking any risks, he had quite a good flair for the tactical aspects of chess, and made some nice combinations in correspondence games. I remember a friend telling me about analysing with Andersson after they had made a draw, that Andersson was coming up with complicated tactical variations he had calculated during the game. My friend was very impressed but also realised that Andersson looked mainly at these tactics in order to avoid risks. We will return to this below, but first let us discuss his style.

We already know that Ulf Andersson is not one to take a loss lightly, which might be why he has such a liking for exchanging pieces. He is a very prophylactic player, seeing all kinds of tactics well in advance and avoiding pitfalls with great skill. As a lot of his energy is spent on this defensive interest he is a less than dangerous player. In fact, unlike many of his grandmaster colleagues, he will never try desperate winning attempts. If he wins it is due to his opponent's mistakes and shortcomings, not because he has put them under a lot of pressure or created problems unknown to them. If people try to beat him he will bite back, but he is not the type to start a battle himself. The famous game Andersson-Basman, Hastings 1975, shows how this can be used against him. Basman proclaimed before the game (or so the story goes) that Andersson did nothing, and that he did not fear him at all. Basman then repeated the position (his own, that is) eight times before Andersson became so annoyed with the situation that he lost his sense of danger. Basman eventually won the game.

But normally Andersson is a very dangerous opponent for anybody below the top ten. Most prefer to draw with him and get on with their lives, but a few want to play him. The following game is a good example of the strength of his style. Yes, he does not do anything, but he is still deeply motivated and interested. His desire is to play the strongest moves, and should the endgame start to go his way, it is very difficult to defend against him, for − unlike most other players − he does not make stupid mistakes. Consequently you cannot afford to make a mistake against him.

The reason why I have selected Andersson as a primary example is that his endgame play is close to perfect, and because there are no good collections of his games available. I will, naturally, be unable to do them full justice, but I will try.

Andersson–Polugaevsky
Haninge 1990
Queen's Indian Defence

1 ♘f3 ♘f6 2 c4 e6 3 ♘c3 b6 4 g3 ♗b7 5 ♗g2 ♗e7 6 0-0 0-0 7 d4 ♘e4 8 ♘xe4

This is typical Ulf Andersson. To most players this line is tantamount to a draw offer, but to Andersson it is a serious alternative to the main lines. I remember discussing this line with a friend after having played 7 ♖e1 in a game and later regretting it slightly. He said: 'True, sometimes I just take a deep look into my opponents eyes, and then exchange everything.' To some people this is a truly destructive way of playing, as the more technical aspects of chess hold little or no interest at all to them. Andersson, presumably, does not see this as destructive at all (although I am only guessing).

After some moves we will enter the part of the game where there is no confusion (tactics), and where a more static understanding of the pieces begins to count.

8...♗xe4 9 ♘e1 ♗xg2 10 ♘xg2 d5 11 ♕a4 c5 12 ♗e3 cxd4 13 ♗xd4 dxc4 14 ♕xc4 ♕c8 15 ♖ac1 ♘a6

A new move at the time. Polugaevsky

claims in his annotations in *Informant* that Black has fully equalised at this point. He is obviously correct but, for Andersson, this is not too important. Playing for an advantage would include taking all kinds of risks anyway, so he would rather just go directly into the endgame and then take it from there.

16 ♘f4 ♕xc4

This gives White a chance to cause Black problems. Better is 16...♖d8! with the idea of ...♕xc4 followed by ...b6-b5, winning material. After 17 ♗e3 ♕b7 Black has equalised according to Polugaevsky.

17 ♖xc4 ♖fd8 18 ♗e3

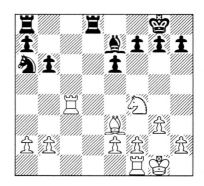

Now Black experiences minor but definite problems with his queenside (this would probably not be the case with the queens still in play). The main cause of irritation is the poorly placed knight on a6 and the threat of ♖a4. Having combined these factors it is not difficult to find the right move.

18...b5! 19 ♖c3 ♘b4 20 a3

Here Polugaevsky also analyses 20 ♖b3 but, according to this book's main argument, such a move would never be seriously considered.

20...e5!

A wise decision, as Black's a-pawn should prove a stronger asset than White's e-pawn. It is only due to the strong performance from Andersson that this does not happen. Less convincing is 20...♘d5!? 21 ♘xd5 ♖xd5 22 ♖c7 ♗f6 23 b4, which might be a little unpleasant for Black because White has control over the c-file, which is clearly much more glamorous than the d-file. Note that 23...♗b2? gets Black nowhere as White has 24 ♖b1! ♗xa3? 25 ♖b3, after which Black is forced into 25...♖d1+ 26 ♔g2 ♖a1 in order not to lose the bishop. It should be obvious that White has enough compensation here, but otherwise one can also analyse 27 ♗d4 ♖a2 (27...♖d1 28 e3 ♗c1 29 ♖bc3 and White wins) 28 ♖f3! and there is no defence for the king: 28...♖f8 29 ♗c5 ♖c2!? 30 ♖fxf7! and Black is mated.

21 axb4 exf4 22 ♗xf4 ♗xb4 23 ♖c7 h6 24 ♖a1

How should Black improve his position?

24...♗d6?!

This move is a little naive, and probably comes from the feeling that the draw is not far away. Polugaevsky probably thought that all he needed to do was exchange a few pieces and then the ending would be so drawn that he could offer without considering a refusal. This is a classic mistake. When the opponent's play seems completely unambitious it is easy to believe he just wants a draw. Yet this is often not the case! When people play on they normally want to win, and if they do not really try they often offer a draw at some point. I know only of one case

where a draw offer was refused with the words: 'Of course it is a draw, but I want to prove it!'

So, always search for your opponent's plans and ideas and do not end up in the same situation as Kasparov did above, and Polugaevsky does here, where they only react when it is to late.

24...a5! is the correct move, when 25 ♖b7 is best met not with the reasonable 25...♖d5, as suggested by Polugaevsky himself, but the far more active 25...♖ac8! with the idea of 26 ♖xb5 ♖c2! and Black might even be (very) slightly better. It is understandable that Polugaevsky wants to protect his d5-pawn, but remembering Dvoretsky's words, it is not difficult to realise that the rook on a8 needs to be activated. Perhaps 25 ♖b7 is not that accurate, and the move 25 ♖ac1 is a possible alternative.

25 ♗xd6 ♖xd6

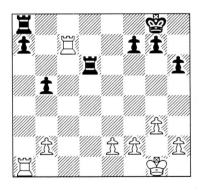

How can White improve his position?

26 ♖a3!

After this White has an edge (Polugaevsky). White will improve his rook in the best possible way by transferring it to e7 (should Black choose to do nothing). Being on his way to time-trouble (where did he spend all this time?) Polugaevsky decides not to wait for White to find his path, and forces pawn trades. Notice how Polu thinks that as soon as Black has problems to solve – even if they might later seem to be straightforward and easy to solve – he thinks White is slightly better. This is because he is a player who cares how games are won in practice, rather than a commentator searching for the truth in the position. Games are won because it is easier playing on one side of the board than the other, and this example is typical.

26...a5

26...a6 is slightly passive in view of 27 ♖e3!. Instead 26...♖d2 is more natural, when play might continue 27 ♖e3 ♖xb2 28 ♖ee7 ♖f8 29 ♖xa7 and Black still has some problems to solve. White will not round up the b-pawn quickly (exchanging a rook along the lines of Piket-Kasparov) but try to advance his king-side pawns and create further weaknesses in Black's camp. The simple plan of e2-e4-e5-e6 is particularly relevant here, although Black should draw without too much difficulty. He can give up the b-pawn without expecting any exchanges in return, re-route his rook from b2 to the eighth rank and perpetually threaten to exchange a rook should White not give up his seventh rank supremacy. This endgame actually occurred in Petrosian-Balashov, Leningrad 1977.

---

see following diagram

White won as follows:
29 ♔g2 h5 30 h3 ♔g7 31 ♔f3 ♔f6 32

h4 ♔g7 33 ♖d5 ♖e8 34 ♖dd7 ♖f8 35 ♖e7 ♔f6 36 e4 ♖d4 37 e5+ ♔f5 38 ♖xc5 ♖d3+ 39 ♔g2 ♖a3 40 ♖c6 ♔e4 41 ♖f6 ♖aa8 42 e6 ♔e5 43 ♖fxf7 ♖g8 44 ♖b7 ♔xe6 45 ♖be7+ ♔d6 46 ♖e2 ♖af8 47 ♖a7 ♖a8 48 ♖ae7 ♖ac8 49 ♖2e6+ ♔d5 50 ♔h3 ♖c7 51 ♖xg6 1-0

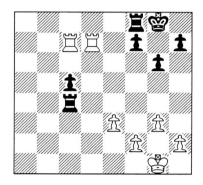

Okay, Black did not defend well in this game, but it does show how some positions are easier to play, and how some players find some positions easier to play.

Returning to the main game, the action is on the queenside.

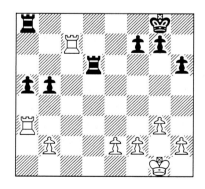

27 ♖b7 b4?

Activating the a8-rook at the cost of a pawn, which seems too big a price. In fact Black has a fairly easy draw, it seems, in 27...罝d2!, when White has a choice. 28 b4 a4 should transpose to the line given below, or it can end in a draw after 29 e4 罝d4 (29...f5? 30 exf5 罝d5 31 g4 罝c8 32 罝e3! favours White) 30 罝xb5 罝xe4 31 罝a5 (31 罝b7 罝e1+ 32 ♔g2 罝b1) 31...罝b8.

This leaves 28 罝xb5 罝xe2 29 b4 a4 30 罝a5 罝b8 31 罝3xa4 罝b2 with a draw. Note that White's 29th move is forcing, which is very unlike Andersson, who would probably have opted for 29 罝b7!, which is also the move that causes Black the most problems because White revives his old plan of doubling rooks on the seventh rank. The best response might then be 29...罝e6!?, which looks strange but has two important ideas – the first is equally strange and might never be relevant, featuring ...罝a8-a6-b6, while the second is simply to meet 罝f3 with ...罝f6. The draw should not be difficult to hold – even in time-trouble – but there are chances (slim) for Black to falter.

28 罝xb4 罝e8! 29 罝xa5 罝xe2 30 罝b8+ ♔h7 31 罝f5 罝d7!

With the rooks somewhere other than d7 and f5 Polugaevsky would comfortably draw this position, but they are there and the f5-rook is the more active of the two if we follow my definition given earlier (attacking=active, defending=passive). Polugaevsky evaluates the position as slightly better for White, probably meaning that Black should be able to draw without too much difficulty.

32 g4!

This is a standard move, intending to combat the defensive structure f7-g6-h5.

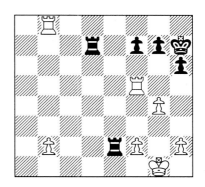

32...g6 33 罝f4 ♔g7 34 ♔g2 罝e5 35 h3 h5

Unlike Khalifman, in the example below, Polugaevsky has the awareness to exchange off his potentially weak h-pawn.

36 b4 hxg4 37 hxg4 g5?

In the long-term this will force Black to play ...f7-f6, after which both the 8th and the 7th ranks will have to be protected (at the moment only the 8th rank is susceptible to invasion). White also gains the f5-square for later exploits, as we shall see in the game. The correct course, as pointed out by Polugaevsky, is 37...罝e2! followed by ...罝b2, and Black will have to do some suffering, but not lose the game.

38 罝c4 罝e2 39 罝b5 f6 40 罝f5 罝b2 41 b5 罝b7 42 罝cc5 罝b4?!

The rook was perfect on b2 but the other rook needs improving. Black will now have to play more precisely to avoid losing. 42...罝e7 was Polu's own suggestion, when the apparently promising 43 罝c6 achieves nothing after 43...罝b7! 44 罝cxf6 罝2xb5, and White will have to enter an easily drawn ending.

43 ♔f3

43...♖b3+?

And this is definitely a mistake. Now White gets his king to the queenside and with it an almost winning position. Forced is 43...♖e7 to cut off White's king, when Polugaevsky offers the following variation: 44 ♖c6 ♖b3+ 45 ♔g2 ♖e4 (45...♖b7!? 46 ♖cxf6 ♖3xb5 also draws, as suggested above) 46 b6 (46 ♖cxf6 ♖xg4+ 47 ♔f1 ♖xb5 with a draw!) 46...♖xg4+ 47 ♔f1 ♖f4 and the endgame is drawn without much difficulty.

After the text drawn variations will not occur again, and it is the non-appearance of winning lines for White that will have to be Black's ambition.

44 ♔e2 ♖b4?!

This is also not in Black's interest. The rook was more damaging to the white king's safety on the third rank, and White's pawn surely wants to go to f3 in order to team up with the g4-pawn. 44...♖a7!, activating the rook, is preferable, when Black still has problems because this rook was supposed to protect the king. Well, things have changed.

45 f3 ♖a7 46 ♔d3 ♖a3+?

Losing by force. After allowing the

king to reach the third rank Black should play 46...♖b7 47 ♔c3 ♖b1 and hope White will not find a way to exploit his advantage. The situation is one of those that balances on the thin line between a win/loss and a draw. To us – practical players – it is of most interest to conclude that White has good winning chances.

47 ♖c3 ♖a5

Polugaevsky gives the following winning line for White: 47...♖a7 48 ♖c4! ♖b1 49 ♔c2! ♖aa1 50 ♖c7+ ♔g6 51 ♖c6 ♖c1+ 52 ♔d2 ♖d1+ 53 ♔c3.

48 ♖c7+ ♔g6 49 ♖c6 ♖axb5 50 ♖cxf6+ ♔h7 51 ♖f7+

Now we see the difference between having a rook on b7 and capturing with the other rook. Black's king is forced to the back rank, and exchanges are enough for White.

51...♔h8 52 ♖xb5 ♖xb5 53 ♖f5! ♖b3+ 54 ♔e4 1-0

In my view this was a brilliant performance from Andersson. Okay, I know he did absolutely nothing to win, but just playing good moves in the endgame, every move, is very difficult. It is easy to find the right move in a specific position if we know that this is precisely the place to look. But imagine that the position is completely harmless and nothing is really going on, and you still have to play the best move each time – this is very difficult indeed!

In the next two games we shall see how Andersson wins against two of his younger countrymen in the Sigeman tournament in Malmö (with a six year interval). In both games the matter of simple, very simple, positional rules suddenly requires excellence from the young players, something they do not have in this phase of the game.

What I really want you to notice is that Andersson does not play for a win in the strict sense of the word, rather he plays the position and sees what happens. Like all top players he knows that he will have his chances, and that all he needs to do is to be alert to them. As Brynell and Hillarp-Persson do not play these endgames well enough, they never really have a chance. It is not that they cannot now understand where they made their mistakes, but that they could not tell with certainty when considering their moves during the game.

Andersson–Brynell
Malmö 1994
Queen's Indian Defence

1 d4 e6 2 ♘f3 ♘f6 3 g3 b6 4 ♗g2 ♗b7 5 0-0 ♗e7 6 c4 0-0 7 ♘c3 ♘e4 8 ♕c2 ♘xc3 9 ♕xc3 c5 10 b3 ♗f6 11 ♗b2 cxd4 12 ♘xd4 ♗xg2 13 ♔xg2 d5 14 ♖fd1 ♘c6 15 ♕c2 ♘xd4 16 ♗xd4 ♖c8 17 ♖ac1 ♗xd4 18 ♖xd4 ♕c7 19 e4 ♕e5 20 ♕d3 dxe4 21 ♖xe4

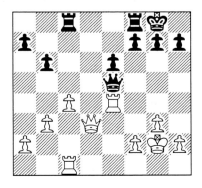

Andersson has played the opening completely without any ambition to prove an advantage, and now Black equalises by forcing a rook ending.

21...♖cd8! 22 ♖xe5 ♖xd3 23 ♖c2 ♖c8

With Black in control of the d-file White can do nothing to seriously harm him. So what does Andersson do? He simply improves his position move by move, knowing that his understanding of how to do this will give him an advantage similar to that of a boxer with the better reach. As we shall see in the game Brynell will make some minor errors, after which he will have to play very accurately in order to make the draw. As so often happens when a player cannot play a relatively simple drawn position sufficiently accurately, he also has problems when it becomes more difficult. Moreover, the knowledge that an easy draw was within reach can have a negative impact on a player.

24 ♔f1

The rooks cannot be much better placed for the time being, so White wisely brings his king into the game. Black decides to do the same.

24...♔f8 25 ♔e2 ♖d6 26 ♖d2

Andersson does not see an exchange of pieces as something that makes a draw more likely. He looks for the best move from an objective viewpoint, and here the d6-rook is better than the one on d2 and should therefore be exchanged.

26...♔e7 27 ♖e3 ♖xd2+ 28 ♔xd2 ♖c5!?

This looks a bit strange, actually, although Black is obviously okay. Krasenkov prefers 28...f6 with the idea of ...e6-e5 and therefore forcing 29 f4, after which Black can play 29...罩d8+ with an easy mind since the pawn ending after 30 罩d3 罩xd3+ 31 含xd3 含d6 must be a dead draw. I am not sure what Andersson would have played; perhaps 30 含e2 in order to keep some life in the position, but he might also have entered this pawn ending, just out of curiosity, trying to find some way to prove an advantage.

29 含c3 罩f5!

Brynell's plan has no faults other than requiring dynamic play. At this point he is certainly showing good form. White is forced to advance his pawn, after which ...h7-h5 and ...g7-g5-g4 will exert pressure on h2.

30 f3 h5 31 b4

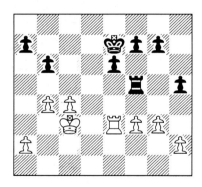

31...a5?

But this move is wrong. The a7-pawn is not really a weakness because it cannot be attacked, and White cannot produce a passed pawn on the queenside for some time to come. In fact there was nothing for Black to worry about over there. Now White might find a way in down the a-file at some point, and the b6-pawn has suddenly become a potential weakness − far more than the a7-pawn. However, Black's position

is basically sound, and the text is a little step in the wrong direction. In reality these little steps decide the majority of games (I know I am repeating myself, but this is very important!). Indeed among Ulf Andersson's wins this is the most common way.

32 a3 含d6 33 含d4 g5 34 罩d3 罩e5 35 含c3+ 含c7 36 含d2 g4 37 罩e3

Tricky, as Black cannot allow the king and pawn ending.

37...罩f5

Forced in view of 37...罩xe3?? 38 含xe3 gxf3 39 含xf3 axb4 40 axb4 f5 (40...e5 41 含e4 含d6 42 含f5 f6 43 h4 含d7 44 g4) 41 含f4 含d6 42 h4 含d7 43 含e5 含e7 44 c5 with a win for White.

38 含e2 axb4

In the event of 38...gxf3+!? Krasenkov gives 39 罩xf3 罩e5+ as a drawing line (he continues 40 罩e3 罩f5 with a repetition), but he does not consider 40 含d3, which seems to be the best move. In fact I prefer White here, although the position must be completely equal from an objective point of view.

39 axb4 含d6 40 罩d3+ 含c6 41 f4

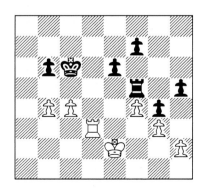

Now Black is beginning to be seriously challenged. His rook is no longer fantastic on the fifth rank and his kingside is becoming slightly fragile. Brynell must have given the position much thought, after which he came up with the right decision: activating the rook.

41...h4! 42 ♔e3 hxg3 43 hxg3 ♖h5 44 ♔d4

White's king does not hiding its intentions! With great ambition it is trying to make its way into Black's kingside. Black has two principally equal opportunities – to prevent this or to proceed with his own plans in the meantime. Brynell chooses the latter. I probably would have chosen the former as I feel it would be easier to play. Never mind that the position is objectively drawn. Black is now forced to find a good plan and, subsequently, to stick to it, and we have seen that this is not always as easy as it sounds.

44...♖h1

The alternative is 44...f6!?, when play might continue 45 ♖e3 ♔d6 46 c5+!? bxc5+ 47 bxc5+ ♔d7!? 48 ♖a3 ♖h1! (48...♖h3? is passive because it attacks the g3-pawn but does nothing else; at the right moment White will give up the in order to help promote his c-pawn – after 49 ♔c4! Black is in trouble because 49...♖h1 50 ♖a7+ ♔c6 51 ♖a6+ ♔d7 52 ♖d6+ ♔e7 53 ♖d3! gives White definite winning chances) 49 ♖a7+ ♔c6 50 ♖a6+ ♔d7 51 ♖d6+ ♔e7 52 ♔c4 ♖c1+ with a draw since after 53 ♔b5 ♖c3 Black has excellent prospects.

In this line 47...♔d7 would most likely be my practical choice as the king and pawn endgame after 47...♖xc5! 48 ♖xe6+ ♔xe6 49 ♔xc5 appears terribly risky to me. Actually it seems to be drawn after 49...♔d7! (the only move due to the standard 49...f5 50 ♔c6 ♔e7

51 ♔d5 ♔f6 52 ♔d6 ♔f7 53 ♔e5 ♔g6 54 ♔e6) 50 ♔d5 ♔e7 51 ♔e4 ♔e6 52 f5+ ♔d6 53 ♔f4 ♔d5 54 ♔xg4 ♔e5 and Black regains his pawn. I would not feel sufficiently confident to go for this line. I would have the feeling that there might be something I had overlooked, and that I was alright anyway. Such practical decisions are an important part of good endgame play. Where do you trust you intuition and where do you have doubts?

45 ♔e5

45...♖c1?

Not yet the losing mistake, but we are getting closer and closer, one mistake at a time. Krasenkov gives the following line: 45...♖f1! 46 ♖d6+ ♔c7 47 ♖d2 ♖g1 48 ♖d3 ♖f1 and the position will be repeated.

I am sure 47...♖f3 is also a pretty good move, just more double-edged. However, against Andersson, in this position, I would no doubt just force the draw.

46 ♔f6 ♖xc4

It often happens that, after you have chosen your plan, you have to stick to it, whether or not it was best. This is the case here. Black can no longer make a draw with 46...♖f1 in view of 47 ♖e3! (preventing ...e6-e5 on ♔xf7), leading to the following variation: 47...♖f3 48 ♖e4 ♖xg3 49 ♔xf7 ♖g1 (49...♖f3 50 ♔xe6 g3 51 f5 g2 52 ♖g4 wins for White) 50 ♖xe6+ ♔c7 51 f5 ♖f1 52 f6 g3 53 ♖e2 ♖f2 54 ♖e3 g2 55 ♖g3 and White is winning.

47 ♔xf7 ♖e4 48 ♔e7 ♔b5 49 ♖d6

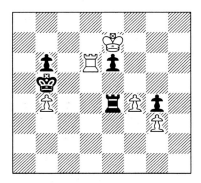

49...♖e3?

Too slow. With White's rook on the sixth rank it is impossible for Black to play ...♔xb4 without losing his key b6-pawn. Consequently Black's king is suddenly misplaced on the queenside and would be better placed on the other flank, helping the g-pawn. A better try is 49...♖xb4! 50 ♖xe6 ♖b3 51 f5 ♖xg3 52 f6 ♖f3 53 f7 g3 54 f8♕ (obviously wrong is 54 ♖f6 ♖xf6 55 ♔xf6 g2) 54...♖xf8 55 ♔xf8 g2 56 ♖g6 ♔c4! (an important point as Black's king will cut off White's) 57 ♔e7 b5 58 ♔d6 b4 59 ♖g4+ ♔c3 60 ♔c5 (60 ♖g3+ ♔c4! and White's king remains cut off) 60...b3 61 ♖g3+ ♔c2 62 ♔c4 b2 63 ♖xg2+ and now Black can even avoid underpromotion (which is also fine) and play 63...♔b1 64 ♔b3 ♔a1! 65 ♖xb2 with stalemate.

50 ♖xe6 ♖xg3 51 f5 ♖f3 52 f6 g3 53 f7 g2 54 ♖g6 ♖e3+ 55 ♔f8 g1♕

Black also loses after 55...♖f3 56 ♔g7 g1♕ 57 ♖xg1 ♔xb4 58 ♖g6, e.g. 58...♖xf7+ 59 ♔xf7 b5 60 ♔e6 ♔c4 61 ♔e5 b4 62 ♔e4 ♔c3 63 ♖c6+ ♔d2 64 ♖b6 ♔c3 65 ♔e3 b3 66 ♖c6+ ♔b2 67 ♔d2 and White wins easily, or 58...b5 59 ♖f6 ♖g3+ 60 ♔h6 ♖h3+ 61 ♔g5 ♖h8 62 f8♕+ ♖xf8 63 ♖xf8 ♔c4 64 ♔f4 b4 65 ♔e3 and White wins.

56 ♖xg1 ♔xb4 57 ♖f1 ♖a3 58 ♔e7 ♖a8 59 f8♕ ♖xf8 60 ♖xf8 1-0

Hillarp Persson-Andersson
Malmö 2000
Queen's Gambit Declined

1 d4 ♘f6 2 c4 e6 3 ♘c3 d5 4 ♗g5 ♗e7 5 ♘f3 ♘bd7 6 e3 0-0 7 ♕c2 c5 8 ♖d1 ♕a5 9 cxd5 ♘xd5 10 ♗xe7 ♘xe7 11 ♗d3 ♘f6! 12 0-0 cxd4 13 exd4!?

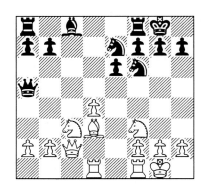

The decision to accept the isolated pawn can be justifiably questioned. The exchange of dark-squared bishops reduces White's ability to develop an initiative and in turn makes it more likely that the d-pawn will prove to be a genuine weakness. Nevertheless 13 ♘xd4 e5

is also good enough for equality for Black.

13...♗d7 14 ♘e5 ♗c6 15 ♖fe1 ♖ad8 16 ♕d2 ♘ed5

Presenting Hillarp-Persson with the opportunity to give Black a weak pawn, too, ensuring that the position is completely equal. I imagine that Black wanted to be careful and prevent the possible rook manoeuvre ♖e1–e3-g3/h3.

17 ♘xc6 bxc6 18 ♘xd5 ♕xd5 19 ♕c3 g6 20 ♗e2

Re-routing the bishop to the most sensible square. The position is completely level.

20...♕d6 21 ♗f3 ♘d5 22 ♕c1 ♖d7 23 h4 ♖fd8 24 g3 ♘e7 25 ♔g2 ♘f5

Andersson, true to his style, decides to exchange the weak pawns, and in this way eliminates losing chances.

26 ♕xc6 ♘xd4 27 ♕xd6 ♖xd6

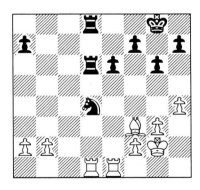

28 ♖d3!

Addressing the threat of ...♘xf3, ♖xd6 ♘xe1+! but at the same time inviting Black to take up residence on the second rank. More natural is 28 ♗e4 f5 29 ♗d3, although I prefer Black in this position. The strong centralised knight and the possibility of pushing the e-

pawn might prove a problem for White.

28...♘xf3 29 ♖xf3 ♖d2 30 ♖c1!

Remember Dvoretsky's rule? The idea of ♖c7 breathes some much needed life into White's rooks. Not 30 ♖b3? ♖c2 followed by ...♖d8-d2.

30...♖8d7

There is no way Andersson will allow the rook invasion. In principle Black is slightly better co-ordinated but, as in the games above, the position is more or less harmless for White.

31 ♖b3 ♔g7

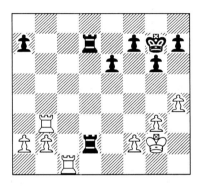

Andersson is improving his position one move at a time, without feeling any kind of hurry. Tsesarsky gives the following line as better for Black: 31...♖e2 32 g4 ♖dd2 33 ♖f3 ♖xb2 34 ♖c7 f5 35 gxf5 gxf5 36 ♖xa7 ♖xa2 37 ♖e7. This is true, but White has a huge improvement in 34 ♖c8+! ♔g7 35 ♖c7 and the tables are turned. This is a nice trick to know, by the way.

32 ♔f3 h6 33 ♔e3 ♖2d5 34 ♖bc3 ♖e5+ 35 ♔f3 ♖f5+ 36 ♔e3 g5

Turning down the perpetual and proof that Andersson really likes to play (without risks).

37 hxg5 hxg5 38 ♖c4

Directed against ...g5-g4 followed by

...♖f3+ and ...f7-f5 with a slight pull for Black.

38...♖e5+ 39 ♔f3 ♖d3+ 40 ♔g2 ♔g6 41 ♖1c2 ♖a5

It is clear here that Black's rooks are the better placed, affording Black easier play. Consequently White should be careful, but that is not as easy as it looks.

42 b3 ♖d1 43 ♖c5 ♖a3

An exchange of a pair of rooks would rid Black of any winning chances.

44 ♖e5 ♖a6

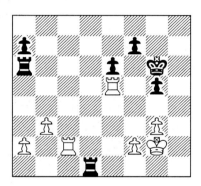

45 b4?

White is not being careful enough. It is better to play 45 ♖ec5 and see how Black responds. Now the b- and a-pawns will become weaker because they are no longer protecting each other, and precise defence is now required from White.

45...♖b1 46 b5 ♖a4!

Here the rook is not necessarily threatening much but it has great potential. Of course it attacks a2, but Black is toying with the idea of ...♖a4-b4. Notice also that the rook covers g4, where Black's g-pawn will be ideally placed, cramping White's kingside and accentuating the weakness on f2.

47 ♖cc5 g4 48 ♖g5+?

Despite the fact that it is not clear whether the game is winning for Black against accurate defence after this move, the text is nonetheless a grave mistake. Black will double rooks on his seventh rank and win the f2-pawn, and thus put White under tremendous pressure. The way I see it is simple – from an equal position Black has made all kinds of small improvements and there is no reason to believe that this trend should not continue, ultimately leading to a win.

The right way to play is with the move 48 ♖e2!, e.g. 48...♖a1 49 ♖cc2 ♖b1 50 ♖c5 ♔f6 51 ♖ec2 ♖a1 52 ♖5c4 ♖xc4 53 ♖xc4 ♖xa2 54 ♖xg4 and White is no worse, or 52...♖1xa2 53 ♖xa2 ♖xc4 54 ♖xa7 ♖b4 55 ♖b7 with a drawish position.

48...♔f6 49 ♖g8 ♖b2!

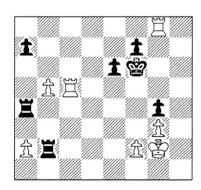

Black is quite happy with his g4-pawn at the moment. He cannot allow White to grab it before the reply ...♖xf2+ is possible, as ♖f4+ would be a factor.

50 a3 ♖d4!

Going to d2.

51 ♖c7 ♖dd2 52 ♖xg4 ♖xf2+ 53 ♔g1 ♖g2+

Black delivers a few checks in order

to avoid drifting into time trouble. Knowing Hillarp-Persson, he might also have been slightly short of time, but when your position is as good as Black's is here, the best thing you can do is forget about the opponent's clock and focus on your own challenges.

54 ♔h1 ♖h2+ 55 ♔g1 ♖bg2+ 56 ♔f1 ♖a2 57 ♔g1 ♖hg2+ 58 ♔h1 ♖gf2

Preventing ♖f4+, which would lead to a winning ending for Black.

59 ♔g1 e5!

Freeing the rook from the responsibility of preventing ♖f4+ and thus introducing ...♖fb2 with mate threats.

60 ♖c1!

White is forced to look after his first rank sooner or later so he wisely decides to do it before the mate theme is used in tactics against him. 60 ♖c6+? ♔f5 61 ♖g7 ♔e4 makes progress only for Black.

60...♖g2+

Tsesarsky proposes the following line: 60...♔f5!? 61 ♖g7 (61 ♖h4 ♖g2+ 62 ♔h1 ♖xg3 nets Black a pawn) 61...♔e4 62 a4 ♖g2+ 63 ♔h1 ♖h2+ 64 ♔g1 ♖ag2+ 65 ♔f1 f5 (it is not easy to propose another way for Black to make any progress here) 66 ♖xa7 ♖xg3, and here he thinks Black is slightly better, and perhaps he is right after 67 ♖c4+ ♔f3! 68 ♖c3+ ♔f4 69 ♖xg3 ♔xg3, when the pawns in the centre are preferable to those on the flank – even if they are further back – because they will come with an attack on the king. Perhaps 67 ♖ac7 is a better move, trying to defend with two active rooks, but nevertheless I believe Andersson would have won this position without too much difficulty.

61 ♔h1 ♖h2+ 62 ♔g1 ♖hg2+ 63 ♔h1 ♖gb2 64 a4 ♔e6

64...♖e2!?, in order to help the pawn forward, is Tsesarsky's suggestion.

65 ♖d1?

Now the last line of defence will be broken down. More chances of survival are offered by 65 ♖h4!? f5 (65...♖e2!? is also good) 66 ♖h6+ ♔d5 67 ♖d1+ ♔c5 68 ♖e1 e4! (maintaining the pressure) 69 ♖h5 ♔d4 70 ♖d1+ ♖d2 71 ♖e1 (71 ♖xd2+ ♖xd2 leaves White with no defence against the e-pawn – 72 ♖h7 e3 73 ♖xa7 e2 74 ♖e7 ♖d1+) 71...e3 72 ♖h7 ♔c4! and White's queenside is in trouble. Still, there are no forced wins for Black, so there is hope.

65...♖e2!

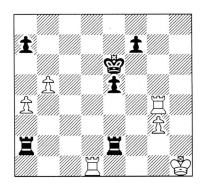

Finally the rook chooses to assist the e-pawn.

66 ♖h4 e4 67 a5

Hillarp-Persson chooses not to wait and see, instead opting to attack.

67...♖xa5 68 ♖h6+

68 ♖b1 ♖aa2 69 b6 axb6 70 ♖xb6+ ♔e7 71 ♖b7+ ♔f8 72 ♖b1 e3 is also very much in Black's favour, but it still might be a better choice. The rest of the game is easy:

68...♔e5 69 ♖h5+ ♔f6 70 ♖d6+ ♔e7

71 ♖a6 ♖xa6 72 bxa6 ♔e6 73 ♖h6+ ♔f5 74 ♖h7 ♔g6 75 ♖h8 ♖a2 76 ♖e8 f5 77 g4 fxg4 78 ♖xe4 ♔f5 79 ♖b4 ♔g5 80 ♖b7 ♔h4 81 ♔g1 ♖xa6 82 ♖b2 ♖a1+ 83 ♔g2 a5 84 ♖c2 a4 85 ♖b2 a3 86 ♖b3 ♖a2+ 87 ♔g1 g3 0-1

There is a funny story from the 1996 Olympiad in Erevan. Ulf Andersson had played exceptionally safely and made more draws than could be expected – even from him. Hillarp-Persson and International Master Hellsten asked him throughout one evening and the next morning questions like: 'Wouldn't it be nice to win a game Ulf?' and finally Ulf became quite frustrated about these questions and their implication. In something close to shouting he exclaimed: 'Alright, alright then, I will play for a win. But under no circumstances will I take any risks.' Here is his next game:

Andersson–Kengis
Yerevan 1996
English Opening

1 ♘f3 ♘f6 2 c4 e6 3 g3 a6 4 b3 c5 5 ♗g2 b5 6 ♘c3 ♕b6 7 0-0 ♗b7 8 ♗b2 ♗e7 9 d4 cxd4 10 ♕xd4 ♕xd4 11 ♘xd4 ♗xg2 12 ♔xg2 bxc4 13 bxc4 d6 14 ♘a4 ♘bd7 15 ♖fd1 ♖c8 16 ♖ac1 0-0 17 ♘b3 ♘e4 18 ♗d4 ♖fd8 19 f3 ♘ec5 20 ♘axc5 ♘xc5 21 ♘xc5 dxc5 22 ♗e3 ♖xd1 23 ♖xd1 ♖b8 24 ♖d7 ♗f8 25 ♖a7 ♖b4 26 ♖xa6 ♖xc4 27 ♔f2 e5 28 g4 f6 29 ♖a7 h5 30 gxh5 f5 31 ♗g5 e4 32 ♗f4 exf3 33 ♔xf3 ♖c3+ 34 e3 c4 35 ♗e5 ♖c2 36 a4 ♖a2 37 a5 ♔h7 38 a6 ♖a5 39 ♗c3 ♖a3 40 ♗d4 c3 41 ♖a8 c2 42 ♗b2

♖a2 43 ♖xf8 ♖xb2 44 ♖c8 ♖a2 45 ♔f4 ♖xa6 46 ♖xc2 ♖e6 47 ♖e2 ♖h6 48 ♔g5 ♖f6

49 h3 ♖f7 50 ♖f2 ♖e7 51 ♖f3 ♖e5 52 ♔f4 ♖a5 53 ♖g3 ♖b5 54 ♖g5 ♖b4+ 55 ♔xf5 ♖h4 56 e4 ♖xh3 57 e5 ♔g8 58 ♔e6 ♔f8 59 ♖f5+ ♔g8 60 ♖g5 ♔f8 61 ♖f5+ ♔e8 62 ♖f7 ♖xh5 63 ♖e7+ ♔f8 64 ♔d7 g6 65 ♔d8 ♖h1 66 e6 ♖e1 67 ♖f7+ ♔g8 68 ♔e7 ♖e2 69 ♔d7 ♖a2 70 ♖f1 ♖a7+ 71 ♔e8 ♖a8+ 72 ♔e7 ♖a2 73 ♖d1 ♔g7 74 ♔e8 ♖a8+ 75 ♖d8 1-0

The game has a lot in common with the three previous games, except that Kengis seemed to be bored. Black was never close to a draw after 29...h5?, yet most of the time he was further from a loss. As an exercise you can go through the game – in the same way I have described in the earlier games – and try to find out where White made progress. I promise that such an exercise will do you a lot of good. It would be even better to study with a friend. Moreover the game Andersson-Leko, Ter Apel 1996, is very instructive and can help you a great deal if you play through it with the intention of understanding where Black drifts.

Andersson-Leko
Ter Apel 1996
English Opening

1 ♘f3 ♘f6 2 c4 c5 3 g3 ♘c6 4 ♗g2
d5 5 cxd5 ♘xd5 6 d4 cxd4 7 ♘xd4
♘db4 8 ♘xc6 ♕xd1+ 9 ♔xd1 ♘xc6
10 ♘c3 ♗d7 11 ♗e3 g6 12 ♖c1 ♗g7
13 f4 0-0 14 ♔e1 e5 15 ♔f2 exf4 16
gxf4 ♗e6 17 b3 ♖ad8 18 ♘e4 ♗d4
19 ♘c5 ♗xe3+ 20 ♔xe3 ♖fe8 21 ♔f2
♘b4 22 a3 ♘d5 23 ♘xe6 fxe6 24 e3
♖e7 25 ♖hd1 ♖ed7 26 ♖d4 ♔f7 27
♗f3 b6 28 ♗xd5 exd5 29 h4 ♖d6 30
♔f3 ♔f6 31 b4 b5 32 ♖c5 a6 33 ♖d2
h6 34 ♔g4 ♖8d7 35 ♖d3 ♖e7 36 ♔f3
♖ed7 37 ♖d1 ♖d8 38 ♖d2 ♖8d7 39
♖dc2 ♖e7 40 ♖c8 ♖de6 41 ♖2c3 ♖d6

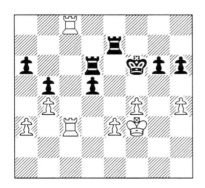

42 ♖d3 ♔f7 43 ♖c5 ♖ed7 44 ♖c2 ♔f6
45 ♖d1 g5 46 fxg5+ hxg5 47 hxg5+
♔xg5 48 ♔e2 ♔f5 49 ♔d3 ♖h7 50
♖g1 ♖hh6 51 ♖c7 ♔e6 52 ♖gg7 ♔e5
53 ♖g5+ ♔f6 54 ♖cg7 ♖c6 55 ♔d4
♖c4+ 56 ♔xd5 ♖c3 57 e4 ♖d3+ 58
♔c5 ♖xa3 59 ♖g8 ♔e6 60 ♔b6 ♔f7+
61 ♔b7 ♖e3 62 ♖5g7+ ♔f6 63 ♖g4
♔e5 64 ♖d8 ♖b3 65 ♖d5+ ♔e6 66
♔c6 ♖c3+ 67 ♖c5 ♖d3 68 ♔b7 ♔e7
69 ♖e5+ ♔f6 70 ♖gg5 ♖d4 71 ♖gf5+
♔g7 72 ♖e7+ ♔g8 73 e5 ♖e4 74 ♔c8

♖c6+ 75 ♔d7 ♖cc4 76 ♖g5+ ♔f8 77
♖f5+ ♔g8 78 ♖g5+ ♔f8 79 ♖e8+ ♔f7
80 ♖f5+ ♔g7 81 ♖g5+ ♔h6 82 ♖g1
♖ed4+ 83 ♔e6 ♖g4 84 ♖h1+ ♔g5 85
♖g8+ ♔f4 86 ♖xg4+ ♔xg4 87 ♔d5
♖xb4 88 e6 ♖b2 89 ♖e1 ♖d2+ 90 ♔c6
♖c2+ 91 ♔b7 1-0

One of the things I have tried to demonstrate with these games of Ulf Andersson is how little is actually required in order to be able to play the endgame well. Andersson does not do anything special at any time, nor does he show skills which cannot be understood. But every move is good – not great, just good. This is the skill one should aim for when studying the endgame. Achieve the level of basic understanding that will facilitate the production of good moves all the time. Playing through theoretical positions alone will never help you do this.

From Andersson we will turn to one of the strongest endgame performances in modern chess.

The Salov–Khalifman Match 1994
In 1994 in Wijk aan Zee Salov beat Khalifman 5-1 in their candidates match, thus making the seventh and eighth games unnecessary. The way Salov won was amazingly simple – thanks to a superior understanding of the endgame he succeeded in winning three drawn endings.

In my opinion there is no doubt that Khalifman is the better player of the two, a view strongly supported by his 1999 world championship title and the fact that, thus far, only reigning FIDE champion Anand has managed to eliminate him from the knock-out tournament (twice – first in 1997, when Khalifman was very close to eliminating Anand before it ended in a play-off). However, in this match Salov was much the superior player due to his excellent technique.

So far we have considered mainly rook endgames. This is where that road ends and another begins, since all three of the following games feature minor piece endings.

Salov–Khalifman
Wijk aan Zee (Game 1) 1994
Grunfeld Defence

1 d4 ♘f6 2 c4 g6 3 g3 ♗g7 4 ♗g2 d5 5 ♘f3 0-0 6 0-0 dxc4 7 ♘a3 c3 8 bxc3 c5 9 e3 ♘c6 10 ♕e2 ♘d5 11 ♗b2 ♕a5 12 ♖fc1 ♗g4 13 h3 ♗xf3 14 ♗xf3 ♘b6 15 ♘c4 ♕a6 16 ♘d2 ♕xe2 17 ♗xe2 cxd4 18 cxd4 e5 19 dxe5 ♘xe5 20 ♗d4 ♖fc8 21 ♘b3

The opening has finished, and the middlegame is almost over, too. A look at the diagram position shows that White has a slight advantage in view of the bishop pair, and later he is allowed to convert this advantage into an extra pawn in a drawn ending. I believe that this decision is objectively correct from Khalifman, but in practice the position can be very difficult to defend.

21...♖xc1+!?

21...♘c6 22 ♗xg7 ♔xg7 23 ♘c5 ♘d8 24 ♗f3 ♖c7 has been suggested by Belov as only slightly better for White. I believe White can improve on that variation with 24 a4!? in order to put some pressure on Black's queenside, and only later play ♗f3. The problem with doing so at once is obvious – Black gets time to double rooks on the c-file, presumably affording him the chance to make an easy draw.

22 ♖xc1 ♖c8 23 ♖xc8+ ♘xc8 24 ♘a5

This wins the a-pawn, but at the price of entering an endgame with opposite coloured bishops.

24...b6 25 ♗xe5 ♗xe5 26 ♘c6 ♗c3 27 ♗a6 ♘d6 28 ♘xa7 ♔f8

It is from this point that our interest really starts. White is a pawn up on the kingside, we have opposite coloured bishops and White has difficulties with his knight. In fact the knight has no way of escaping a7 without being exchanged (note how the bishop on c3 is covering a number of important squares), when the resulting endgame is immediately drawn. So how does White intend to win this? First he will bring his king to the centre, a basic rule of the endgame because the king is a strong piece (as long as it is not mated...) and should take part in the action. Black does the same. I have a theory that in the endgame the activity of your strongest piece should be your main concern since this is the piece that can dominate all others in head-to-head meetings. This means queen over rook, rook over king, king over minor pieces. But, as I said, this is just a theory.

28...h5 is an interesting suggestion from Grandmaster Lars Bo Hansen. The key idea is that White will need to play g3-g4 sooner or later, when Black will exchange his h-pawn and both avoid getting a distant weakness and simply limit White's chances for victory with an exchange of pawns. Yet this is not the most important factor here. In fact it is quite important to be the first to occupy the centre, as otherwise White's knight escapes from its imprisonment. The following line shows that Black reaches only e6 when d5 is the necessary target: 29 ♔f1 ♔f8 30 ♔e2 ♔e7 31 g4 hxg4 32 hxg4 ♔e6 33 ♔d3 ♗b2 34 ♘c6 etc.

29 ♔f1 ♔e7 30 ♔e2 ♔e6 31 g4 ♔d5 32 ♔d3 ♗b2 33 g5!

This is a standard move, fixing the h7- and f7-pawns, which are now constant weaknesses. It is well known that in endgames with opposite coloured bishops the attacker will put his pawns on the same colour squares as the opponent's bishop, serving to both restrict the piece and attack the enemy pawns.

33...♔c5

Dominating the knight. I assume that the endgame would be drawn were the players to exchange colours.

34 a4 f6?

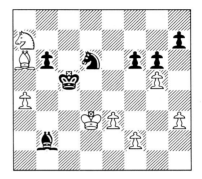

I feel certain that this is a mistake, and I cannot support the text with any fancy variation or argument. Quite simply the e-pawn has now been elevated to passed pawn status. I much prefer Grandmaster Hansen's suggestion of 34...♗g7, planning to exchange the h-pawn, which I believe is a potential weakness and never a source of counterplay here. This is because White has control of the position, and I do not see a serious threat of a pawn reaching h1.

Black's 34...f6 is designed to do something about White's idea of f2-f4 followed by e3-e4-e5, when f7 will become a target. Belov gives the following illustration of how dangerous this can be for Black: 34...♔b4? 35 f4 ♔xa4 36 e4 ♔a5 37 e5! and Black is in trouble because f7 is more than awkward to defend. Yet after 34...♗g7!? 35 h4 h6 36 f4 hxg5 37 hxg5 f6! the situation is not the same as in the game. The distant h3-pawn has been exchanged and Black is coming much closer to a draw.

35 gxf6 ♗xf6 36 ♗b5 ♗h4

This move looks like a product of time trouble. Lars Bo Hansen suggests the correct 36...g5! with the idea of 37 f4 h6. White then has a route into the kingside using the light squares, but this takes time and it seems likely that Black's king can do damage to the white pawns when White is otherwise engaged on the h-file.

37 f3 ♗f6 38 ♗d7 ♘c4 39 ♗b5 ♘d6 40 ♗d7 ♘c4 41 ♗e8 ♘d6 42 ♗b5

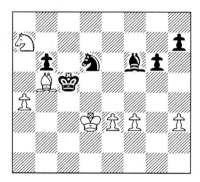

Black to move. What now?

White has made some progress. He has a passed pawn on e-file and Black must be a little careful. The pawn cannot progress at the moment because it would be blockaded immediately, but there is always the prospect of its advance. If the knight comes back into play victory will be seriously within reach for White, so Black will have to prevent this...

42...♘f7?

After this the knight finds a path into freedom via b8 and d7. Better moves are 42...♗h4, to keep things floating, or Hansen's 42...g5 43 f4 h6.

43 f4

With the enormous threat of 44 e4.

43...g5 44 ♘c6

This would not have been possible had Black's knight kept an eye on b5.

44...gxf4 45 exf4 ♗h4

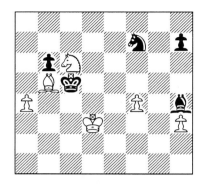

46 ♘b8!

To freedom, along the way causing Black problems with the b6-pawn.

46...♔d6

Belov criticises this move and suggests that Black has more chances to draw with 46...♘d6 47 ♘d7+ ♔b4 48 ♘xb6 ♘xb5 49 axb5 ♔xb5 50 ♘d5 ♔c5. But this line seems unlikely because White can improve with 48 ♗c6!, when Black will have to play 48...♗f2 and remain passive since the endgame after 48...b5?! 49 axb5 ♘xb5 50 ♗xb5 ♔xb5 51 ♘f8! h6 52 ♘g6 ♗f2 53 ♘e5 is easily winning for White (Black will not be able to defend his h-pawn forever). Note that after 48...♔a5 49 ♔d4 White wins more or less on the spot. Remember that the king is a strong piece in these endings and should be active. I believe Belov overlooked this line for White because he was looking for something that wins by force, but White is positionally winning anyway, so he does not need to think along these lines. The game will be won by normal moves.

47 ♘d7 ♗d8

47...♗f2 48 ♘f6 wins a pawn for White as 49 ♘e4+ is a threat.

48 ♘f8 h5

Forced in order to have a square for the knight.

49 ♗c4 ♘h6 50 ♔e4

Now it is Black's knight that has problems. White is winning.

50...♔c5?!

A more stubborn defence is 50...♗f6.

51 ♘e6+ ♔xc4 52 ♘xd8

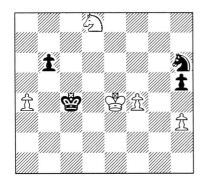

52...♔b4

52...b5 53 axb5 ♔xb5 54 f5 ♔c5 55 ♔e5 and the h3-pawn wins. Remember Lars Bo Hansen's desire to exchange the h-pawns? I have known Lars for more than ten years and have also played him a few times. I have come to the conclusion that he 'does not see anything tactically' – of course this is an exaggeration, but for a Grandmaster close to 2600 his calculation is poor. Yet he *is* close to 2600, and that as a happy amateur. I am sure that this is because he has great talent for schematic thinking and a strong feeling for the general technical aspects of chess. One of these is that such an h-pawn

should be exchanged if you are defending. Khalifman did not have this sense of danger here, and nor in the next game, as we shall see. But let us not get ahead of ourselves. First Salov must catch Black's b-pawn.

53 f5 ♔xa4 54 f6 b5 55 f7 ♘xf7 56 ♘xf7 b4 57 ♔d3 ♔a3 58 ♘e5 ♔b2 59 ♔d2 b3 60 ♘d3+ ♔a3 61 ♔c3 1-0

Salov–Khalifman

Wijk aan Zee (Game 3) 1994
English Opening

1 c4 ♘f6 2 ♘c3 e6 3 e4 c5 4 e5 ♘g8 5 ♘f3 d6 6 exd6 ♗xd6 7 d4 cxd4 8 ♕xd4

This was a new move at the time. Whether Salov had prepared beforehand a policy of going for the endgame as often as possible, or whether this was something he sensed during game 1 do not know, but it appears to be the appropriate strategy nevertheless.

8...♘f6 9 ♘b5!

The exclamation mark is solely for psychological reasons. White has no advantage whatsoever.

9...♗b4+ 10 ♗d2 ♕xd4!?

This is very interesting. Black will just have time to play ...♔e7 and ...♘c6 without being bothered with the threat of ♘c7+.

11 ♘fxd4 ♗xd2+ 12 ♔xd2 ♔e7!? 13 ♗e2

Salov decides to take it slowly and believe Black's sacrifice. Actually, after 13 ♘c7 ♖d8 14 ♘xa8 ♖xd4+ 15 ♔e1!, with the idea of 16 ♖d1 and later a2-a3 and b2-b4, the position is far from clear. However, as Game 1 is an important aspect of White's thoughts here, he decided that there was no need to go for something like this. My guess is that Black will have more than enough play in this practical struggle to compensate for the exchange, although intensive analysis might prove that the sacrifice is incorrect.

13...♖d8 14 ♔e3 e5 15 ♘b3 ♘c6 16 ♖hd1 ♗f5

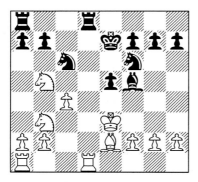

Black is now fully mobilised. His knights are ideally placed on f6 and c6, his bishop is active and he might be able to expand in the centre and on the kingside. White enjoys less harmony. It is not at all clear that his knight is well placed on b5, and it seems quite clear that the one on b3 will have to be repositioned at some point if it is to have an impact on the game. Overall White is on the verge of being slightly worse, and thus decides to exchange rooks.

17 ♖xd8 ♖xd8 18 ♖d1 ♖xd1 19 ♗xd1 ♘g4+!

I am not sure that the bishop is better than the knight in this position – certainly as the game develops it is inferior. But if Black wants to play for an advantage he needs to make this exchange because it unbalances the situation slightly, and the knight – currently re-

stricting a pawn advance on the kingside – has no other good square.

20 ♗xg4 ♗xg4 21 ♘c5 ♗c8?!

I do not like the look of this move. It is too passive. More normal is 21...b6 22 ♘e4 ♗e6 23 b3 f5 with a double-edged position in which Black does not appear to be any worse. Khalifman must have been a little unsure about his a-pawn, which does become rather vulnerable after ...b7-b6, but that is missing the point. The a-pawn will later go to a5 in order to free the knight. In the game Khalifman puts his pawns on the same colour squares as the bishop, and for this he is severely punished.

In this variation 22 ♘d3 meets with 22...♗e6 23 b3 g5! and Black has good chances to generate pressure on the kingside. Note that Black's initiative on the kingside is superior to White's in view of two factors: his bishop is active on both sides of the board and his pawns will advance with a hint of an attack on the white king, thus provoking weaknesses.

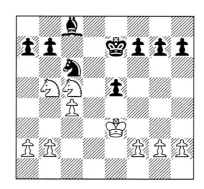

You are White. What do you do?

22 f4!

There are two main advantages to the

text since White gains a little space and Black no longer has the possibility of creating a powerful centre. Now it is Black who must fight for equality.

22...exf4+

22...b6 23 ♘d3 exf4+ 24 ♘xf4 ♗e6 25 ♘d5+ ♔d7 might be the best way for Black to play. Although White is a little more active it is difficult to see how he can make serious improvements, while each of Black's pieces finally has a function.

23 ♔xf4 h6?!

Principally Khalifman is right in putting this pawn on a dark square but he loses much of his kingside mobility in doing so. Additionally g7 is on its way to becoming a serious weakness, a factor to which Khalifman does not pay serious attention.

24 h4!

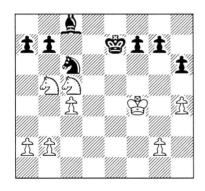

24...f6?

This is a serious mistake, probably due to a miscalculation (I am sure that Khalifman underestimated the impact of White's next move), and now Black's kingside is a collection of weaknesses. However, on the other hand, I have the feeling that real chess players avoid playing ugly moves at all times. I cannot

see a player like Kramnik or Karpov playing this move. 24...b6 and 24...g6 are both okay.

25 h5!

The finest move of the game. White secures himself a superior structure, the downside being that the h-pawn is a short-term weakness. However, too many resources are required to attack the pawn, so White will have his cannons ready in time.

The alternative is allowing ...g7-g5, after which Black is fine, a factor which has helped Salov in making his decision.

25...a6

As the coming tactics are all in White's favour Black should avoid putting a pawn on the bishop's colour. Of course Khalifman must have believed otherwise, but there are numerous signs that he should be worse and he ignores them, most likely due to the desire to level the match.

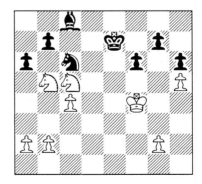

26 ♘c3 ♘e5 27 ♘d5+ ♔d8

Wolf offers the following amazing line, which seems to prove an advantage for White: 27...♔d6 28 ♘e4+ ♔c6 29 ♘e7+ ♔d7 30 ♘xc8 ♔xc8 31 b3 ♔d7 32 ♘c5+ ♔c6 33 ♘e6 g6 34 ♘d8+ ♔c7 35 ♘f7!! g5+ 36 ♔f5 ♘xf7 37 ♔xf6

♘d6 38 ♔g6 ♗d7 39 ♔xh6 ♔e7 (39...♘f7+ 40 ♔g6 ♔e7 41 h6 ♘f8 42 h7 ♘h8+ 43 ♔f6 and the extra queen-side pawn wins) 40 ♔xg5 and Black is in great difficulties.

28 b3 b5 29 cxb5 axb5

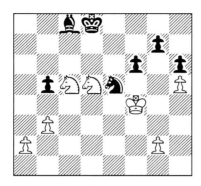

How should White play?

30 b4!

An excellent move that demonstrates a good understanding of the position. Black's king is terrible and Black will not be able to capture the h5-pawn without losing g7 in return. Thus White has all the time he wants and fixes the b5-pawn so that the bishop will never be able to attack White's queenside.

30...♗g4 31 a3 ♔c8

31...♔e8 32 ♘c7+ ♔e7 33 ♘xb5 ♗xh5 34 ♔e4 looks very dangerous for Black, as does 31...♗xh5 32 ♘e6+ ♔d7 33 ♘xg7, when both h6 and f6 are weaknesses.

32 ♘e7+ ♔c7 33 ♘g6!

This gives Black a chance to get rid of the h-pawn without weakening his kingside. But my preference 33 ♘f5 is only a draw: 33...♗xh5 (forced because 33...♗xf5 34 ♔xf5 ♔d6 35 ♘e6 wins for White) 34 ♘xg7 ♗g6 35 ♘ge6+

♔d6 36 ♘d4. While this appears very promising for White, with Black's pawns weak and White's knights far superior, it turns out that Black has a forced draw with 36...♘d3+! with the idea of 37 ♘xd3 ♗xd3 38 ♘f5+ ♔e6 39 ♘xh6 f5!, and White cannot get his knight back into the game without exchanging pawns on the kingside, after which Black will make the draw. So, although understanding is important, calculation is also necessary. Salov's choice presents Black with more serious problems.

33...♗xh5

The only move as Black loses the knight ending after 33...♘xg6+ 34 ♔xg4! ♘f8 (34...♘e5+ 35 ♔f5 ♔d6 36 ♘e6) 35 ♔f5 ♔d6 36 a4!, creating the passed pawn on the kingside in order to divert Black's king. After 36...bxa4 37 ♘xa4 ♔c6 38 ♘c3 ♔b6 39 g4 ♔c6 40 ♘e4 ♔b5 41 ♘xf6 ♔xb4 42 ♘e8 ♔c5 43 ♘xg7 ♔d6 44 ♔e4 the h-pawn falls – 44...♔e7 45 ♔e5! (45 ♘f5+ ♔f6 46 ♘xh6 ♔g5 is a draw) 45...♘d7+ 46 ♔f4! etc.

34 ♘xe5

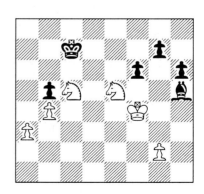

34...fxe5+?

Losing. After 34...g5+! 35 ♔f5 fxe5

36 ♔xe5 Black has a free move compared to the game. I still believe Black is in dire straits – at least from a practical point of view – but this is nonetheless the way to play. Note that for the tournament player it is of less importance knowing where the game could still be saved compared to knowing where mistakes have been made. It is eliminating the latter that makes you a better player (I know I am repeating myself, but this is really important!).

35 ♔xe5 g5 36 ♘e6+!

Forcing the king into passivity as 37 ♘d4 is an important threat.

36...♔b6 37 ♔f6 ♗e2 38 ♔g6 ♗f1 39 g3 ♔c6 40 ♔xh6 ♔d5

40...g4 41 ♘f4 does not improve for Black.

41 ♘xg5 ♗e2 42 ♔g6 ♔c4 43 ♘e6 ♔c3

43...♗g4 44 ♘c7 ♗d7 45 ♔f6 ♔b3 46 ♔e7 and White has won all Black's pawns!

44 ♔f5 ♔b2

45 ♘c5!

White's knight will only have one job – to take care of the b-pawn; meanwhile the king wins the bishop.

45...♔xa3 46 ♘a6 ♗d3+

Or 46...♗f3 47 g4 ♗b7 48 g5 ♗xa6 49 g6 ♗b7 50 ♔e5 and White wins.

47 ♔f4 ♔b2 48 g4 ♔c3 49 ♔e5 ♔c4 50 g5 1-0

These losses might seem unnecessary, but not in the same way as the final game of the match. To be fair to Khalifman we need to remember that he was trailing 1-4 and thus had no realistic chance of a comeback. This cannot avoid damaging your ability to play serious chess on a short-term basis. Nevertheless the game is quite instructive, and Salov certainly plays very well.

Khalifman-Salov

Wijk aan Zee (Game 6) 1994
Queen's Gambit Accepted

1 d4 ♘f6 2 ♘f3 e6 3 e3 b6 4 ♗d3 ♗b7 5 0-0 d5 6 c4 dxc4!?

Salov does not want to play the main line of the Queens Indian Defence, instead transposing to something very close to the Queen's Gambit Accepted.

7 ♗xc4 a6 8 ♕e2 ♘bd7

8...b5 9 ♗b3 c5 is a normal position in the QGA.

9 ♖d1 c5 10 a4 ♗d6 11 ♘c3 0-0 12 b3 cxd4!

Accurate. White's last move does not fit in well with an isolated d-pawn and 13 ♘xd4 is met with 13...♘e5!, securing the two bishops. Perhaps 13 ♖xd4!? is a reasonable alternative.

13 exd4 ♖e8 14 ♘e5 ♘d5 15 ♗b2 ♕c7

Practically forcing a series of exchanges. 15...♘7f6 might offer Black a slight advantage according to Salov, but remember he has no need for any more than a half point.

16 ♘xd7 ♛xd7 17 ♗xd5 ♗xd5 18 ♘xd5 exd5 19 ♛d3 b5!

Salov secures a draw and Khalifman is clearly no longer interested in a fight.

20 axb5 ♛xb5!

Good not just because it brings the win of the match closer, but also because the b5-pawn would be weak had he played 20...axb5. Now this is no longer a problem, as only the queen was able to attack the pawn.

21 ♛xb5 axb5 22 ♖xa8 ♖xa8 23 ♖a1 ♖xa1+

Probably played out of primary considerations for the overall result. Salov's 23...♖e8!? 24 ♔f1 ♗b4 is slightly better, when it is not clear how White will untangle himself. He could try to play the rook to c1 and follow up with ♗c3, but Black might just play ...♖e4 and draw attention to the d4-pawn.

24 ♗xa1

This is a good place to take stock, now that the position has transformed and will remain the same for some time. At first sight Black looks slightly better, and this is due to the bishop and nothing else (if we altered the positions of the bishops to b1 and d7 Black would, perhaps, even be slightly worse).

Black has only one genuine winning plan, namely bringing the king to the centre and mobilising the kingside pawns. He can then hope that his bishop's superiority will offer some chances (note that Black's bishop will be superior for a long time). Salov's next is appropriate to this plan because he wants to bring his king to f5 and push his pawns to h4 and g4. If White plays h2-h3 Black's king retreats and makes way for ...f7-f5 and ...g5-g4. Generally the fight revolves around the important e4-square. If Black succeeds in getting his king there White will be very close to losing (or simply losing). However, I believe that White's next is not best.

24...h5!?

Wolf gives this an exclamation mark but, in my opinion, it lacks precision. If we investigate White's chances of improving his king we quickly discover that he will not get further than f3, so Black will always be able to come to f5 in time. So what does White want to do? The most accurate course is to activate the bishop as soon as possible and, for this reason, Black should prefer 24...b4! with the general idea of 25...♗f4-c1-a3, keeping White's bishop caged in the corner. Later Black's bishop will be able to return to battle at a moment when it appears to have the impact of an extra piece.

Wolf is probably happy with the move played because it prevents 25 ♔f1 and 26 ♔e2 due to 26...♗xh2! 27 g3 h4! and White's pawn structure is ruined. But White has a more solid line of defence, which Black should have taken into account.

25 h3?

25 ♗c3! ♚h7 26 g3! has been proposed, with convincing lines leading to a draw: 26...♚g6 (This is the test; 26...f5 has also been analysed to a draw) 27 ♚g2 ♚f5 28 ♚f3 g5 29 h3 g4+ 30 hxg4+ hxg4+ 31 ♚e3 ♚e6 and now White can keep the equilibrium with both 32 ♚d3 f5 33 ♗d2 f4 34 ♗xf4 ♗xf4 35 gxf4 b4 36 ♚e2 ♚f6 37 ♚d3 and the simpler 32 f4!?.

The position can still be defended after Khalifman's move, but it requires more good moves from White.

25...♚h7 26 ♚f1 ♚g6 27 ♚e2 b4

Sooner or later this will have to come.

28 g3

White now realises that this move will have to be played sooner or later, as otherwise Black will play ...h5-h4 at some point, aiming for the set-up with the king on h5 and pawns on f5 and g4, giving White some problems in view of the prospect of a black passed pawn on the h-file. In such a position only Black can improve his lot, although I believe that White should still be able to hold a draw.

28...♚f5

To illustrate the poor quality of White's bishop look at the following line given by Salov. The sacrifice does not work but it is very close (and the price is merely one pawn): 28...h4 29 ♚f3 hxg3 30 fxg3 ♚f5 31 ♗b2 ♗xg3? 32 ♚xg3 ♚e4 33 ♗c1 ♚d3 (33...♚xd4? 34 ♗d2! is an easy win for White) 34 ♚f4 ♚c2 35 ♚e5 ♚xc1 36 ♚xd5 ♚c2 37 ♚c4 f5 38 d5 f4 39 ♚d4 and White is winning.

29 ♗b2 g5

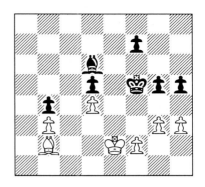

You are White. What do you play?

30 ♗c1?

This is a grave error which costs the game. Now Black will either be allowed to come to e4, after which the push ...f7-f5-f4 decides the game, or, as in the game, get a passed pawn on the h-file. Necessary is 30 ♚d3!, taking control of the e4-square and saving White with tactics. After 30...h4 31 g4+! ♚f4?? 32 ♚e2!! Black will soon be mated, e.g. 32...♚e4 33 f3+ ♚f4 34 ♚f2 f5 35 ♗c1 mate, or 32...f5 33 ♗c1+ ♚e4 34 ♗e3 fxg4 35 hxg4 followed by 36 f3 mate. After the alternative 30...g4 31 h4! the position is completely blocked after 31...♚e6 32 ♗c1 f5 (the only winning attempt, but even a defence like ♗d2-e1 is an easy draw) 33 ♗f4!, and the draw is a fact.

30...g4 31 hxg4+

31 h4 ♚e4 and White has no more lives left.

31...♚xg4!

With this move Black decides the game. Now White can no longer prevent him from achieving a passed pawn on the h-file due to ...f7-f5-f4, which White will have to capture. It seems

Khalifman overlooked 32 ♔e2!! (see the note above) and thus felt he had to go for this. The finish is beautiful in its simplicity.

32 ♗d2 f5 33 ♗e1 ♗e7

Probably just gaining time on the clock. I believe it was Petrosian who, if he did not introduce it, then at least supported the idea that it is good to repeat the position with no other intention than to show the opponent who is in control. If you feel that it can be hard to make progress in a position then this can also provide a 'break', and at least you have the satisfaction of actually playing some moves.

34 ♗d2 ♗d6 35 ♗e1 f4!

This is, in effect, a pawn sacrifice. Either White will have to accept the creation of a strong passed pawn on the h-file after 36 gxf4 ♔xf4, or do so by winning a pawn on the way. White's choice is therefore easy.

36 f3+ ♔h3 37 gxf4

37...♔g2!

But Black is not just losing a pawn, he also prepares the promotion of his h-pawn. The position now clearly illustrates the superiority of Black's bishop and king. The end of the game shows

that Salov has calculated everything perfectly.

38 f5 ♗e7

Black would naturally prefer to win the f-pawn in this fashion, allowing him to hit d4 and help the h-pawn.

39 f6

White's only counterplay comes from the b-pawn.

39...♗xf6 40 ♗xb4 h4 41 ♗d6 h3

With the idea of ...♗f6-h4-g3, after which the h-pawn can no longer be stopped. This idea does not work after White's next, but there are other resources.

42 b4 ♗e7! 0-1

Of course Black would never play 42...♗h4? when after 43 b5 ♗g3 44 ♗xg3 ♔xg3 45 b6 h2 46 b7 h1♕ 47 b8♕+ the tables are turned and suddenly White is winning.

Having studied these nice wins from Salov I have come to the same concluded as with the Ulf Andersson games, namely that Salov did not win by any special means or achievement. There were no moves that I could not have played, yet the difference is that I could not have played them all. A basic understanding of how the pieces should play in the endgame was enough to eliminate one of the strongest players of the modern era from the Candidates tournament.

And this is my argument. If you want to excel at chess, you should have solid endgame technique. Such technique is not a deep knowledge of theoretical positions – although this certainly helps – but rather a good feeling for simple positional elements. Khalifman, Georgiev, Brynell, Polugaevsky, Kasparov and Hillarp-Persson did not show this in the games above. Andersson and Salov did and they were rightfully rewarded.

In my opinion the best way to study the endgame is illustrated in this chapter. Solve exercises. Personally, I work with a friend. We find exercises and then act as each other's trainer. I suggest you take one of the exercises featured in this chapter, give yourself fifteen minutes and then 'solve' it as if you were playing a real game. This is training in the purest sense of the word. Dvoretsky, who I believe invented this rather obvious method, calls it play-out of positions.

The other part of endgame training comes from playing through endgames, preferably annotated, of very strong technical players, although just believing the annotations will not be enough. Anyway, I am thinking of Rubinstein, Alekhine, Botvinnik, Smyslov, Petrosian, Larsen, Korchnoi, Andersson, Karpov, Salov and others. Remember not to examine these games quickly, but slowly. Try to find mistakes and see how their accumulation leads to defeat. See how these great players are always slightly more accurate in their play than their opponents. Try to understand what they do by introducing a credible line of thought to their moves. Speak your thoughts out loud so you will not only become a commentator, but also a have the wisdom of the listener. If you do this you will find that you learn a lot. And when you feel it is time to move on to something more advanced, you should be able to find your own way.

CHAPTER SIX

Attitude at the Board and other Tips

Do you think Clint Eastwood does the dishes? – Esben Lund

Many players want to do well at the board but fail to consider how other influences affect their results. In my ten years in international chess I have heard so many *bad* excuses for losses. There are always players who are going to be stronger. There are players who are always unlucky – I am sure you know some of them yourself. What you rarely meet is a professional who knows what is good for him and what is bad in terms of his behaviour at the board. In this chapter I will argue for a more effective frame of mind, based on a year of study and almost 3,000 pages of established performance psychology books and similar, relevant material.

Believe in yourself

You got to roll with it
You got to take your time
You got to do what you do
Don't let anybody get in your way
'Roll with it' – Oasis

The most important thing is self-confidence. So many people will doubt your abilities in life – never listen to them. If you do not truly believe that you can make it to the Grandmaster title, for example, you will never do so. My favourite television commercial features a NBA basketball player preparing for a shot, while all around him there are monsters, representing the people who doubt his abilities. They whisper things to him like 'so you think you can make it all the way to the NBA' and so on – all of them negative inputs. When he shoots there is no sound, and he scores. Afterwards he says 'Just believe in yourself.'

Later I saw a new commercial with Roberto Baggio, the Italian soccer international, in which he talks about his failed penalty in the 1994 World Cup final against Brazil, right at the end of the tournament. He says: 'In 1994 I made a mistake' and then goes on to talk about 1998, when he took another important penalty for Italy, also in the World Cup. He says something like:

'How many people believed I could do it?' Then you see the ball go into the net. 'The important thing is that I believed it.'

Such examples are all around if you just look, and most successful people say the same thing. The famous magician David Copperfield once said something along the lines of 'The greatest magic I have seen was when I started saying *I will* instead of *I wish*.' In his autobiography Garry Kasparov, undoubtedly the greatest player in chess history, says that as a child he had a poster over his bed which read: 'If not me – then who else?'

I know many people who would say: 'Okay, that is all very nice, but you also have to be realistic.'

These people are just nicer versions of the monsters in the basketball commercial. I would like to ask them: 'Why?' Or maybe even better: 'What is it to be realistic?' The problem with the frame of mind of these people is that they are afraid of failing. I will return to the question of excuses later. First I will give some examples of what it would be to be realistic. A twelve-year-old boy visits a chess club for the first time. He is not a big talent in the eyes of the people in the club. Nine years later, in 1954, he has the highest score on the top board in the Moscow Olympiad, and consequently is awarded the Grandmaster title. His name is Bent Larsen, perhaps the best player in the world in the late sixties but, unfortunately, never a great match player, and therefore never a serious contender for the world title. For years it was Larsen's policy always to play for a win against anybody in order to develop the right frame of mind, being both optimistic and aggressive. There is also the idea that playing with maximum effort will teach you a great deal about chess. Larsen did not believe he was one of the greatest players in 1954, despite his high level of self-confidence. A much older Danish player, Jens Enevoldsen, told him: 'Now you have proved you can draw with the Grandmasters, now it is time to prove you can beat them.' After this Larsen won against Gligoric.

Here is another example. Together with my best friend Coach, I have set up, without any ambitions, a rock band. We are four people aged between twenty-five and twenty-seven. Coach and I are clearly the worst musicians in the group. He has played the guitar for two years now, and he does not really enjoy practising. However, I believe he is quite talented as a songwriter. He has the ability to write from the heart, as they say. I want us to become as good as we possibly can.

Playing alone is hard enough, but playing with three other people is a nightmare – or a dream. Although it is clearly something he wants, were it up to Coach we would not have begun a band in the first place. Why? Because he is so focused about being realistic. He sees so many people who have played instruments for fifteen years and simply failed to attain success. Why should we be different? Well...

In the year 1999-2000 I was quite serious about chess. I tried with everything I had. I wanted to become a Grandmaster. This is where Coach earned his name. With previous experience in Neuro Linguistic Programming (*NLP*), he knew a little something about trance-theory. I hired him as a trainer for a year and took him around to the tournaments. I failed in my ambitions for several reasons – which we will investigate in this chapter – but I am happy that I tried. And at one time I had a performance of 2587 over 25 games...

Coach also played at some of the tournaments in order to pass the time. His fighting spirit was very much influenced by mine, and he began to believe that if you really want to win, you can. In that one year he improved from 1750 to 2150, earning himself the top board for his club team and doing well, even against IMs, despite the fact that he lacks the ability to remember opening theory beyond move six.

But what will happen to the band? Well, we will not be rich and famous. We will have a lot of fun and we will learn to play together. Maybe we will even make a record one day and, I guess, I will pay for it myself. That is not really important. We love music and we will be able to play it together and enjoy it.

Finally, while we are still on the subject of musicians who start late – working as a 'roadie' for a small English band on their world tour, 24-year-old (approximately) Noel Gallagher was taught to play the guitar by the band's guitarist. Returning home a year later he joined his little brother's band, Oasis. Four years later they had made what some critics acclaimed as the best record of the 1990s, *What's the story (Morning Glory)?* – from where the lines at the

beginning of this chapter come.

Anyway, here we are talking about chess. Chess and attitude. The stories above are fairly accurate, but I have not found it necessary to check all details again. The point is what matters. You should believe that you can do what you want. Always. If people criticise what you do, and nothing positive comes from them, tell them to stop doing so or to leave you alone. Criticism tends to be valuable only if it is welcome; otherwise the damage to self-esteem can be far more significant than any advice or shared knowledge.

The Will to Win

Together with a strong self-belief, you need the will to win, for without this you are not going to get very far. Fischer once said that 'a very strong will' was the most important factor for success in chess, and he was right. You need to want to win in order to do so, of course. And we all want to win, but how much do we want it?

It is quite clear that our results are closely linked to the effort we put into the game – during training, tournament preparation and the actual time at the board. And we cannot just count hours here. Ten hours of work will not automatically give you ten Elo points, for example. What matters is the quality of the work you do. Is it the right thing you are working with? Are you sure this is what you need to work with in order to improve your chess, and not just what you get the most pleasure from?

One thing is for sure – you cannot spend a lot of time working at home and then expect the results to come by themselves, nor will results come without putting in the hours. It is very important how much you want to win when you are sitting at the board. Only then can you benefit from the work you have done at home. This is why training to achieve the right frame of mind is imperative if you are to fight for your dream – and I mean fight. Later in this chapter I we will look at how this can be done.

But how important is this *will*, actually? Well, it is the thing that will take you further than you believed possible when you started on your journey. It is that which will make you work on your endgame rather than watching the *Simpsons*. It is the will that will make you go to bed at a more sensible time because you have an important game the next day. It is your best chess trainer because it will make you learn to trust yourself. And this is very important because you, like all humans, have enormous resources at your disposal. Or as Henry Ford said: 'There is no person living who isn't capable of doing more than he thinks he can do.'

Here is another anecdote that might illustrate very well what the right attitude is, and how a strong will can take you far. A young television soccer commentator lost his dream job but, instead of being negative, he decided that on his last performance he would give everything he had, just to see how good he actually was. Someone from another television channel watched the game and was so impressed he offered him a job. The young man realised something which should have been obvious to him all

along – he should have given his all each and every time he worked. This is not to say that all your performances should be your best, but that you should try to perform as well as you possibly can under the circumstances.

Respect your Opponents

One of the main drawbacks of those having very high self-confidence is that they start to believe that other people do not have the same potential for success. This is not only quite unsympathetic, it also restricts performance. The number of players who do well against very strong opponents but poorly against lesser opposition is enormous and, of course, this is something you cannot afford if you want to excel at chess.

I believe you should always prepare for your opponents – no matter who they are – with an attitude that the game is absolutely crucial. This is as much to be in the right frame of mind as it is to be well prepared. In this way you will always do well, and the mistake of playing inferior moves purely because you underestimate your opponent can be avoided. Remember that if you really are the better player you will – more often than not – win the game anyway. You do not need to set silly traps; normal play should be enough. More importantly, there is a reason if you are stronger than your opponent. Perhaps it is not because you are able to play quickly and superficially against weaker players, rather because you understand chess much better, *when you really try*. Remember that your strength will diminish – and the probability that you win – if you do not try as hard as usual.

When people start getting interested in performance psychology they change from the social *I am not so good,* to *I am the king of the world.* They go from thinking something is impossible to believing that it is something which can *just* be done. Anybody can achieve anything (how much do you want it?). But things can be pretty difficult anyway.

Almost all of us are aware of the phenomenon from practical play when, in an unclear position, we play very well and with a high level of adrenaline. Our hands might be sweating, the heart beats faster and so on. But when we emerge from the tension, when the battle is in some way over, we lose our interest and fighting ability. Below, in the passage *Look ahead,* you will find a short story about a friend of mine who suffers heavily from this problem.

The following example is illustrative of what I am talking about.

Aagaard-Danielsen
Copenhagen 1997

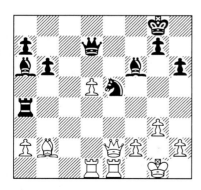

28 ♕h5 g6 29 ♕xh6 ♗g5 30 ♖xe5 ♗xh6 31 ♖e6 ♖xa2 32 ♗c3 ♗e2 33 ♖d4 ♗f3 34 ♖xg6+ ♔h7 35 ♖f6 ♗xd5

36 ♖h4 ♗e4 37 ♖hxh6+ ♔g8 38 ♖h8+ ♔xh8 39 ♖d6+ ♔g8 40 ♖xd7 ♖c2 41 ♗d2 a5 42 f4 a4 43 ♔f2 a3 44 ♔e3 ♗f5 45 ♖a7 ♖a2 46 ♗b4 ♖xh2 47 ♗xa3 ½-½

Of course this game ended in time-trouble. But still... White had only an exchange for the queen! I am sure that Danielsen, who had to make the last ten moves in one minute, would never let me escape something like this again. The amazing player that he is, he quickly realised after the game that he had underestimated my chances of creating counterplay. In other words, he was waiting for me to resign. As this horrifying example shows (I am sure you will have similar examples of your own!) something can always happen. The difficult task is to stay emotional until the game is finished, and not until you think your opponent should resign.

In Wijk aan Zee 2001 I succeeded in easily winning the following endgame:

Aagaard-van der Berg
Wijk aan Zee 2001

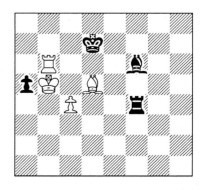

My opponent had defended very well

in the opening and the middlegame but, later, after declining a draw, I managed to create problems for him in the ending with opposite coloured bishops. Missing a very complicated win I had to exchange most of the pawns to maintain some kind of an initiative.

The position is now objectively drawn, but I was very determined to win. My long-term plan consisted of winning the a-pawn, winning the bishop for my pawn and, eventually, winning with rook and bishop against rook. Let us evaluate the position. I will not win the a-pawn, I will not win the bishop and, even if I did, the position would still be a theoretical draw. That would be the objective evaluation.

Real life experience, however, tells us something completely different – if Black is bored he might do something silly. And rook and bishop against rook wins in 56% of the games on my database. So why not play on a little longer?

61...♗d8?!

It is not of great importance but, objectively speaking, I believe 61...♗c3 is better.

62 ♖h6 ♖h4 63 ♖g6 ♖h7 64 ♗e4 ♖h5+ 65 ♗d5 ♖h7 66 c5 ♗c7 67 ♗e4 ♖f7 68 ♗d5 ♖h7 69 ♗f3 ♔e7 70 ♖c6 ♔f8?

Black's decision to bring his king to the kingside is unwise. It avoids the tricks including threats on the king but gives White a chance to win the a-pawn by forcing the bishop off the diagonal.

71 ♗d5 ♖d7 72 ♗e6 ♖e7 73 ♖a6 ♔g7 74 ♗d5 ♔h7? 75 ♔c6 ♖g7

At this time we required new scoresheets and I noticed that my opponent was missing two moves. When I

pointed this out he replied that he was not that interested any more. I laughed – I was now sure that he would make a mistake and that I would win the game.

76 ♖a8 ♔h6 77 ♗e6 ♗f4

Black gives up the a-pawn. Despite the fact that he is now drifting into trouble his psychology is set – it is only when the game is beyond salvation that he is aware of his plight.

78 ♖xa5 ♖c7+ 79 ♔d5 ♗e3 80 c6 ♗f4

Permitting the rook to be trapped. This is possibly a very good decision, but now Black must be extremely careful.

81 ♗d7 ♔g6 82 ♖a4!

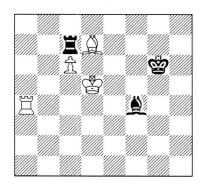

82...♗g5?

A blunder. Earlier Black should have returned his king to the centre, but even after 82...♔g5!, White has no way to make real progress. Now it's over.

83 ♔d6 1-0

The lesson here is simple. Even the simplest position has some tricks, and if your opponent is playing on, he is hoping·to make use of one. Furthermore, your opponent is not stupid. If you believe that, then you are making a big mistake.

Be Positive

Later I will talk about how language influences us, and it will seem a bit abstract. So first I will be more general. In order to be able to win a game you first need to believe you can win. Do not joke about losing the game, or something along these lines – this will only prepare you for losing. You need to tell yourself that you can win – not that you will, but that you can. You need the tension and uncertainty in order to be fully alert. Also, as I said earlier, you need to respect the opponent's abilities, or they *will* surprise you.

Recently I saw an interview with the athlete Michael Johnson on Swedish television. They were talking about his fantastic world record in the 1996 Olympics in Atlanta, where he ran 200 metres in 19.32 seconds. He said about this performance that if anybody had asked him before the Olympics if he believed he *would* run in this time, he would have said no. But if he had been asked if he *could*, he would have said yes: 'I do not believe in putting limits for myself' was his sensible logic. Watching this I realised that there are basically three attitudes to a challenge. The first is filled with disbelief – the challenge is a mountain you cannot see yourself climbing, let alone conquering. The second attitude is filled with respect for the mountain but also with the belief that it is possible to climb it. The third is the state where there is no doubt in your mind that you will beat the mountain. Over time I have come to believe that only the second attitude is fruitful. The first will fail without any doubt. When you do not believe you can meet the challenge you will, of course, find it impossible to prepare yourself for it. The third suffers from a similar problem. When you are sure you will win you do not respect the challenge and you cannot motivate yourself to do the necessary work. The second attitude will help you motivate yourself all the way. You are nervous because the challenge is difficult, but you are also confident and believe that you can meet it. You are not setting any boundaries on yourself, but at the same time you do not take anything for granted.

Knowing that you can beat your opponent, but that it will be hard, and that there are no promises, no justice or fairness, only the game, will undoubtedly make you nervous before the game. This feeling might seem intimidating to you, or wrong, perhaps. However, fortunately, it is not.

Moreover it has been discovered that people who have a lot of nervous tension before their performances do better. They get what is called positive stress when they are actually performing. They experience much emotion when performing but this is by no means damaging. In fact such emotions are stimulating. It is when the body reacts with adrenaline that you feel so alive, so alert, like walking across a thin rope between two buildings, not really believing you can fall, even though you still watch your steps. Preparing for your game an hour or two in advance will help you to attain this frame of mind, as the game seems real.

There are many who have been intimidated by their pre-performance emotions. Some have tried to calm these emotions down with alcohol, for example, which is obviously not a good path. Instead you should learn to respect these emotions and not fear them. Once you are not afraid of the fear you might feel before a game, once you know that it is natural, then it loses a lot of its 'scary' faces and becomes a high performance engine rather than something unwanted.

People who feel little or nothing before the game will experience problems when playing. They will either be unable to properly motivate themselves when their best is needed, or they will falter when the fear of losing arrives like a new-born baby, craving attention when it is time to find the best move.

No Excuses

An important part about trying your best is to say goodbye to all kinds of excuses. You need to take full responsibility for the level of your performance. Your opponents are only lucky the day you agree with yourself that this or that was something you would never be able to see. That day is also the day you stop believing in improving your level. Your opponents win because they play well enough to beat you, and because you made a mistake you possibly could avoid committing in the future. This mistake can be a lot of things of course, one being underestimating your opponent.

The main point here is that if you really want to be as good at chess – or, indeed, anything – as you possibly can be, you will need to put in maximum effort. If you do that and still fail, then the reason for failing can only be one thing: that you are not good enough. That you did not yet train yourself enough. And if you did not train enough, or did not train the correct way, then you know there are no excuses.

Now, while you read this, is probably the best moment to ask yourself if you are afraid of failing. Personally, I had to ask myself the same question in 1999 before going for the Grandmaster title. I discovered that I had been, but only because I had not thought properly about what would happen if I did fail. As is often the case I was just afraid of the unknown.

Now I have failed. For me that is, in itself, not so interesting. Rather I am happy to know what I did wrong. I expected too much of myself. I lost respect for some of my opponents due to such high confidence and, consequently, I lost some again! I sat thinking at the board for three hours but could not focus after that. All these things mean more to me than the rather remote pain I might have felt the moment I realised I was not going to make it this time around.

Failing and losing is as much a part of life as winning and succeeding. Every game of chess has a loser if it has a winner. Of course you can take the approach of Grandmaster Ulf Andersson and believe that a draw is happiness for both, but then you should not play at all, as this does not lose rating points (as Andersson once remarked in an interview).

Failing and losing hurts, but then you move on and say to yourself – so what? You lose and you feel like sitting in a corner with your head in your hands, just diving into the pain. Respect that and do it. Why not? Some people might look and think whatever. So what? What can they think that can be as bad as it is for you to keep these emotions inside and be dishonest to yourself? As long as you do not abuse people verbally or misbehave when you lose, people are not really going to care a lot. Deep down they know that they feel the same way when they lose. They just try to hide it because they are ashamed of it. Once you learn to respect your emotions you will also learn that there is no shame connected to honesty.

Now, why am I talking so much about losing and failing when this is a book about excelling? Mainly to make one point – that failing is possible. If you did not do what you could to succeed it will hurt, but if you really tried it is okay. The thing that will hurt is the knowledge of what you could have done, what you could have become. However, you will regret what you did not do much more.

You can have it all – but how much do you want it? Know yourself.

Look Ahead

Okay, you lose a terrible game. It happens to everyone. Or you miss a big chance for a win that you would normally see in any blitz game. It happens. Here is one example.

Kasparov-Kramnik
Wijk aan Zee 2001

In this position Kasparov played 25 ♘g5?? yet, as he later indicated, the simple 25 g4! gives him an almost winning positional advantage because 25...hxg3? 26 ♘xg3 followed by 27 ♖xd4 wins material thanks to the fork on f5.

How does someone like Kasparov deal with such a mistake? With humour – 'g4 and we can go home, it is unbelievable' – and then a lot of hand movements, rather like an unknown form of martial arts. It is truly absurd that the two best players in the world both overlook this simple trick. But how do they think about it when they go home? They still treat it with humour, I am sure. Why not? It is better to laugh than to cry!

But if they want to avoid this mistake in the future it is not enough to realise it was there. It is much more important to decide what kind of mistake we are talking about. Of course it is not due to any lack of ability, so it must be something else. Could it be that the slow positional nature of the position made the players forget about tactics? Let us assume so. Still, such a realisation is not enough to settle for and move on – the weakness should be eliminated through training.

We then figure out how to increase

our alertness for tactical tricks in positional positions, and work on it. In this way mistakes will only hurt for a short while, because soon you will be doing something. And pain most often comes from inactivity. When you are doing something you are at least involved in a process. When you are doing something you feel happy.

I have been talking a lot about pain and disappointment. Now it is time to talk about success. Have you ever had a genuine success? Have you ever achieved something you truly wanted? Do you know the feeling that accompanies it? If not, then I can assure you that it is worth it.

Also, the feeling of working for something, that you have a purpose with your everyday life, is invaluable. To feel yourself developing on this level from something close to nothing, into something, is bliss.

Of course risk plays a very important role in all of this. If you try to win you risk the chance of losing. If you do not try to win, you risk less but you can still lose – always. This is very, very true. But the best way to look at it is: *Risk winning*.

One book I read about performance psychology pointed to a very important factor in self-projection. If you want to be a winner you have to see yourself as a winner – not in the future, but the present. To the mind time is a very abstract phenomenon, with which it does not work well. Therefore you should not see yourself as a winner in the future, but in the present. You should behave like a winner, because why should you be different when you achieve your goals? Be

who you really are, here and now.

Another book I have read offered some very good advice about self-projection – drawing pictures (even if, like me, you are limited in talent). Draw pictures of yourself in the situations you are aiming for. Draw a picture of yourself making the winning move in a crucial game, thinking deeply on the top board in the league or receiving first prize. Get used to seeing yourself in successful situations.

But before you speculate too much about drawing a picture of yourself winning the world championship you should formulate your goals, of which there are normally three kinds – short-term, middle-term and long-term.

Short-term goals are connected with the near future – winning the next tournament, achieving a title norm or whatever you feel is possible in the near future.

Middle-term is something you feel you can achieve over a year or so. It can be an International Master norm or perhaps the title. Again it is your personal situation that defines what your goals should be. Often you will achieve your goals sooner than you expect or your ambitions might alter somehow, when it will be time to adjust your goals to the new situation.

Long-term goals are those you see at the end of the long and winding road. It can be the Grandmaster title, the top board of the club team or something else. Such a goal is the place where you want to be at the end of your journey towards mastery. Usually a long-term goal is not something you can realistically achieve within the time of the short and the middle term periods, but something that requires a lot of improvement – the reason why you are doing all that you do.

Once you have established your goals there is one good exercise I recommend. Take your goals and write two lists for all three of them. Compile a list of all the things supporting you in reaching your goals, then another list of all the things preventing you from reaching them. Do not be alarmed if your 'negative' list is longer than your 'positive' list – this is quite normal. You take your positive sides for granted, while the hurdles you need to overcome have a tendency to come to the forefront of your attention. Never mind. What you do then is write down what you need to do about the different items on your negative list. Then you erase them. Soon your negative list will diminish and include only a few items you can do nothing about. Erase them, there is no reason to think about them.

You are then left with a list of positives and a 'to do' list. In this way you have framed your situation and also experienced, in part, the feeling of overcoming your obstacles.

Different Frames of Mind

A young writer once asked Hemingway what books he should read if he wanted to achieve a high level of skill. Hemingway gave him a very long list of classics, indicating that this was actually only a third of the list. The young writer replied that reading all the great masters might make you lose your nerve, to which Hemingway said that if it does, it should. By this Hemingway made it very clear that your own confidence is essential. If it can

be easily shaken you will not make it. When you look at the great you should see the potential for you to be one of them, not try to find and therefore extend the distance between them and you. That is why your attitude is the first thing you should try to improve.

A very good friend of mine had two easily winning positions in the 2000 Danish Club Championships. After achieving these positions he played miserably and made only a draw. While his play was bad, what he then did was worse – he said that by improving just once he would have won. He could have played a better move fifteen times, yet only the final mistake seems important to him! He would never have had the chance to make this mistake if he had played slightly better earlier. Now, suddenly, it was hard to find the right moves. Now it was understandable that he made a mistake, whereas earlier a mistake that would throw away the full point would be difficult to consider. Of course he is correct when he claims that he could still have won the game, but in practise it is a different matter. We need to evaluate mistakes that make life more difficult for us as similar to those that change the overall evaluation of the position.

Ups and Downs

Life is created by movement – by change. If nothing moved there would be no life. Something similar goes for the human being. We need to change between stress and relaxation. When we 'stress' our muscles we know that they need rest later. When we do not we know that they will lose strength. The same goes for the mind.

Many chess players think that they can be social and active for sixteen hours a day when they play tournaments. They prepare in the morning, go and play, and between the moves they talk with their friends, or opponents from previous rounds. After the game they often go in groups to restaurants, where they chat and eat and drink. Later they might go somewhere for a game of pool or cards or perhaps just a drink. They practically collapse at their hotel at midnight or later, and do not understand why they reach only a certain level of performance.

If we want to win we cannot only think of what we do when we are at the board, but also of what we do between games. It is deliberate that I have mentioned this before turning to what actually happens when in the tournament hall, because I think this is where a lot of people can improve considerably. And it does not take a lot, in fact. Look at it this way – during the game you use a lot of energy, of which you need to regain most or all in order to do just as well the next day. You do not want to be exhausted after just five games. The way to do this is not by sitting alone in your room all evening, watching television or reading (unless this is what you normally do). But an hour of rest between the game and dinner could do you good, and perhaps a short nap two hours before the game. Learn to listen to your body and find your own way. As individuals we are so different that it would be worthless to propose general rules for recharging the batteries. Finally, remember that being bored or being serious all the time is very hard for both body and mind. Go out and have a few laughs, please. Nothing can replace being happy when it comes to positive mantras!

At the Board

In an Open in Pardubice in 2000 I had fantastic energy, having prepared for the tournament in a way I had not done before. This should have been the best tournament of my life if we only judge from my form. As it was I lost ten Elo-points and, almost, all my self-esteem.

My main mistake was this: I had so much power and energy that I would sit at the board thinking hard for three hours, yet after this I would miss something. I was simply growing tired. I believe that three hours of full concentration is pretty terrifying, and if I get to this level again, I am going to use it better. But here I did not.

Later, when I have thought about what went wrong, I have read about tennis. Tennis is a sport that in some ways is very similar to chess. Much of it is monotonous, the ball being sent back the same way it came. There is nothing exciting about it. Then at other times every ball is played to win, every shot is a potential winner. Chess is like that, too. Often you need only to avoid mistakes and care about accuracy, while at other times inaccuracy means losing. But this is not the closest resemblance. In a five set tennis match the actual playing time seems to be something between twenty and thirty minutes! In chess the actual playing time is most often around fifty percent of the total duration. When the trainers in tennis discovered that the actual playing time was such a small part of the game the next conclusion came easy to them. What the players did the rest of the time was highly important. By observation it was discovered that the best players all had a similar pattern of behaviour. They corrected the strings and talked to themselves. They said a lot of positive things about their fighting spirit and kept focused. From their emotions they created new energy, and this extra energy would prove very crucial by the time the game came to the third set, when the hard physical stress started to drain the players.

In the 1992 Olympic Games in Barcelona Mike Powell broke the legendary world record in the long jump. He felt fantastic but also knew that, after him, Carl Lewis had one final shot at the medal. He was actually convinced that Lewis would beat him. As he said: 'Lewis has the strongest competitive edge in the world.' Lewis did jump a lifetime best, but this was not enough to beat Powell. However, it is remarkable that when the pressure increased, Lewis' abilities did likewise.

With this knowledge I went to Wijk aan Zee 2001 to take a look at the behaviour of the best players. I expected to be able to observe something similar to what has been observed in tennis. I was not disappointed. Kasparov, Anand, Morozevich, Ivanchuk and Kramnik all did the same thing. They walked up and down on the stage, staring down at the floor. They occasionally glanced at the other games, but never with true interest. The only one of these who was not totally focussed was Anand who,

occasionally, would talk with Piket or another player. Anand, by the way, did not have a strong tournament, and it is quite well known that he is not a very patient person. In his youth he played very quickly, living only on his enormous talent. He never became the great player he could have been, and I predict he will not be. He is now the FIDE world champion, but Kramnik and Kasparov can both claim to be better players.

Shirov behaved differently, sitting at the board for most of the time. After six or seven games he was leading by a point. Then he lost some games through terrible play and went astray, even self-destructing in his game with Ivanchuk. He was not the same player we saw at the beginning of the tournament. Not at all.

In tennis they talk about an ideal performance zone, the state where you are doing all you possibly can. It is not something they practically pray for, but something they try to reach every time they play. We should do the same in chess, and it is not impossible.

Be on the Outside what you want to be on the Inside

It is not possible for me, in the limited constraints of this book, to fully cover the mental training that can be performed in order to improve the level of concentration and fighting spirit. If you feel inspired to pursue this line of work you should go to your local bookshop or library and find your way from there. Personally I contacted the Danish Sports Committee and, through their website, I acquired some tapes and books, which was a start for me. I also worked with professional NLP therapists and did cognitive studies. All this in order to find something that would work for me. As no one has my personality but me I think it would be best for others to find their own way and their own methods.

Nonetheless, here is some advice:

Be on the Outside what you want to be on the Inside

This is a simple rule. Jesus was the first who said that no kingdom could live being at war with itself (when he was accused of being Satan). You should not believe that your ambitions and confidence will be the same if they exist only on the inside. When people ask you about your ambitions, tell the truth. You should not care about what they think, but nor should try to promote yourself as something that you are not (yet). Find a balance – 'I believe I can win this championship' or 'I believe I can become a Grandmaster' etc.

Positive Language

This is going to sound abstract, but trust me, it is true... You should always use what I choose to call positive statements. Say to yourself when you are waiting for your move 'I can draw this position' rather than 'I can avoid losing this position' (most players think like this). In the second example the line of thought is connected to losing, in the first to drawing. And yes, it is more than just a linguistic difference. If you relate yourself to losing you will be more willing to accept it and less ready to put in maximum effort. If you relate yourself to drawing, this will be the only thing

you are thinking of. This goes for everything. Do not answer the question 'How are you?' with the negative 'Not bad' – as many do. Focus on being positive, 'Good' being a nice answer.

Confront your Fear of Losing

In order to be able to win you need to be able to lose. Winning means taking risks. Taking risks introduces the possibility of losing. You should confront your fear of losing in advance. One easy way to do this is by thinking about what will happen if you actually lose the game, fail your goal or whatever is your ambition. Most often you will realise that nothing will happen or, if something bad does, then it is not as bad as you initially felt.

A lot of players have never confronted their fear of losing, and when they play their game can suddenly be influenced by it, thus losing much of their strength because they are not focused on playing their best chess but on serving this useless feeling.

Make a list of your Future Qualities

This is a very simple exercise. Write down on a piece of paper ten positive things that you aspire to. Mine would include the following:

- I love to play chess
- I attack
- I play for a win
- I respect my opponents

And so on. You write this short list of mantras and stick it on the door of your freezer, for example, and every morning you say them out loud. In this way you will soon begin to change your attitude towards this list.

Learn Three Things from Every Game

After every game try to think of three new things you have learned. You will find that this is not always so easy, but it is a very useful exercise nonetheless. Write them down in a book, on your computer or in some kind of special chess diary – but do keep such a book.

Listen to your Inner Voice

Today psychology is moving away from an interest in the subconscious and into more practical psychology. The idea is simple – not only the ill can improve their mental health, but we all can. In this process things like social intelligence and its enormous influence on our lives have been discovered. A new thing that has recently emerged is the idea of subconscious intelligence, the theory that we have more than one way to solve problems. For the last one and a half centuries there has been a praising of the logical mind, with feelings being rated as less important – I am sure this will not last for another decade.

Your inner voice is a voice that only you can listen to. It will hardly ever lie to you. It is perhaps not really good at playing chess but it can tell you for sure when you are about to do something you do not really believe in. You are about to play a piece sacrifice, and it is not at all clear. You ask you inner voice and it might say 'I think it is good' – then you should go for it. On the other hand it might also say 'Hmm...' – then you should do something else. When you learn to talk to your inner voice you will soon start to do something else. Something very important.

Pose Questions

Here we are simply talking about everything in life. When we reach the age of ten we rapidly lose our open mind. This is a neurological fact. I will not delve deeply into the details, but instead offer an example.

We know that we live with the caveman's body, but we do not really appreciate that we also live with his mind and emotions. When you are a hunter and will not live more than twenty years you need to learn some basic things and then do them for some years. Life is not a constant development, but a hard fight for survival. For this reason a lot of the open connections in our brain are lost at the age of ten. Our possible worlds decrease rapidly. We begin to lose our ability to look at everything without having made our conclusions in advance.

In order to develop we need to pose questions in places where we previously did not. Most improvements are not only new knowledge but also replacement of old knowledge. If we approach chess (and life) with the determination to ask one question every time we meet one fixed truth, we will be better for it. Just think of the revolutions in chess. First the best attacker won through his genius. Then came positional chess. Then hypermodern. Around 1980 Karpov's style was believed to be the only correct style, but then Kasparov blew this theory away. He was eventually beaten by Kramnik, who did not fight for equality with him in the opening, but controlled his inferior positions with great elegance.

All this happened through something

novel – a replacement of fixed ideas. Believe in something, but always have your doubts when you are too sure. This is when you limit yourself.

Meditation and Hypnosis

If you are serious about improving your concentration and confidence, then sooner or later you will end here. But first a brief anecdote.

In the 1976 Olympic Games the Eastern Europeans did very well. It was for a long time thought that this was mainly due to doping and, although this might partly be true, it was definitely not the only reason. Through the space program in the 1950s and 1960s the Soviets had discovered how methods of relaxation from Asia could improve levels of physical performance enormously. They included this throughout the eastern bloc in preparation for the 1976 Games, and for that reason won many medals.

In chess this can also be very useful. As this does not directly improve muscle performance but the brain's ability to be more open, then it is obvious that it can do a lot for concentration and confidence. It can also help in terms of the general level of energy and the will to win.

A programme should be made for the individual and by a professional, so here I will only say that it is worth it. It will improve your chess and, perhaps even more important, it will make you feel happier than ever before. There is a reason why people in the Far East spend years of their lives meditating...

Through hypnosis you will also learn about visual imagery and the impact it can have on your results. Here another nice function in the brain is used. The brain does not differentiate between what is seen in the mind and what is seen in reality – these have the same emotional impact. This is why we like fiction so much, although we know it is not real.

Now, imagine a basketball player who, in practise, makes four out of five penalties. Compare him with the basketball player who imagines five out of five for 25% of his training. Now imagine that both players have made 4 out of 4. Who do you think has the best chance to make the fifth shot? The second, of course. The first is emotionally prepared to make four only. The second is prepared to make five. His odds are better.

This influence cannot be underestimated. In shooting it has been noticed that if someone already has 4/4 and has to attempt a fifth shot, the his odds of success are worse compared to what they would be of he stopped and then started again later. Then he will make what is now the first shot easily.

If you still are interested in psychological preparation, then go to your National Olympic Committee or National Organisation of Sports Federations. They will very likely be able to help you. In Denmark that would be Dansk Idræts Forbund.

One final thing before we turn from the mind to the body. Have high aspirations, but do not expect yourself to be perfect. Disappointment will come, even to you. Accept it as a challenge to go further, rather as the end of the world. You need to be happy too.

Get your Sleep – Every Day

One of the biggest crimes of our age in the western world is the pressure put on children. A child or teenager needs, on average, ten hours of sleep every night, yet they are asked to go to school at eight o'clock in the morning (or earlier). No wonder they do not learn very much – their minds are still at home, on the pillow...

You should not do the same damage to yourself. An adult generally needs eight or nine hours every night (as we grow older and as our body stops rebuilding itself this requirement diminishes). We need to wake up at approximately the same time every morning and we need to go to bed at the same time every night. If for one night we get less sleep than usual, we should catch up by going earlier to bed on the following night, not by getting up later. The body does not understand the concept of the weekend! People often get six hours of sleep throughout the week, and then sleep for ten or eleven hours at the weekend, waking up much later than usual. Then they go to bed at midnight or later and get up on Monday morning at seven or earlier. There is no wonder they are yawning all week.

In chess tournaments we should not sleep more or less than we normally do. If we sleep more our body will go into a relaxed mode where it is trying to create energy for later. We will literally be sleeping at the board. If we do not sleep as much as we usually do, then we will soon find ourselves drained and tired. The best thing is to get your sleep every day, all of your life. The worst thing is to have a significant change in your sleep pattern at a tournament.

The kind of sleep we normally will not get enough of is Rapid Eye Movement, or *REM*, so called for obvious reasons. This is where the majority of our dreams take place. Even though there is no certainty concerning what happens in REM sleep, today's theories offer a pretty good guide and are worth paying attention to.

If we think of all the inputs we receive throughout the day as physical objects, then what we do during the day can be seen as throwing them into an enormous box in the basement. During REM the night team then classifies the information and emotions and puts them on their appropriate shelves. If this process is terminated early by an alarm clock, day after day, we will be able to function physically, but mentally our condition will be imperfect. Our ability to remember things and the level of our reasoning will be considerably impaired. And our emotions will be in an uninterpreted state. We will be less in peace with negative inputs, as they have not been processed. We will easily become impatient and angry with others in situations which would usually not bother us. When we get bored we get sleepy, instead of the normal irritation. Behind the wheel of a car sleepy people are potential killers. In chess, for sure, they are just losers.

'I have no problems sleeping. I just lay my head on the pillow and I am gone' – this is an important myth about people's sleeping habits. Does it sound healthy? Really, you think so? Well you are wrong. If you literally pass out the second you lay down you are most likely suffering from sleep deprivation. Your body is so tired that it collapses the moment you allow it.

The following list of symptoms can be indications of sleep deprivation:

- You are in need of an alarm clock to get up in the mornings
- You have trouble concentrating and remembering
- You fall asleep watching TV or even at boring meetings and lectures
- You fall asleep when relaxing after dinner
- You fall asleep within five minutes of going to bed
- You sleep longer in the morning at the weekend

Food and Drink

There are many amateur experts on *the right diet* in the western world. As much as I hate to add myself to the list, I would like to briefly comment on the subject. First, your general diet does influence your level of capability at the board. Of course it does. Your mind lives from your body, as, indeed, do your emotions. So a healthy diet is important.

As for food and playing, some general points should be noted. You should not eat a heavy meal during the hour before you play. The digestion will influence the amount of blood going to your head. Secondly, you should be careful what you eat and drink during the game. Besides avoiding heavy and fatty food you should also avoid food containing a lot of sugar. For example if you drink a Coca-Cola and eat a chocolate bar the level of your blood sugar will be such that for fifteen to twenty minutes you will feel a great boost of energy. The body will not be happy with this sudden boost, which is too much too soon, and it will believe that something is wrong. Soon your blood sugar will fall drastically and you will lose all the energy again. Your body has stabilised itself and you are on the way to doing worse than you should have done.

So simply have something natural. Eat some fruit or a fat free sandwich. Do not get full. You need to feel light, not heavy, you need your blood for your head, not for your stomach. The best kind of food during the game is bananas, which have much natural sugar. Also good for you are pears, grapes and so on – just choose.

And drink water. During the game I like to drink a litre (or even more – it depends on the length of the game). If you get bored with water, then drink juices, preferably without added sugar. You should also be aware of the way caffeine and alcohol affects your sleep. You might be able to fall asleep quicker with a sharp drink before you go to bed, but it also damages the level of your sleep. The same goes for such things as coffee, tea, Coca-Cola and similar things drunk during the last three hours before sleeping. Small amounts will not be so important and can be beneficial in that they put you in a good mood, but you should be aware of what they do to you.

Physical Condition

There are so many good arguments for getting some exercise that I will not try to come up with more. Only I will ask you – do you think the level of your blood circulation affects your brain? Do you think your physical strength affects your energy level at the board? The final, convincing argument I have seen in favour of doing exercise was that the brain cells grow, and thus we probably have an increase in intelligence.

Again I would suggest that you consult a professional to guide you if you wish to improve your physical well-being. Find a gym close to where you live. That is a good start.

If you decide to start running there is one thing you need to know – the body does not like sudden changes (as with blood sugar and sleeping). With running, this means that the body should not be asked to reach full speed too soon. It will most likely hurt somewhere and feel wrong. And it is. It takes ten to twelve minutes of light exercise to warm up the body. You can do that even before you go out running, or by starting running at a slower tempo. The first is preferable, but if you choose the latter, then you should try to run at a tempo you can maintain for all twelve minutes. The body does not like to be jump-started.

If you decide to go to a gym you will be given great exercises, including interval training, which is now considered the superior form of training. But first and foremost you should find the kind of exercise you like.

Do not Expect Perfection

Small improvements. A small step every day. This is the way to go far. Every long journey consists of many small steps. You are not a space rocket! Rather you are a human being. You live from your emotions and moods. You can affect and control them, but you should also respect and follow them. You cannot love every minute of training. Perfect happiness does not exist. Of course you should not train if you hate every minute of it. If you have to fight yourself before you fight your opponents they already have an edge, and you are better off doing something else.

But why not give it a try. You love chess and you want to excel in it. You can do it. I believe it, you believe it. What else do you need? Not much, actually. Patience is the answer.

Most people who have ambitions can accept the failures and shortcomings of others but they cannot forgive themselves their own mistakes. This can, over time, prove destructive. You should be ambitious and expect a lot from yourself, but you should also give yourself room to be a human being. Grandmaster Eran Liss once said that the best thing to do after losing a game of chess was to go to the cinema, see a film and be happy thinking about something else. And he is right. Why should we punish ourselves when we fail? We already know that children who are punished do not learn to behave well, while those who are loved and supported will believe in themselves and have the ability to go far.

Most ambitious people do not have this frame of mind, but need to train it. Those who do will succeed.

Social Considerations

An important aspect of working on

your personality to become a natural winner is its social implications. You will need your friends to work for you rather than against you. Why would they work against me, I am sure you are thinking. They will. Not out of ill intentions, but nevertheless they will. They will make silly jokes when you are not successful, which can limit your confidence. They will try to make you go out for a beer when you really want to rest and prepare. They will tell you to be realistic and not invest too much of yourself, as you will probably become disappointed.

As we now know their attitude is wrong. But what shall you do? You do not want to argue with your friends just because you want to improve your chess. The solution is simple. Tell them that they should let you find your own way. Do not try to educate them on the general impact of negative language (nobody likes a know-all!), instead tell them how it affects you. Tell them they should respect your boundaries. Do not tell them all the time how great you are going to be. Only that you think you can do it. You want to stay positive, but also aware of the hurdles you need to overcome, and it is no shame to let your friends be like that too.

The ambitious approach to things is more acceptable in a masculine environment. I know I am risking an accusation of being sexist by saying this, but in feminine surroundings being alone and wanting to win is emotionally less acceptable. This is in our hormones and chromosomes. Of course I am talking tendencies, and there are exceptions but, basically, women do not feel the same about competitive sports as men.

This introduces social implications on people who want to be winners. These disappear once success is attained, but until then they remain. Everyone has a unique situation, and to provide general guidelines is not within my ability. I just wanted to make you aware that this is normal. This will probably make you feel much better when you one day find yourself in a similar situation.

Those who try to excel in chess, soccer or their work will always be targets for humour and jealousy. It is a package. Just ignore people who cannot accept that you are trying to achieve something. This way you will not regret choosing your path.

CHAPTER SEVEN

Be Practical

Not so long ago I observed two players, who are stronger than I am, analyse their short draw. It was mainly a discussion of opening finesses. At one point they were discussing the position after **1 d4 d5 2 ♘f3 ♘f6 3 c4 e6 4 ♘c3 c6 5 cxd5 exd5 6 ♗g5 ♗e7 7 ♕c2 g6 8 e3 ♗f5**

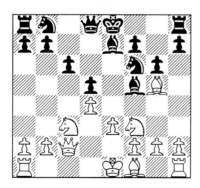

This is probably the easiest way to equalise with Black in the QGD, and the player with White was slightly frustrated that there seemed to be no decent way to fight for an advantage. After some time he suggested the following move:
9 ♕d2

I thought this was a little joke until they started discussing the move. 'Yes, this is possible,' said Black, and they started discussing moves. 'Come on,' I said, 'You cannot be serious!' But indeed they were, and they analysed the position for some minutes (analysing by just moving the pieces around to get a feel for the position – not serious analysis, but not without benefits) before agreeing that this was not dangerous for Black. I was really shocked by this. Both of them know the QGD far better than I, and both of them were aware of the plans in the following position:

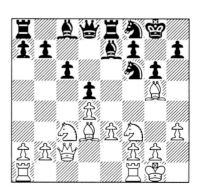

Here Black has just played 11...g6 with the two ideas ...♘f6-h5-g7 and ...♘f8-e6-g7. Both plans include the idea ....♗c8-f5 (among others, of course). So Black is ready to go through all this trouble in order to play ...♗f5. And when we look at the position we see that this is in fact the only decent square for the bishop. So Black really wants to play ...♗f5.

The move 9 ♕d2 suggested above clearly shows a lack of respect for Black's light-squared bishop. White will play 10 ♗e2 and take it easy. Our player with White was beginning to get a little sceptical when he realised that avoiding the exchange of bishops included this, too, and was not just the loss of a tempo.

My reasoning was quite simple. We were not discussing whether 9 ♕d2 was playable, but whether it was useful for White. And there was simply nothing suggesting any kind of improvement. There was no genuine idea from the players associated with the move, except not playing the main move 9 ♗d3, as this exchange is principally good for Black.

Actually I did find a game where 9 ♕d2 was played against a strong player, and Black had no problems at all in equalising.

Galakhov–Novikov

Ukraine 1991

Queen's Gambit Declined

1 d4 d5 2 ♘f3 ♘f6 3 c4 e6 4 ♘c3 c6 5 cxd5 exd5 6 ♗g5 ♗e7 7 ♕c2 g6 8 e3 ♗f5 9 ♕d2 0-0 10 ♗e2 ♘bd7 11 0-0 ♖e8 12 h3 ♘e4 13 ♘xe4 dxe4!

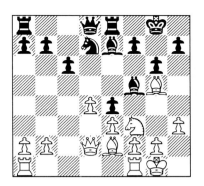

The correct decision. After 13...♗xe4 White's strategy might finally begin to make a little sense. The bishop on e4 will not control any important squares and it has no prospects of getting to another useful diagonal. After the text the a2-g8 diagonal is the where the bishop belongs, away from the constant danger of being pushed back by White's pawns. In fact the bishop can later become quite powerful.

To some it might not be that apparent that the bishop is better on e6 than e4, but the Grandmaster is in no doubt. I believe that the safety of the e6-square is the main reason why this is the best move, but also the strength of the e4-pawn is important. From being a potential weakness on d5 it now limits the possibilities for White on the kingside. What is certain is that White had no success with his opening idea.

14 ♗xe7 ♕xe7 15 ♘h2 a5 16 ♖fc1 ♗e6 17 ♗c4 ♘f6 18 ♗xe6 ♕xe6 19 ♖c5 b6 20 ♖e5 ♕d6 21 ♖xe8+ ♖xe8 22 ♕c2 ♘d5 23 a3 h5 24 ♖c1 ♖e6 25 ♘f1 g5 26 ♕e2 ♘f6 27 ♕a6 ♘d5 28 ♕e2 ½-½

When I say 'Be practical' this is one

of the things I am thinking of. Be aware of what you are trying to do and how you should do it. One thing I have noticed about many chess players – including those who are far stronger than I could ever become – is that they waste time because they do not know where they are going and because they are lying to themselves. The latter point requires some explanation. Many players experience much emotion when involved in a game, and after the game is finished they are often left with the impression that they played well – if they won – or that they just overlooked something – if they lost. Of course this is not the true picture. People tend to lose because they do not play very well, and win because they play better than their opponents (not necessarily well, of course). Your emotions want to do this to you, will you allow them?

There are two sides to being a practical chess player – at and away from the board. The first is related to situations such as the one above. Involve basic logic in your frame of mind and you will never go completely off the track. Being practical at the board also means accepting that chess is a game, a struggle between two people, and not a mathematical exercise. At times there will be games that are difficult to win by normal play and something will have to happen. Here a sense of being practical will be helpful. Below are some useful practical tricks.

1) When you have a drawn endgame against a weaker player, doing nothing is often the best policy. Your opponent will feel less sure of the draw than you

and, at some stage, trying to force the draw as his patience runs out will involve a certain risk. This has won me many points over the years. See the example below, as well as Pedersen–Aagaard in Chapter 4.

2) Another good tip for beating weaker players is exchanging knight for bishop, or the other way round. Championed by Smyslov, the idea is that when the pieces in the two armies have different properties the outcome is less likely to be a draw. This is, of course, the technical player's approach. Someone like Kasparov would rather create an imbalance by sacrificing a pawn, an exchange or two minor pieces for a rook, for example.

3) Bore your opponent. Often, if a position is in deadlock, you can lull your opponent into boredom before jumping to action. This can be done by repeating a position several times in different manners. Again, see the aforementioned Pedersen–Aagaard. If your opponent does not know when to be alert, the chances that he will commit an error increase.

4) A very interesting idea comes from Swedish Grandmaster Tiger Hillarp-Persson and is based on psychology. As he is a person who is good at dealing with pressure, he rarely exchanges pieces himself, but leaves this for his opponent. The pressure on the opponent has many times proved strong and in Tiger's favour. This, again, owes much to personality.

5) When your opponent is in time-trouble and you would like to achieve a better result from the position than normal play would grant you, then a

good idea is to voluntarily grow short of time yourself. Aagaard–Danielsen is a good example of how effective this can be.

But being practical at the board is not only about playing logical moves and using different legal tricks. It also has to do with managing yourself correctly. I had one pupil who could use thirty minutes calculating completely irrelevant lines, and then decide between two moves on feeling alone. He would very often be afraid of going into tactical lines and sacrificing material, of which he was generally afraid. But then when he went into time-trouble and had insufficient time to solve the problems he was confronted with, he would always make some violent sacrifice, rarely gaining from doing so. We looked at his scoresheets after two tournaments where I had asked him to write down how much time he spent on each move. The facts were clear to him and the pattern quite evident. In the next tournament, by paying attention to what he was thinking about, he escaped his fears; as well as improving his time management, he also sharpened his style. This also had something to do with performance psychology I had introduced him to, but the practical approach to time management was the main factor in his almost immediate jump from 2250 to 2330.

As my pupil had problems with his time management, others are unaware of what they are really doing, and why. I will return to this in more generic terms below, but first here is an illustrative example.

Nielsen–Aagaard
Ribe 2001

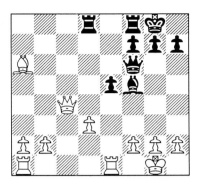

White is two pawns up and should now concentrate on freeing his queen and bishop from the commitment they have on the queenside.

22 ♖e3?

The practical approach involves returning the weak d-pawn in order to get the rest of the army organised. This is best done with 22 ♗b7! ♗xd3 23 ♕c3 and White wins easily.

22...♖d4 23 ♕c5?

My opponent saw 23 ♕b5 ♗d7 24 ♕b7 ♗c8 25 ♕xc8 ♖xc8 26 ♗xc8, which probably leads to a draw, and decided to be 'smart' – a notion that often leads to an outright blunder.

23...♕xa6 24 ♖xe5?!

I had missed 24 ♕xe5 ♕f6!, when I am a piece up but with a damaged pawn structure. My opponent, on the other hand, had missed something much simpler.

24...♕xd3!

Black is winning.

25 ♖e3 ♖d5 26 ♕xf8+ ♔xf8 0-1

White resigned without playing a few moves of the endgame.

White should have been more attentive to the actual situation on the board than to calculating variations. Clearly he got lost in his calculation where simple logic would have brought him to the conclusion that the d-pawn was not doing him any good, and that the harmony of his pieces was more important.

Make Decisions at Home

Of course being practical about chess also has to do with how you approach the game from your home. There are three kinds of situation in chess – between tournaments, between games in a tournament, and at the board. To me it is obvious that an ambitious player should *make as many decisions as possible at home*. This means doing your opening preparation at home between tournaments and then refreshing it between games. Create special files with your opening repertoire so that you are prepared for this kind of preparation and therefore do not need to start at the beginning every time. Of course you will also need to prepare different lines at the tournament, but they should be extensions of your home preparation, not replacements. And when you have selected something, stick with it. Do not get nervous or have second thoughts at the board. The decision you made in your personal, calm environment will most likely be correct. There is a well-known anecdote about an International Master who prepared the Advance variation of the French Defence for several hours before a game, yet after 1 e4 e6 lost his confidence and spent forty minutes (!) thinking before playing 2 e5?. Whenever you think of abandoning your home preparation, think of this

guy. Is there something of him in you?

But making decisions from home is not only about opening preparation. Also important is your strategy at the board. What are you playing for? Know it! The Danish Tour de France winner Bjarne Riis spoke about how his career changed one day. He was in a minor Dutch race and thought of how many of the cyclists really knew why they were there, concluding that only two or three did so – those who really wanted to win the race or those preparing for another event. The rest were just doing what they did without really having decided why.

The moral here is: know where you are going when you sit down at the board. If you do not know, then you should go through the previous chapter once again and settle on some ambition of yours.

When I was trying to become a stronger player in 1999-2000 I had a clear image in my head of what kind of player I wanted to become. I wanted to be a fighter, a creative player, with little interest in draws. I rather wanted to take risks rather than peacefully share the point. I also knew that I could do this considerably against a weaker player and still play for a win as long as I showed the required will to do so. The game below is an example of how this decision helped me at the board.

The day before my opponent had drawn with a 2450 International Master who was sitting next to us, playing another opponent rated approximately 2200. He drew in seventeen moves with Black, being slightly worse. I wonder if he knew what he was doing at the tournament. I presume he did not.

Lahlum-Aagaard
Hamburg 1999
Nimzo-Indian Defence

1 d4 ♘f6 2 c4 e6 3 ♘c3 ♗b4 4 ♕c2 0-0 5 a3 ♗xc3+ 6 ♕xc3 d6 7 ♗g5 ♘bd7 8 e3 b6

I was not afraid of equal positions without immediate dynamical winning chances because I trusted in my superior powers as a chess player. Moreover I knew I could win even the simplest endgames.

9 ♗e2 ♗b7 10 ♗f3 ♗xf3 11 ♘xf3 c5 12 dxc5 bxc5 13 0-0 ♕b6 14 ♖fd1 a5 15 b3 ♖fb8 16 ♖ab1 a4 17 b4 cxb4 18 ♖xb4 ♕c5 19 ♗xf6 ♘xf6 20 ♖db1 ♖c8 21 ♕d4 h6 22 ♕xc5 ♖xc5 23 ♖b8+ ♖xb8 24 ♖xb8+ ♔h7 25 ♖b4 d5 26 ♘d2 dxc4 27 ♖xc4

White has played quite defensively and tried to exchange all the pieces, clearly with the hope of a draw. But I was not in the mood to split the point, and experience has taught me that exchanging pieces is not a genuine drawing method, but more a way of altering the nature of the game. However, the exchanges performed by my opponent were very effective, and the position before us has become rather dull. I decided to take a few risks in order to improve my prospects of winning. This involves a sacrifice.

27...♖b5!?

This is obviously a trick. By sacrificing the a-pawn Black hopes that White will let his rook be passive on the a-file, while Black attacks on the kingside.

28 ♖xa4 ♖b2 29 ♘f1

Forced. 29 ♖d4 e5 30 ♖d3 ♘e4! illustrates the weakness of the first rank.

29...♘d5!

Threatening ...♘c3. Now White wisely activates his rook.

30 ♖c4! ♖a2 31 a4 g5

Simply gaining space on the kingside and awaiting my opponent's actions.

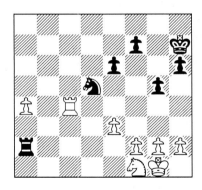

32 g3?

A grave error, although not enough to bring White into serious trouble. I was very pleased when I saw my opponent make this move, as I knew that the weakness on f3 should later fall into my possession. The right move is 32 h4!, creating breathing space for the king and exchanging a pawn, both useful defensive measures for White.

32...♔g6 33 e4?!

I am also sceptical of this move as the e-pawn now becomes weak. Moreover, Black's knight had no intention of staying on d5 for long anyway. My opponent was, apparently, under the impression that he was forcing a draw, but this is far from the truth.

33...♘b6 34 ♖c6 ♘d7!

34...♘xa4 35 ♖a6 is drawn, although I could find a few tricks for Black (there is always a trick or two left...). But why should Black do this? The knight does not belong on the a-file, but on f3. Hence Black's next.

35 ♘e3

A waiting move, showing that White is aware that he is on the verge of being worse. He is not afraid of returning the a-pawn if he can save the rest of his position. 35 ♖a6 ♘c5! already favours Black.

35...♘e5!

Black is playing to win and this can only happen if he attacks on the king-side.

36 ♖a6

Forced as after 36 ♖c2 ♖xa4 the e-pawn will fall, and Black will have a serious advantage.

36...g4!

Setting up the mating net. Let us be serious – there is no mate. But just setting up the threats and seeing what happens, this is what works. Maybe there will be some way to advance the attack beyond perpetual check, and maybe not. But it certainly feels much better taking this risk on Black's side compared to how it must feel for White, left with nothing but the hope

that there are no surprises beyond the horizon. As so often happens in tournament chess, the threat is stronger than the execution. Here it prompts White to go into panic (inducing a loss) instead of playing his own trump card.

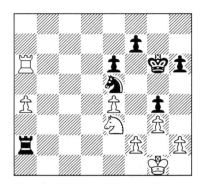

37 ♔g2?

After this move White appears to be losing. The correct continuation consists of advancing the a-pawn as far as possible: 37 a5 h5 38 ♖a8 ♖a1+ 39 ♔g2 ♘f3 40 ♘f1 ♘e1+ 41 ♔h1 ♘f3 42 ♔g2.

37...h5 38 h3

I was surprised by the text as I was unsure whether 38 ♖a8 ♘d3 39 ♘d1 ♖d2 40 ♘c3 would give White a chance to save the game. Now I can see that this is rubbish, since Black wins after 40...♖xf2+ 41 ♔g1 ♖c2 42 ♘b5 ♘e5 with a winning attack. Black's kingside pawns are by now stronger than White's a-pawn.

38 ♘d5!?, to defend the kingside, is an alternative, but I feel that he is already in a lot of trouble. There is also 38 ♖d6!?, giving up both the a- and e-pawns. It is better trying to defend an endgame where the pawns are all on the same side of the board than losing your

head and half of your pawns.

38...gxh3+ 39 ♔xh3 ♖xf2 40 ♘g2

40 ♖a8 ♘f3 41 g4? (41 ♘g2! – see next note) 41...h4 42 ♘g2 ♘g1+ 43 ♔h2 h3 44 ♔xg1 ♖xg2+ 45 ♔h1 ♔g5 with the plan ...♔g5-h4-g3 with a winning position. After 46 ♖h8 ♔xg4 47 ♖g8+ ♔f3 48 ♖xg2 hxg2+ 49 ♔g1 ♔xe4 the king is close enough to the far corner to prevent the a-pawn from queening.

40...♘f3

41 ♘h4+?

Loses immediately. The only chance is 41 ♖a8 ♘g5+ 42 ♔h2 ♘xe4 with a clear advantage for Black.

41...♘xh4 42 gxh4 ♖f3+ 43 ♔g2 ♖e3

Now the rook endgame is easily winning.

44 ♖a8 ♖xe4 45 ♔g3 ♔f5 46 ♖g8 f6 47 a5 ♖e3+ 48 ♔f2 ♖a3 0-1

For me this game was easy to play as I had already decided from home to take the kind of risks I did. There was no reason to become nervous about whether or not I had chosen the right path, as this had already been decided in advance. Instead I did what my job was there and then: I did what I could to win.

When Bent Larsen advanced in the chess world in the late 1950s and early 1960s he decided to always take chances. His goal was to become the best player in the world, and in some way I think he achieved this by the late 1960s, when he won so many tournaments. In his learning period Larsen took so many risks and learned a great deal about chess as a competitive game. He later said that he probably had worse results for some time than he could have had if his style had been less risky, but that he was aiming at improving his chess rather than winning only the next game. In the same way I advise you to know where you are going and to find out what will take you there (see the previous chapter), and then play according to your plan. Be practical.

CHAPTER EIGHT

Openings, Calculation and Analysis

In this book I argue for a development of practical chess ability based on positional understanding. Over time I have come to believe that this is the fastest path to chess mastery. However, although we have not delved into opening analysis and calculation I do not underestimate their importance. But nor do I overestimate their impact on results. In this chapter I will give a brief introduction as to how I would approach openings, calculation, analysing your own games and the feeling for when the position is turning. A ghost in all of this will be computer programs such as *Fritz 6*.

Opening Preparation

There are different ways to prepare for the opening. Different styles. If you are a young aggressive player you might like to play 1 e4 and violent Sicilians. If you have a more quiet temperament you might prefer 1 d4 and the Petroff. We are all different in our taste for openings.

Some people with a great memory play sharp Sicilians where remembering complications is essential for survival. If this is your playing style you will face a lot of work. The problem is often that if your opponent settles for less ambitious lines with Black, refraining from any attempts to equalise, you will not have developed the skills for playing with a small advantage because you need to use so much time preparing long and complex variations. This is a very demanding opening style, but it does pay off with quick wins from time to time. If this is the way you want to play, then go for it. Just be aware that the costs are great.

I propose another way of preparing, which consists of three stages and is based on positional understanding rather than memory. It requires a good database and a less ambitious opening style, but in practise it should not appear any less dangerous for the opponent.

The first phase to be investigated when you decide on an opening is the endgame. You create a database file of relevant games in the opening of your choice. I recommend that you consider only games with players rated over 2350 as relevant material, and you should be aware that some games between Grandmasters are entered into the data-bases as unrated, particularly old games.

You then search for endgames only and study those. Draw some general conclusions from your studies and keep them in mind when you continue your work. And please, do not just flick through the games at high speed. Invest some time and pay especial attention to annotated games. Personally I used to print out the games and play through them using a real chess set to get a pleasant experience from the work.

For a good illustration of what I am talking about you can see the chapter on the Classical Endgame in my Panov-Botvinnik book.

When you have concluded your work on the endgame you continue to the middlegame. You start by playing through the 100-150 highest rated games in the opening. Every time you encounter a positional concept you write it down on a piece of paper. After some time there will be longer and longer between a new element, and in the end you will only see variations of the same theme. You then search in *ChessBase* or *Chess Assistant* for positions in your opening where these concepts occur. It takes some practise, but is not so difficult. You will then learn a lot about these concepts from playing through seven or eight games in which they have occurred. Make a file of your favourite examples for later repetition. You might like to look through the in-

troduction chapters in my recent books on the Dutch Stonewall and Meeting 1 d4 (published early in 2002) to get a good idea of this, and you might even go further than I did and invest more time before you turn to the final step of the process.

Finally it is time to look at the actual theory. Most likely you already have some idea of the value of the lines you have spent a few working days on, or you would not have put in the hours, but still you want to be accurate. You build up a repertoire in the usual manner, learn the critical lines by heart and maybe even find some new ideas. You will be much more prepared for this now that you already understand the opening. You will easily find improvements in the less frequently played lines. Here is one Esben Lund and I came up with for our book on the QGD Tarrasch entitled *Meeting 1 d4*:

1 d4 d5 2 c4 e6 3 ♘c3 c5 4 cxd5 exd5 5 ♘f3 ♘c6 6 g3 ♘f6 7 ♗g2 ♗e7 8 0-0 0-0 9 dxc5 ♗xc5 10 b3 ♗g4 11 ♗b2

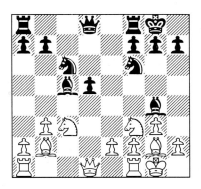

This is a well-known theoretical position in which the main lines feature something like 11...♖e8 12 ♖c1 followed by 13 ♘xd5 ♗xf2+ with complications. But we are already so happy with Black's position that we suggest a simple alternative.

11...a6! 12 ♖c1 ♗a7

Black is in no respect worse here. Esben has studied the Tarrasch in detail and he arrived at this idea without much trouble. Later we discovered that some games had been played here, but we found no reason why this should not be the main line, and in our book it is. The book is due to be published early in 2002. When we worked on the book together we both wrote introduction chapters to main lines, and we both discovered a number of obvious improvements. Not deep subtle ideas, just good moves. It could be you.

Fritz can be a good companion in opening analysis, especially when you need to work quickly and effectively. It will probably not offer many useful new ideas but it will shoot down your poor ones. It is common these days for authors of opening books to rely quite a lot on *Fritz* in their judgement, and some books even claim to be completely computer checked. However, you can fall upon a gem occasionally...

McShane-Hansen
Copenhagen 1999
Sicilian Defence

1 e4 c5 2 ♘f3 d6 3 d4 cxd4 4 ♘xd4 ♘f6 5 ♘c3 g6 6 ♗c4 ♗g7 7 0-0 0-0 8 ♖e1 ♘c6 9 h3 ♗d7 10 ♗g5? ♘xd4 11 ♕xd4 h6 12 ♗d2

12 ♗xf6 is the lesser evil, when Black is quite comfortable, with complete

domination on the dark squares.

12...♘g4 13 ♕d3 ♘e5 14 ♕e2

This line was suggested in *Nunn's Chess Openings*. Unfortunately the authors had not anticipated what *Fritz* found very quickly.

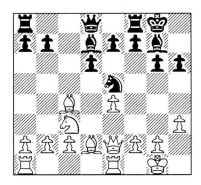

14...♗xh3!! 15 gxh3 ♕c8 16 ♗b3 ♕xh3

The check on f3 is deadly, so White has only one reply.

17 f4 ♕g3+! 18 ♔f1

18 ♕g2 ♘f3+ 19 ♔f1 ♕xg2+ 20 ♔xg2 ♘xd2 amounts to the same thing.

18...♘g4 19 ♕g2 ♘h2+ 20 ♔g1 ♘f3+ 21 ♔f1 ♕xg2+ 22 ♔xg2 ♘xd2

Winning.

23 ♗d5 e6 24 ♖ad1 exd5 25 ♖xd2 ♗xc3 26 bxc3 ♖ac8 27 ♖xd5 ♖xc3 28 ♖xd6 ♖xc2+ 29 ♔g3 ♖fc8 30 f5 ♖8c6 31 ♖d7 ♖xa2 32 ♖xb7 ♔g7 33 ♖d1 g5 34 ♖d3 ♖c1 35 ♔f3 ♖f1+ 36 ♔e3 g4 37 ♔d4 ♖a4+ 38 ♔d5 h5 39 ♖c3 ♖a5+ 40 ♔d4 ♖f4 41 ♖c8 ♖a4+ 42 ♔d5 ♖axe4 43 ♖cc7 ♖d4+ 0-1

Calculation

Calculation is obviously an important part of chess. Sometimes it is only a check for blunders before you execute a positional idea, while at other times it is a precise juggling of complicated lines. No matter what style you have you will need to improve your calculation at some point in order to achieve your goals. I will not go too far into the subject here as it is beyond the boundaries of this book. Rather I would like to guide you to very good books on the subject. My two favourite books are Mark Dvoretsky and Artur Yusupov's *Attack and Defence*, which should be on its way in an improved translation, and the first two chapters in Jonathan Tisdall's *Improve your Chess now*.

However, I do have one improvement over the current theory on how to calculate most effectively. I have discovered that I – and therefore most others, since I am no special case – have a tendency to overlook my opponent's defences. So when you calculate a line you should always end on a move from your opponent. This will save you a lot of grief.

But before you spend a thousand hours on calculation exercises you should sort out your personal style, your endgame and your openings. I believe that calculation will take you the last step up the ladder, but it will not help your the first step. In other words it is easier to improve on positional style with calculation than it is to improve on calculation with positional style. First things first, as they say.

When you practise calculation it can be good to compare your results in an exercise with those of the book and those of *Fritz*. In this way you will be more aware of your worst weaknesses, and you will eventually eradicate them.

Analysing your own Games

An important way to improve is to understand why you make the mistakes you do. To address this I suggest that you create your own tournament reports. Analyse your games in detail and single out the mistakes. Then go over the mistakes and try to find similarities in the same way as you would look for middlegame concepts, as in the paragraph on opening preparation, above. You will probably single out five or six different types of mistake that are common for you, and this gives you an opportunity to direct your training.

When you analyse your games, start by doing so yourself – do not ask *Fritz* to find your mistakes for you. You will not benefit from this. Instead do it yourself and later briefly check with *Fritz* to see if there was something you missed. Remember that *Fritz* does not 'understand' chess and cannot explain anything, but from time to time it might see something you did not. It is particularly good at uncovering where you should have played in a less forcing manner. A good book about analysing your own games (and other things) is Alexander Yermolinsky's *The Road to Chess Improvement*. Highly recommended.

Good luck to you, wherever you are going.

CHAPTER NINE

Exercises

Just the other day I had a very interesting conversation with a close friend. He told me that he often realised how he could obtain his ambitions, and that he then lost his motivation. I disagreed with him on one particular detail – I do not believe that we can foresee the nature of the problems that will meet us on our journey to mastery, no matter how experienced we might believe we are. You can only truly understand how difficult it is to climb the mountain if you have succeeded. If you failed or lost your motivation on the way, you will never know the half of it.

So if we want to know, we need to work and, as Mark Dvoretsky so has so rightly said, there is no better way to improve than training. If you want to be good at playing chess, knowing a lot about the game is not enough, you also have to train the abilities you need to make strong decisions at the board. This chapter has been designed to help you do so.

I have selected twelve exercises where conceptual judgement is required,

as well as good old-fashioned thinking. The exercises have been chosen quite randomly, as I, too, like to test my theories constantly. By choosing exercises from my database I have also tried to avoid too many known examples. However, as I use games between top players from the last decade there will probably be a collision or two with your memory.

A few of the examples have been taken from my personal collection of exercises because I enjoy them a great deal. By a miracle, only one of them is from a game I played, while one is from my favourite pupil Finn Nøhr, since he has helped me so much, reading the proofs and providing so many suggestions, and I think he deserves this exposure.

There is no guarantee that the move suggested in the solutions is the only serious move in the position. It has not been my intention to give straight exercises where the solution has been cut in stone. Rather I have sought out some more open material, where the suggested solution is not necessarily the only or the best one. Feel free to over-rule my conclusions. Actually you will probably learn something from trying to argue both sides of a decision, with my suggestions on one side, with you leading the counter argument.

Again I recommend going over these exercises together with a trainer or a friend. There is nothing better than having someone to discuss the positions with. Nothing more fruitful. And please do not turn to the solutions before you feel you have complete confidence in your own judgement. You need to compare the solutions – not just read mine!

The struggle for perfection is the only thing that will truly develop your chess. If you do not try to push yourself beyond what you can already do, your development will be slow and, ultimately, stop completely. Talent will only take you so far. I remember Botvinnik saying about Reshevsky: 'He is the most talented player in the world. But it doesn't really matter as I worked so much harder.' Botvinnik, of course, was the world champion for fifteen years (and this was so short due to WW2), while Reshevsky never came close.

Anyway, here are the exercises. I hope you enjoy them.

Exercise 1
White to move

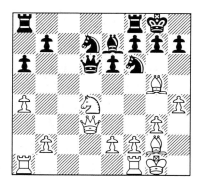

Exercise 4
White to move

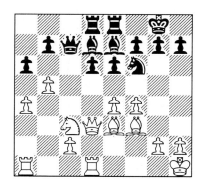

Exercise 2
White to move

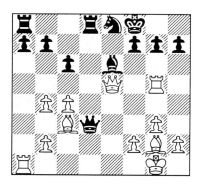

Exercise 5
Black to move

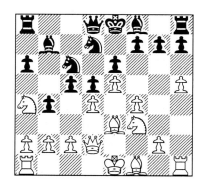

Exercise 3
Black to move

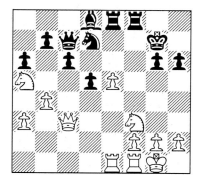

Exercise 6
White to move

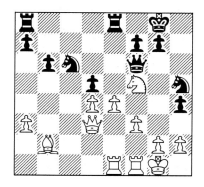

Exercise 7
Black to move

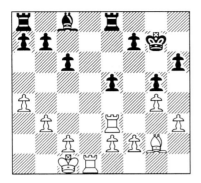

Exercise 10
Black to move

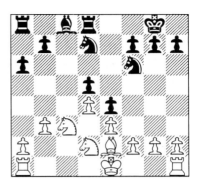

Exercise 8
White to move

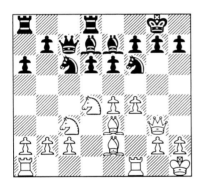

Exercise 11
White to move

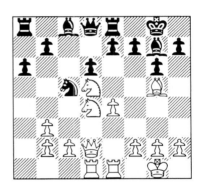

Exercise 9
White to move

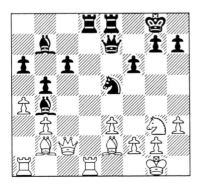

Exercise 12
White to move

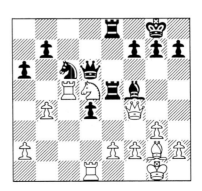

CHAPTER TEN

Solutions to Exercises

As I mentioned earlier, and as indicated in the preamble to the exercises, these solutions are not final, and were never intended to be. Rather they are good starting points for discussions and evaluations. As far as the annotations are concerned, where relevant I have followed the game to the end.

Exercise 1
Karpov-Beliavsky
Linares 1994
Catalan Opening

1 d4 ♘f6 2 ♘f3 d5 3 c4 e6 4 g3 ♗e7 5 ♗g2 0-0 6 0-0 dxc4 7 ♕c2 a6 8 a4 ♗d7 9 ♕xc4 ♗c6 10 ♗g5 ♗d5 11 ♕d3 c5 12 ♘c3 cxd4 13 ♘xd5 ♕xd5 14 h4 ♘bd7 15 ♘xd4 ♕d6

After having compared the pieces it is not difficult to see that White is better. His g2-bishop is superior to any black minor piece and Black has some problems with his queen. If you have compared the queens properly you will most likely have noticed just how much his queen is a problem for Black, being slightly exposed on d6 and without a suitable resting place. The concept of ♘f5 with the intention of meeting ...♕xd3 with ♘xe7+ comes to mind, as does the exploitation of the unprotected b7-pawn. But neither works – the former because Black's queen is protected and the latter in view of ...♘c5. While it seems difficult to add to the pressure on b7 the target is not really running away. Anyway, development has not been completed yet.

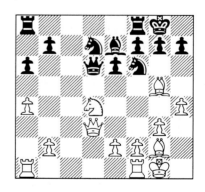

16 ♖fd1!

This is the right move for a number of reasons. First the rook was inactive on f1 and on d1 it is very active. Secondly the d4-knight was not as safely protected as the rest of White's pieces, and therefore might need some backup. Finally, White now threatens the ♘f5 trick.

16...♘c5?

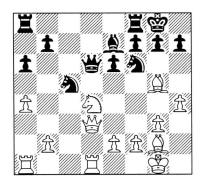

Black has to do something, but not this. After 16...♖ac8 White will execute his plan and have a winning endgame after 17 ♘f5! exf5 18 ♕xd6 ♗xd6 19 ♖xd6 ♖c2 20 ♗xb7 ♖xe2 21 ♗xa6 ♖xb2 22 ♗b5 (Donev), when the two bishops and the passed a-pawn are sufficient to net the full point. Black has difficulties avoiding tactics because 16...♕b6 17 a5! illustrates the missing squares for the queen. But Black can still fight after 17...♕a7, when White is clearly better but still has to work for it. 16...♔h8!? is another way for Black to avoid the tactical twists and turns.

The text is wrong for several reasons, but mainly because it only postpones the problem on the d-file, while simultaneously creating new problems. It is true that the knight jump prevents ♗xb7, but c5 is not a good square for the knight, which is not going anywhere, and is too exposed.

17 ♕c4!

White maintains the pressure, which would be diminished by tangling himself up in tactics.

17...♖fd8

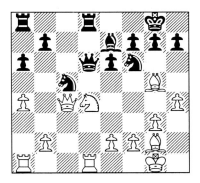

A natural move, pinning the knight.

18 b4!

Immediately exploiting the misplacement of the knight, a sensible kind of tactic which offers the opponent little by way of response.

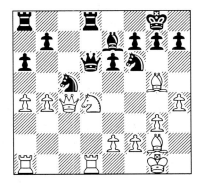

18...♘xa4

This tactic does not work, but nor does any other. No good is 18...♘cd7 19 ♘c6! bxc6 20 ♖xd6 ♗xd6 21 ♗xc6, when the extra pawn on the queenside will win. Black could consider playing 18...♘ce4, but after 19 ♗xf6 ♘xf6 20

♗xb7 ♖ab8 21 ♘c2! ♕xd1+ 22 ♖xd1
♖xd1+ 23 ♔g2 ♘d5 24 ♗xd5 exd5 25
♕xa6 White has a decisive advantage,
although it will require a little effort to
convert to a full point. Note that recap-
turing on f6 with the bishop leads to an
easy technical win for White after
19...♗xf6 20 ♗xe4 ♗xd4 21 e3 ♗xa1
22 ♖xd6 ♖xd6 23 ♗xb7, when Black's
bishop is worthless and the two pawns
will run to promotion.

19 ♕b3 ♕b6

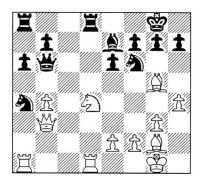

19...♘b6 20 ♗xb7! and White is an
exchange up. 19...♕xb4 is also useless
in view of 20 ♕xb4 ♗xb4 21 ♖xa4 ♗c3
22 ♗xb7 ♖ab8 23 ♖d3.

20 e3 1-0

Exercise 2
Anand-Speelman
Geneva 1996
English Opening

**1 ♘f3 d5 2 c4 d4 3 g3 ♘c6 4 ♗g2 e5
5 d3 ♘f6 6 0-0 ♘d7 7 e3 ♗c5 8 exd4
♘xd4 9 ♘bd2 0-0 10 ♘b3 ♘xb3 11
axb3 c6 12 ♗d2 ♘f6 13 ♘xe5 ♗d4
14 ♗c3 ♗f5 15 ♖e1 ♕d6 16 ♕f3 ♗e6
17 ♕f4 ♖fd8 18 b4 ♗xe5 19 ♖xe5
♕xd3 20 ♖g5 ♘e8 21 ♕e5 ♔f8**

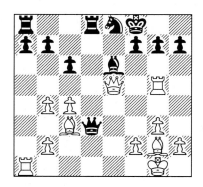

This is a tactical position that concerns king safety.

22 ♖xg7!

This move is obviously correct.
White obtains full domination over the
dark squares and removes the only effective defender on the kingside. It is
tempting to try to improve the position
before sacrificing the exchange with 22
♖e1? but, unfortunately for White,
Black has a defence in 22...♕xc4! 23
♖xg7 f6! and the position is less clear
than in ought to be.

22...♘xg7

Now 22...f6 23 ♕xe6 ♔xg7 24 ♕e7+
♔g8 25 ♕xb7 offers no resistance.

23 ♕xg7+ ♔e8 24 ♖e1!

This is, of course, correct. 'Invite all
your friends to the party' is what my
pupil Finn Nøhr always says about such
moves. The trick in this exercise is actually that there seems to be nothing immediately winning for White, yet Black
is completely lost here. The pawn for
the exchange is more than enough
compensation, and the ugly king in the
middle will be the deciding factor.

24...♕g6

Black needs to fight for control over
his king position. After the alternative

24...♛xc4 25 ♗h3! (the only piece not helping in the attack...) Black's defence ceases to exist.

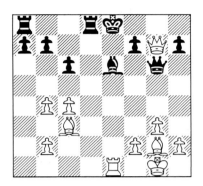

25 ♛e5

Black has no way to improve his position. He would love to exchange a set of rooks but White will obviously not let him do so. Soon White will nudge his h-pawn forward to leave h2 free for the king, after which he can bring the rook to the fourth rank or some other place where it can join the attack.

25...♚f8 26 b5!

Creating weaknesses.

26...♜ac8 27 bxc6 bxc6 28 h4 ♜e8 29 ♚h2! f6 30 ♛d6+ ♚f7

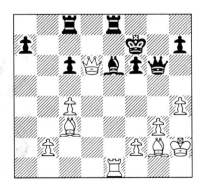

31 ♜xe6! ♜xe6 32 ♛d7+ ♜e7 33 ♛xc8 1-0

Exercise 3
Anand-Karpov
Tilburg 1991
Caro-Kann Defence

1 e4 c6 2 d4 d5 3 e5 ♗f5 4 ♘f3 e6 5 ♗e2 a6 6 0-0 ♘d7 7 ♘bd2 ♗g6 8 a3 ♘h6 9 c4 ♗e7 10 ♘b3 0-0 11 ♗xh6 gxh6 12 ♛d2 ♚g7 13 ♘a5 ♛c7 14 cxd5 exd5 15 b4 f6 16 ♜ae1 ♜ae8 17 ♛c3 ♗d8 18 ♗d3 fxe5 19 ♗xg6 hxg6 20 dxe5

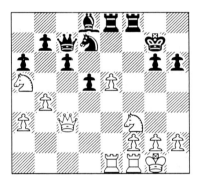

The first thing I notice in this position is the discovered check and Black's slightly weak kingside. I also notice that the discovered check is, in fact, irrelevant, as it does not win a piece as I feared at first. Again simply looking over the pieces tells us a lot about where the position is going. In the end we arrive at the a5-knight as a focus of attention. White will have an advantage if he succeeds in bringing this knight back to b3 and then taking control of the kingside, with ♘f3-d4 at the right time followed by f2-f4. So time is an issue. The knight is only one move away from assuming an important role in controlling the centre, but right now it is stuck on the edge out of play. It is a good time for Black to alter the pawn structure.

20...c5!

Threatening both ...c5-c4 followed by ...b7-b6, winning the knight, and also ...d5-d4 winning the e-pawn. White is actually without choice in his list of replies.

21 e6+ ♘f6 22 ♘b3

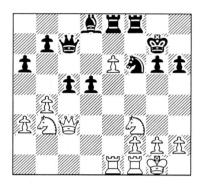

22...cxb4!

To me this is quite a remarkable move. Karpov correctly sees that White will have problems protecting the queenside, an important factor being the superiority of bishop over knight. The bishop will soon stand on e7 now that it is of no use on d8, and the weaknesses on the a3-f8 diagonal will then be under pressure.

23 ♕xb4

23 ♕xc7+ ♗xc7 24 axb4 ♗d6 also wins a pawn for Black, White having nothing better than 25 b5!? since after the alternative 25 ♘c5 ♗xc5 26 bxc5 ♘e4 he is a pawn down for absolutely nothing.

23...♗e7 24 ♕d2 ♗xa3

Black is a pawn up in a complicated position and thus has clearly the better chances. However, Anand is not easy to

beat...

The rest of the game went 25 ♕d3 ♗d6 26 ♘bd4 ♕c4 27 ♕b1 ♕b4 28 e7 ♖f7 29 ♘e6+ ♔h7 30 ♘f8+ ♖exf8 31 exf8♘+ ♗xf8 32 ♕d3 ♕c4 33 ♕e3 ♕e4 34 ♘e5 ♖g7 35 ♕b6 ♕f5 36 ♘f3 ♖f7 37 ♖e5 ♕f4 38 ♖e6 ♘d7 39 ♕b1 ♕g4 40 ♖e3 ♗c5 41 ♖d3 ♕f5 42 ♘d4 ♕h5 43 ♖h3 ♕g4 44 ♘f3 ♗e7 45 ♕xb7 ♕c4 46 ♕b2 h5 47 ♖g3 ♖e2 48 ♕a1 a5 49 ♘g5+ ♔g8 50 ♘h3 ♘e5 51 ♕xa5 ♗e7 52 ♕a7 ♘g4 53 ♖f3 ♘e5 54 ♖e3 ♔f7 55 ♕b7 ♔f6 56 ♖xe2 ♕xe2 57 ♘f4 1-0

Exercise 4
Anand-Kasparov
PCA-World Ch., New York 1995
Sicilian Defence

1 e4 c5 2 ♘f3 d6 3 d4 cxd4 4 ♘xd4 ♘f6 5 ♘c3 a6 6 ♗e2 e6 7 0-0 ♗e7 8 a4 ♘c6 9 ♗e3 0-0 10 f4 ♕c7 11 ♔h1 ♖e8 12 ♗f3 ♗d7 13 ♘b3 ♘a5 14 ♘xa5 ♕xa5 15 ♕d3 ♖ad8 16 ♖fd1 ♗c6 17 b4 ♕c7 18 b5 ♗d7

This is, of course, a famous position in which Anand improved on a previous game – with which he was unfamiliar. In that game White played without any plan and was nowhere near an advantage. One of the first concepts that comes into mind is opening up the position for the bishops with e4-e5, but this creates a problem on the d-file, so we will keep the idea on ice for later. If we then take a look at the weaknesses we realise that b7 is a major problem for Black, and that we should try to attack it. We are already well placed to do so with the bishop on f3 and the advanced queenside pawns.

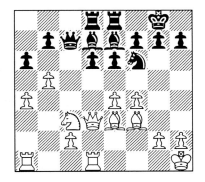

19 ♖ab1!

This rook was doing very little on the a-file. It is true that the file might be opened later with ...axb5 when White could recapture with the a-pawn, but for several reasons he is not interested in doing so. First he is trying to attack b7, and an open b-file is far more in his interest than a permanently closed one. Additionally White wants to maintain his a-pawn because he has a potentially strong influence over the promotion square on a8. The text also aims at the weak b6-square and thus forces Black to do something. Having said all this, we have a case of an inactive piece being brought to a better square – a major part of positional chess.

The other game, Cuijpers-De Boer, Hilversum 1988, went 19 ♘e2?!, which is just passive. There followed 19...♖c8 20 bxa6 bxa6 21 ♕xa6 ♖a8 22 ♕d3 ♖xa4 23 ♖xa4 ♗xa4 24 ♘c3 ♗c6 25 ♘b5 ♗xb5 26 ♕xb5 ♖b8 27 ♕a4 ♖c8 28 ♖d2 ♘d7 29 ♕d4 ♖b8 30 g3 ♘b6 31 ♗e2 ♕c6 ½-½.

19...axb5

This is more or less forced as the alternative runs into concept number one: 19...♖c8 20 e5! dxe5 (20...♕xc3 21 exf6 ♕xf6 22 ♗xb7 and White will win on the queenside) 21 fxe5 ♕xe5 (21...♘d5 22 ♗xd5 exd5 23 ♘xd5 ♕xe5 24 ♗f4 with a clear advantage to White – Anand) 22 ♗d4 ♕c7 23 ♗xf6 (23 b6? ♕b8 24 ♗xf6 ♗xf6 25 ♕xd7 ♖e7 might favour Black) 23...♗xf6 24 ♕xd7 and White will create a dangerous passed pawn on the queenside, with good chances to win the game.

20 ♘xb5!

20 axb5? clearly works against everything White wants, the rook being silly on b1 and the knight stuck on the poor square c3. After all, it is clearly the worst white piece.

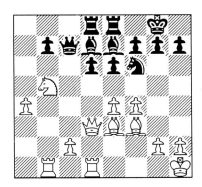

20...♗xb5?

Anand was surprised by this move,

and I can understand why. Black gives up the light squares where White was planning to win the game. Instead Black should go for 20...♕a5! 21 ♘xd6 (anything else allows Black to play ...♗c6 with a fine position – Anand) 21...♗xa4 22 ♗b6 (22 e5 ♗xd6 23 exd6 ♘d5 24 ♗xd5 ♖xd6! is fine for Black) 22...♖xd6. Then Anand gives 23 ♕xd6 ♗xd6 24 ♗xa5 ♗xf4 25 ♖xb7 ♗xc2 26 ♖d8 ♖xd8 27 ♗xd8 ♗xe4! 28 ♖b4 ♗xf3 29 ♖xf4 ♗d5 30 ♗xf6 gxf6 31 ♖xf6 and White cannot win the endgame. Best is 23 ♗xa5! ♖xd3 24 cxd3 ♗xd1 when White retains some pressure, although this is still preferable to the game.

21 ♕xb5

Anand later believed that 21 ♖xb5!? is even stronger. The idea is to improve the position of the rook on d1 and assist in the attack on b7.

21...♖a8 22 c4 e5

Black is forced to try to close off the f3-bishop which can otherwise threaten the black queenside.

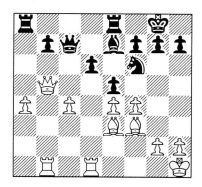

23 ♗b6!

A very nice move. By maintaining the tension in the centre for a moment White reduces Black's defensive capa-

bilities. Inferior is 23 fxe5? dxe5 24 ♗b6, when Black can defend more actively with 24...♕c6!.

23...♕c8

Now 23...♕c6 is different because there is still a battle to be fought in the centre, a factor that White exploits with 24 ♕xc6 bxc6 25 c5! etc.

24 fxe5 dxe5 25 a5 ♗f8 26 h3 ♕e6 27 ♖d5!

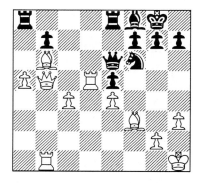

27...♘xd5??

This is hard to understand if one thinks only along the lines of chess and forgets about psychology. Garry Kasparov never had the temper for passive defence, which is a requirement of this position. Instead of trying to improve his position and wait for White to attempt to break through, he gives his opponent two passed pawns in the middle, just to get some counterplay with the e-pawn. Only this is clearly not going to bring him much happiness, and after this grave error the game cannot be saved. 27...h5!? is better according to Anand.

28 exd5 ♕g6 29 c5 e4 30 ♗e2 ♖e5

Trying to get his pieces into play. Another possibility is 30...♗e7 31 d6 ♗f6 32 d7 ♖f8 with the idea of an attack on the b8-h2 diagonal, but White has 33 ♗c7! and he emerges with a decisive advantage.

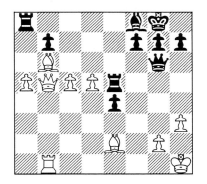

31 ♕d7! ♖g5 32 ♖g1 e3 33 d6 ♖g3 34 ♕xb7 ♕e6 35 ♔h2 1-0

Black has no attack.

Exercise 5
Anand-Dreev
Candidates Match, Madras 1991
French Defence

1 e4 e6 2 d4 d5 3 ♘c3 ♘f6 4 e5 ♘fd7 5 f4 c5 6 ♘f3 ♘c6 7 ♗e3 a6 8 ♕d2 b5 9 h4 ♗b7 10 h5? b4 11 ♘a4

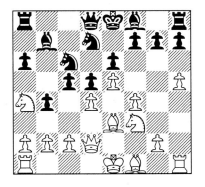

11...cxd4?!

This is wrong for one simple reason – White will not have to recapture at

once. Black was probably expecting something like 12 ♘xd4 ♘xd4 13 ♗xd4 ♗c6 and Black is much better, but Anand has an idea. 11...♘xd4! is much stronger, vacating the c6 square for the bishop no matter what. After 12 ♘xd4 cxd4 13 ♗xd4 ♗c6 Black is much better, while 12 ♗xd4 cxd4 13 ♘xd4 ♕a5 14 b3 ♘c5 15 ♘xc5 ♗xc5 gives Black a large advantage since White is very weak on the dark squares, where the bishop will dominate.

12 ♗f2!

Anand wrote in *NIC* that he played this quickly, pretending that it was home preparation. Actually it is the only move, as we have seen above.

12...♕c7 13 ♗d3

Ignoring the d4-pawn. Black cannot keep it protected forever anyway.

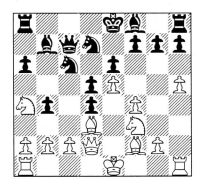

13...♘a5?

This is very slow. Black should exploit White's diminished control in the centre with 13...f6 14 0-0 fxe5 15 fxe5 ♗e7, with the better position. Now White has time to assume the initiative.

14 ♘xd4 ♘c4 15 ♕c1 ♗c6 16 ♘xc6 ♕xc6 17 b3 ♘a3 18 0-0 ♖c8 19 ♕e3 g6 20 ♕h3 ♗h6 21 ♗e3 ♘b5 22 ♖f3 ♘c3 23 ♘xc3 ♕xc3 24 ♖af1 ♕c6 25

♔h1 ♗g7 26 ♗d4 ♘c5 27 ♗xc5
♕xc5 28 g4 ♖c6 29 ♖1f2 ♕d4 30 ♕f1
♔e7 31 ♖h2 a5 32 h6 ♗f8

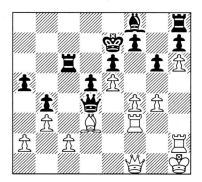

33 f5 gxf5 34 gxf5 ♖g8 35 fxe6 fxe6
36 ♗xh7 ♖c3 37 ♗xg8 ♕e4 38 ♖hh3
♗xh6 39 ♕g2 ♕e1+ 40 ♕g1 ♕e4 41
♕a7+ 1-0

Exercise 6
Botvinnik–Kurajica
Hastings 1966
Nimzo-Indian Defence

1 c4 ♘f6 2 ♘c3 e6 3 d4 ♗b4 4 e3 0-0
5 ♗d3 d5 6 a3 ♗xc3+ 7 bxc3 c5 8
cxd5 exd5 9 ♘e2 b6 10 0-0 cxd4 11
cxd4 ♗a6 12 f3 ♗xd3 13 ♕xd3 ♖e8
14 ♘g3 ♘c6 15 ♗b2 h5?! 16 ♖ae1
h4 17 ♘f5 ♘h5 18 e4 ♕f6?!

White has a strong and powerful centre. Soon he will attack with e4-e5 and f3-f4, attacking on the kingside, something Black will find difficult to address with normal play. But you should have noticed that Black is planning to play ...♘h5-f4 and that this should be prevented. Right now the knight looks rather awkward on h5 and it is very much in White's interest that it stays that way.

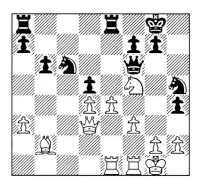

19 ♗c1!

Belov gives the following line to illustrate the importance of this move: 19 e5 ♘f4 20 ♕c2 ♕g6 21 ♗c1 ♘e6 and Black is better placed to resist White's advance. Note that 19 ♗c1 also improves the worst placed white piece. After e4-e5 this will not have any future on b2.

19...♖ed8 20 e5 ♕g6 21 f4

White has a significant positional advantage and went on to win the game without too many difficulties.

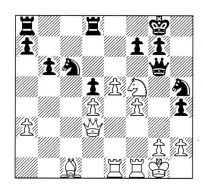

21...♕g4 22 ♖f3 ♖e8 23 ♖ef1 ♖ad8
24 h3 ♕g6 25 ♘xh4 ♕e4 26 g4 ♘xd4
27 gxh5 ♘xf3+ 28 ♕xf3 ♕xf3 29
♘xf3 d4 30 ♗d2 ♖c8 31 ♘xd4 ♖ed8
32 ♗e3 ♖c3 33 ♔f2 ♖xa3 34 ♖g1

♔h7 35 ♘f5 ♖g8 36 ♖c1 ♖b3 37 ♖c7 a5 38 ♖xf7 a4 39 e6 a3 40 ♗d4 a2 41 ♗xg7 1-0

Exercise 7
Polugaevsky-Tal
Leningrad 1971
Queen Pawn Opening

1 ♘f3 ♘f6 2 g3 g6 3 b3 ♗g7 4 ♗b2 d6 5 d4 0-0 6 ♗g2 e5 7 dxe5 ♘g4 8 h3 ♘xe5 9 ♘xe5 ♗xe5 10 ♗xe5 dxe5 11 ♕xd8 ♖xd8 12 ♘d2 ♘d7 13 0-0-0 ♖e8 14 ♘e4 ♔g7 15 g4 h6 16 ♖d3 ♘f6 17 ♘xf6 ♔xf6 18 ♖hd1 c6 19 ♖f3+ ♔g7 20 ♖e3 g5 21 a4

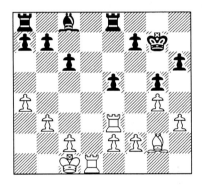

This is actually a remarkably easy exercise. White cannot invade and he cannot create any threats – at least not in any other way than he is trying to.
21...♔f6?
Yet Tal made this highly unusual slip. I guess he was never too strong in dull positions. Forced is 21...a5, when Black's position can be considered worse only from an academic point of view. Now White is allowed to force the creation of weak squares on the queenside.
22 a5!
Threatening the strong 23 a6, so Tal

decides to accept the weaknesses. However, I feel that this is a poor decision, as the position's static nature accentuates the importance of these weak squares. Perhaps 22...♖b8!? is now the lesser evil.
22...a6?!

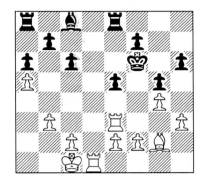

It is possible that Tal had not fully appreciated the impact of the coming infiltration.
23 ♔b2 ♗e6 24 ♔c3 ♖ac8 25 ♔b4!
Black must now decide if he wants b7 to become a target or to allow White's king to enter. He is probably lost either way.

25...h5 26 ♗f3 hxg4 27 hxg4 ♖cd8 28 ♖xd8 ♖xd8 29 ♔c5 ♖d4 30 c4 ♗xg4 31 ♗xg4 ♖xg4

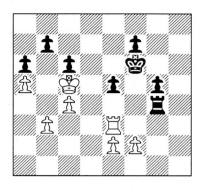

32 ♔b6 ♖f4 33 f3 e4 34 ♔xb7 ♔e5 35 ♔xa6 ♔d4 36 ♖xe4+ ♖xe4 37 fxe4 g4 38 ♔b7 g3 39 a6 g2 40 a7 g1♕ 41 a8♕ c5 42 ♔b6 ♔c3 43 ♕d5 ♕g8 44 ♔xc5 ♔xb3 45 ♕d3+ ♔b2 46 ♕d6 ♔b3 47 ♕b6+ ♔c2 48 ♔b5 ♕g4 49 ♕d4 ♕xe2 50 ♔b6 ♕h2 51 e5 ♔b3 52 c5 f6 53 c6 fxe5 54 ♕d5+ ♔a4 55 ♕b5+ ♔a3 56 c7 1-0

Exercise 8
Aagaard-Baramidze
Hamburg 1999
Sicilian Defence

1 e4 c5 2 ♘f3 ♘c6 3 d4 cxd4 4 ♘xd4 ♘f6 5 ♘c3 d6 6 ♗e2 e6 7 0-0 ♗e7 8 ♗e3 ♕c7 9 f4 a6 10 ♔h1 0-0 11 ♕e1 ♗d7 12 ♕g3 ♖fd8

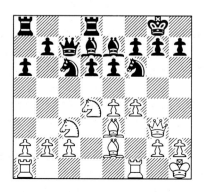

The old theory for this position was 13 e5, but I felt that this was not the right move. I disliked the fact that White's queen's rook was still not in play. I am not sure that my move was the best, but I am sure it was not inferior to what others play. But judge for yourself...

13 ♖ae1!

If you are going to have a party, invite all your friends! Finn is so right. At the board I realised that e4-e5 was possible, but I did not want to start an attack without inviting the rook first. 13 ♗d3!? also makes a lot of sense. Instead of bringing the rook immediately into play White indirectly hits h7. Then 13...♘b4! is the usual and correct decision, but in Illescas-Also, Las Palmas 1989, Black went astray: 13...♘xd4? 14 ♗xd4 ♗c6 15 e5 ♘e8 16 ♕f2 ♕b8 17 ♗b6 ♖c8 18 ♖ae1 g6 19 f5 exf5 20 ♗xf5 f6 21 ♗e6+ Black resigns.

13 ♖ad1 is the real alternative to 13 ♖ae1, White deciding that the rook is better placed here than on e1. He might be right – 13...b5 14 e5 ♘e8 15 ♘e4 f5 16 exf6 ♘xf6 17 ♘g5 ♘xd4 18 ♗xd4 ♖f8 19 ♗d3 h6 20 ♘h7 gave White a winning attack in Luecke-Meier, Germany 1993, while Klovans-Wieser, Graz 1998, saw Black improve but White still had a plus after 13...♔h8 14 ♘f3 ♗e8 15 ♕h3 d5 16 e5 ♘d7 17 ♗d3.

Black was by no means worse after 13 f5?! ♘xd4 14 ♗xd4 e5 in Christensen-Reiter, Bayern 1997.

13...b5

13...♗e8!, as played in Apicella-Kochiev, Budapest 1991, is probably the best move, defending f7 and giving the knight access to d7. However,

White's position seems preferable.

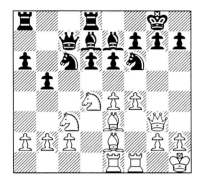

14 e5!

White needs to react immediately if he wants to use his advantage in development. Slow and unnecessary is 14 a3?!, when Lopez del Alamo-Baramidze, Oropesa del Mar 2000, continued 14...♖ac8 15 ♗d3 g6 16 ♘xc6 ♗xc6 17 ♗d4 ♕b7 18 ♗xf6 ♗xf6 19 e5 ♗g7 20 ♘e4 dxe5 21 fxe5 ♗xe4 22 ♗xe4 ♕b8 23 ♗d3 ♖d5 24 ♕f3 ♕a7 25 ♕h3 ♖xe5 26 ♖xe5 ♗xe5 27 ♖e1 ♗xb2 28 ♖xe6 ♕c5 29 ♖xa6 ♖e8 30 g3 ♖e1+ 31 ♔g2 ♕g1+ 32 ♔f3 ♕e3+ White resigns... It is amazing that my opponent repeated this line! At least he did not lose a miniature this time!

14...dxe5?

Losing by force. Black has to play 14...♘e8, after which *Fritz* evaluates the game as equal. Actually in the line 15 ♗d3 b4 16 f5!? ♘xd4 17 ♗xd4 bxc3 18 f6 ♗f8 19 ♗xh7+ ♔xh7 20 ♕h4+ ♔g8 21 ♖f3 it prefers Black all the way until here! Now, suddenly, it realises it is going to be mated...

15 fxe5 ♘d5

The weakest of three ways to lose. The other two are 15...♘xe5 16 ♗f4 ♗d6 17 ♗f3! ♘xf3 18 ♗xd6 ♘h5 19

♕xf3 ♕xd6 20 ♕xh5! ♕xd4 21 ♕xf7+ ♔h8 22 ♖d1 ♕a7 23 ♘e4 ♕c7 24 ♘f6! gxf6 25 ♕xf6+ ♔g8 26 ♖d4 e5 27 ♕f7+ ♔h8 28 ♖h4 ♕xc2 29 ♕f6+ ♔g8 30 ♖h5 and White wins, and 15...♘e8 16 ♘xc6 ♗xc6 17 ♕f2!, winning an exchange, which is the most difficult to see (even in the post-mortem). I guess I had not paid much attention to the weakness on b6, as Illescas Cordoba did above...

16 ♘xd5 exd5

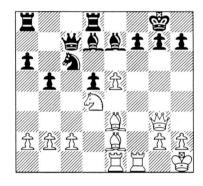

17 ♖xf7! g6 18 ♘xc6 ♗xc6 19 ♕h3! 0-1

Exercise 9
Karpov-Shirov
Biel 1992
Semi-Slav Defence

1 d4 d5 2 c4 c6 3 ♘c3 ♘f6 4 e3 e6 5 ♘f3 ♘bd7 6 ♕c2 ♗d6 7 ♗e2 0-0 8 0-0 dxc4 9 ♗xc4 b5 10 ♗e2 ♖e8 11 ♖d1 ♕c7 12 b3 e5 13 h3 ♗b7 14 ♗b2 a6 15 dxe5 ♘xe5 16 a4 ♖ad8 17 ♘g5 ♕e7 18 ♘ce4 ♘xe4 19 ♘xe4 ♗b4 20 ♘g3 f6

This position looks complex but calls for a simple assessment. Black is weak on the light squares on the kingside and the e5-knight is his only well placed minor piece. The logic is difficult to argue with.

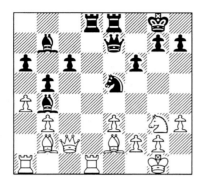

21 ♗xe5! ♕xe5

21...fxe5 gives White control over e4 and with it a clear advantage.

22 ♗d3 h6

Before the exchange the following line probably went through Karpov's mind: 22...g6 23 ♗xg6! hxg6 24 ♕xg6+ ♔h8 25 ♕h6+ ♔g8 26 ♘h5! and wins.

23 ♗g6!

Save the check for later.

23...♖f8

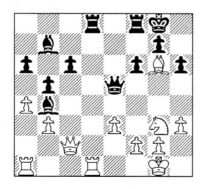

24 ♘f5!

With the plan ♘f5-h4-g6, winning the exchange – at the very least and probably much more.

24...c5

24...♗c8 25 ♘h4 ♕g5 26 ♗h7+ ♔f7 27 ♘f3 also wins for White.

25 axb5 axb5 26 ♖a7

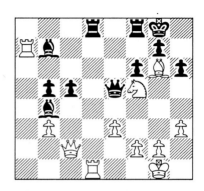

26...♕c7

Black has alternative ways to lose: 26...♕e4 27 ♕xe4! ♖xd1+ 28 ♔h2 ♗xe4 29 ♖xg7+ ♔h8 30 ♖h7+ ♔g8 31 ♘xh6 mate, 26...♖xd1+ 27 ♕xd1 ♕b8 28 ♕d5+ with mate to follow and 26...♕b8 27 ♘e7+ ♔h8 28 ♗f5 ♕xa7 (28...♖xd1+ 29 ♕xd1 ♖d8 30 ♕g4 ♕xa7 31 ♕g6) 29 ♘g6+ ♔g8 30 ♗e6+ lead to the same result.

27 ♘h4 ♖xd1+ 28 ♕xd1 ♖a8

28...♖d8 29 ♕g4 ♕b6 30 ♖xb7 ♕xb7 31 ♕e6+ ♔f8 32 ♗h5 followed by ♘h4-g6+.

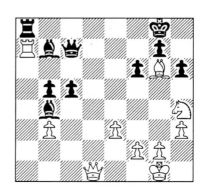

29 ♕g4! ♕c6

29...♖xa7 30 ♕e6+ and mate.

30 ♖xb7! ♕xb7 31 ♕e6+ ♔h8 32 ♗e4 1-0

33 ♘g6+ will easily decide, e.g. 32...♕a6 33 ♘g6+ ♔h7 34 ♘e5+ ♔h8 35 ♘f7+ ♔g8 36 ♘xh6+ ♔h8 37 ♕g8+ ♖xg8 38 ♘f7 mate.

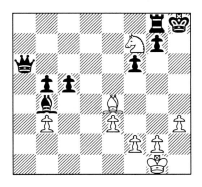

Exercise 10
Adamski–Nøhr
Denmark 2001
Semi-Slav Defence

1 c4 c6 2 ♘f3 d5 3 e3 ♘f6 4 ♘c3 e6 5 d4 ♘bd7 6 ♕c2 ♗d6 7 ♗e2 0-0 8 b3 e5 9 cxd5 cxd5 10 ♘b5 ♗b4+ 11 ♗d2 ♗xd2+ 12 ♘xd2 e4 13 ♕c7 a6 14 ♕xd8 ♖xd8 15 ♘c3

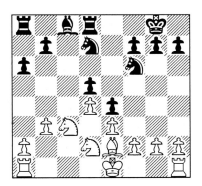

What now? 15...b5 or 15...b6?

15...b5?

This is a strategic error. The b5-pawn will prove weak, even if the bishops are exchanged. On the other hand b4 will not be weak because *Black cannot attack it*. This is a very important property regarding weaknesses – they are significant only if they can actually be attacked. Otherwise there is no reason to worry. 15...b6 is the correct move, when play would most likely proceed along the lines of 16 0-0 ♗b7 17 ♖ac1 ♖ac8 18 ♘a4 ♖xc1 19 ♖xc1 ♖c8, with a level endgame.

16 a3 ♘b6 17 b4

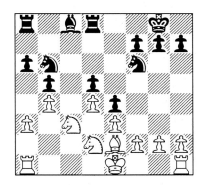

White now has the advantage. In the future he can attack Black's queenside structure with a well timed advance a3-a4.

17...♘a4?

Black has a number of good intentions with this move, including ...♗c8-d7-b5, but he has overlooked how White can prevent this idea. The only way to play is 17...♗g4 to exchange light-squared bishops. Then after 18 f3? ♖ac8! time becomes the issue and Black is better, so the appropriate 18 ♗xg4! ♘xg4 19 ♘b3 gives White the advantage as

Black will have problems with b5 – unlike White with b4.

18 ♘xa4 bxa4

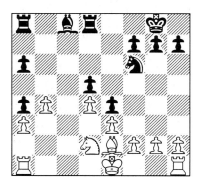

19 ♘b1!

The knight is going to the ideal c3-square, and Black has serious problems with both a4 and a6. White later converted his structural advantage to the full point.

Exercise 11
Aagaard–Jensen
Denmark 2001
Sicilian Defence

1 e4 c5 2 ♘f3 d6 3 d4 cxd4 4 ♘xd4 ♘f6 5 ♘c3 g6 6 ♗c4 ♗g7 7 0-0 0-0 8 ♖e1 ♘c6 9 ♗b3 a6 10 ♗g5 ♘a5 11 ♕d2 ♖e8 12 ♖ad1 ♘xb3 13 axb3 ♘d7 14 ♘d5 ♘c5?!

After the exchange of his light-squared bishop White has been playing exclusively on the light squares. In general Black should not be too intimidated by this, just careful. However, his last move is wrong. Instead 14...♘e5, with the idea of repositioning to c6, more or less maintains the balance. Now the knight has gone astray and no longer has an influence on the dark squares in the centre. Consequently I felt that it had to be right to compromise Black's pawn structure on the dark squares, and analyses later proved me to be right in this judgment.

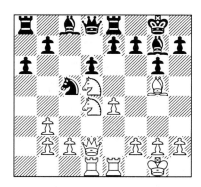

15 e5!

This move is based on feeling and a few variations.

15...♗g4?

Losing, as does 15...dxe5 16 ♘c6! bxc6 17 ♘xe7+ ♕xe7 18 ♗xe7 ♖xe7 19 ♕d6! etc. Forced is 15...♗xe5!, after which White will have to play 16 ♘f3!. Instead the fight on the dark squares with 16 ♘xe7+? ♖xe7 17 ♖xe5 dxe5 18 ♘c6 ♖d7 19 ♗xd8 ♖xd2 20 ♘e7+ ♔f8 21 ♖xd2 ♘e4 sees Black emerge with a decisive advantage. My original plan was 16 ♖xe5?! dxe5 17 ♘c6 bxc6 18 ♘xe7+ ♔g7! (a key difference from 15...dxe5) 19 ♕xd8 ♖xd8 20 ♖xd8 ♗b7 with equality.

Returning to 16 ♘f3, White is winning after 16...♗g4 17 ♘xe5 ♗xd1 18 ♘xg6! hxg6 19 ♗xe7. This leaves the forced 16...f6 17 ♘xe5 fxg5 (17...fxe5 18 ♘xe7+ ♖xe7 19 ♖xe5 ♘e6 20 ♗xe7 ♕xe7 21 ♕xd6 gives White a much better endgame) 18 ♘c4 with a slight advantage to White.

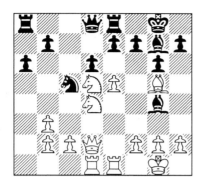

16 f3

Black wanted to force this for later use but, as we shall see, it does not work.

16...♗e6

16...dxe5 17 ♘c6! is still bad.

17 ♘xe6 ♘xe6

17...fxe6 18 ♘xe7+ ♖xe7 19 exd6 ♕b6 20 dxe7 ♘e4+ 21 ♕e3 wins for White.

18 ♘xe7+!

18 exd6!? ♘xg5 19 d7 ♘xf3+ 20 gxf3 ♖f8 21 ♖xe7 also looks very good.

18...♖xe7 19 exd6 ♖d7?!

A form of resignation. Black originally counted on 19...♗d4+ 20 ♔h1 ♕xd6 21 ♗xe7 ♕xe7 but had overlooked the simple 22 ♕xd4!, when White has an exchange and a pawn.

20 ♗xd8 ♖axd8 21 c3

White won without problems.

Exercise 12
Ladeira-Eugenio
Brazil 1997
Queen's Gambit Declined

1 d4 d5 2 c4 e6 3 ♘c3 c5 4 cxd5 exd5 5 ♘f3 ♘c6 6 g3 ♘f6 7 ♗g2 ♗e7 8 0-0 0-0 9 dxc5 ♗xc5 10 ♗g5 d4 11 ♗xf6 ♕xf6 12 ♘d5 ♕d8 13 ♘d2 a6 14 ♖c1 ♗a7 15 ♘e4 ♖e8 16 ♘c5 ♖e5 17 ♕b3 ♘a5 18 ♕f3 ♗f5 19 ♖fd1 ♗xc5 20 ♖xc5 ♘c6 21 ♕f4 ♕d6 22 b4 ♖ae8

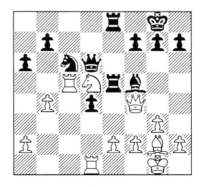

White would like to profit from all the black pieces that are somehow in trouble. There are ideas involving attacking the f5-bishop, and others with ♗xc6 to undermine the protection of the rook on e5. Somehow in this position White should also be able to exploit the pin theme.

But applying our Christmas technique with the pieces is the solution to this very simple exercise. Where does White's knight want to be? Well, most of all: c4. So then the answer starts to come through...

23 a3?

23 ♘e3!! wins. Black has nothing better than 23...♕xc5 (23...♗e6 24 ♗xc6 is final) 24 bxc5 dxe3 25 ♗xc6 exf2+ 26 ♔xf2 g5! 27 ♕xg5+ ♗g6, and now there are numerous options, e.g. 28 ♕d2 or 28 ♕xe5!? ♖xe5 29 ♗xb7 ♖xc5 30 ♗xa6 and White is two pawns up in the endgame.

23...♗e6?

23...♕g6 secures equality.

24 ♘c3?

24 ♘c7! is stronger.

24...♖d8 25 ♘e4 ♕b8 26 ♔f1 ♗d5 27 ♖dc1 h6 28 ♖xd5 ♖exd5 29 ♕xb8 ♘xb8 30 ♘f6+ ½-½